The Collected Works of W. B. Yeats
Richard J. Finneran and George Mills Harper
General Editors

THE COLLECTED WORKS OF W. B. YEATS
VOLUME VII

W. B. YEATS

Letters to the New Island

EDITED BY

George Bornstein

AND

Hugh Witemeyer

Macmillan Publishing Company

NEW YORK

Macmillan Publishing Company
866 Third Avenue, New York, NY 10022

Library of Congress Cataloging-in-Publication Data
Yeats, W. B. (William Butler), 1865–1939.
Letters to the new island.
(The Collected works of W. B. Yeats; v. 7)
Includes index.
1. English literature—Irish authors—History and
criticism. 2. English literature—19th century—
History and criticism. 3. London (England)—Intellectual
life—19th century. 4. Ireland—Intellectual life—19th
century. I. Bornstein, George. II. Witemeyer, Hugh.
III. Title. IV. Series: Yeats, W. B. (William Butler),
1865–1939. Works. 1989; v. 7.
PR5900.A2F56 vol. 7   821'.8 s   88–27366
[PR8750.Y4]   [820'.9'89162]
ISBN 0-02-513722-0

Macmillan books are available at special
discounts for bulk purchases for sales
promotions, premiums, fund-raising, or
educational use. For details contact:

Special Sales Director
Macmillan Publishing Company
866 Third Avenue
New York, NY 10022

10 9 8 7 6 5 4 3 2 1

Printed in the People's Republic of China

CONTENTS

EDITORS' TEXTUAL
PREFACE

The textual history of *Letters to the New Island* is not complicated.
All of Yeats's contributions first appeared in one of two American
newspapers, the Boston *Pilot* and the *Providence Sunday Journal*,
with the exception of the retrospective Preface which he provided
expressly for Horace Reynolds's 1934 edition. That edition, done
for Harvard University Press in the United States and distributed
by Oxford University Press in the United Kingdom, was
reprinted once, in 1970. Reynolds intended his edition to include
all of Yeats's prose contributions to the two journals, and shared
his intention with Yeats himself. Nonetheless, in collecting the
fugitive pieces Reynolds missed two from the *Providence Sunday
Journal*, which are reprinted with the other letters for the first
time in the present volume as items 19 and 21. Except for those
two essays and the Preface, then, the items in the present volume
exist in two previous textual forms – the versions in the journals,
and those in the Reynolds edition. The only known surviving
manuscript is the typescript of the Preface, apparently prepared
by George Yeats and corrected in hand by W. B. Yeats.

We have chosen the Reynolds edition as our copy-text for
three main reasons. First, that edition constitutes the only book
version of the text and provides a principal rationale for treating
the items as a separate volume. Second, although Yeats apparently did not delegate the same authority to Reynolds that he
did to Thomas Mark at Macmillan for other texts, he did
sanction the edition both by giving Reynolds leave to prepare it
and by composing a preface for the occasion. Yeats obviously
had no control over the newspaper versions, with their many
typographical errors, whereas he had at least a distant partici-
pation in the Reynolds volume, including the nomination of

T. Sturge Moore to design the cover. And, finally, the Reynolds text is thus the last version approved by Yeats in his lifetime. For the two items omitted by Reynolds, we have, of course, followed the *Providence Sunday Journal* text as the only one possessing authority, but we have profited from the text and annotations to "The Arts and Crafts: An Exhibition at William Morris's" (item 21) as reprinted in the first volume of John P. Frayne's edition of *Uncollected Prose by W. B. Yeats* (1970).

Reynolds grouped the essays according to the newspaper in which they originally appeared. Thus, the Boston *Pilot* pieces precede the *Providence Sunday Journal* ones in the copy-text. That plan has the additional merit of reinforcing a difference in kind between the two sets of essays, with those for the *Pilot* mostly being literary *causeries* and those for the *Sunday Journal* mostly being extended reviews. Within each grouping, Reynolds followed the chronological order of publication. We have retained his arrangement, inserting the two unreprinted items (19 and 21) at the appropriate points in the *Sunday Journal* series. For readers who wish to view all of the letters in historical sequence, we have provided a chronology in Appendix I. Appendix II reproduces Reynolds's introduction, which describes the genesis of his edition and clarifies the nature of his interest in the work of Yeats. It is incorporated into the present volume because Yeats sanctioned it as part of the original edition of *Letters to the New Island*. Its inclusion here, together with reproductions of the original cover design and frontispiece (see pp. xxiii and xxiv), ensures that no important ancillary material from that edition is missing from the present one.

Despite the general superiority of the copy-text over the earlier versions, we have followed *Pilot* and *Sunday Journal* readings in the following cases: where the accidentals make the sense clearer; where Reynolds added or omitted words not evidently necessary to the sense, or where his transpositions affect rhythm or parallelism; where the earlier text follows Irish syntax; where it contains information omitted by Reynolds; or where Reynolds made an obvious typographical or other error. For example, where Reynolds regularly omitted publication data on current books discussed by Yeats, we have restored it from the *Sunday Journal* text on the grounds that it both contains information and reminds the reader of the occasional nature of Yeats's pieces. Again, where Reynolds includes the typographical error "Willis" for "Wills" or where he substitutes "artist" for "aurist" (meaning a specialist in treatment of the ear) we have emended back to the correct newspaper text. In a few instances where both the newspaper and book texts appear to be in obvious error, we have made emendations on our own authority. For Yeats's Preface, the surviving typescript has served the same purpose that the journal texts have for the other items. All emendations indicated above are marked with a superscript dagger (†) in the text and are listed in the Emendations to the Copy-Text at the back of the volume, together with the authority or rationale for each.

The titles and dates of Yeats's texts pose a particular problem. Yeats did not provide the titles for the book version and may not have supplied those for the newspaper version either. Nevertheless, we have emended back from the copy-text to the earlier version because the earlier titles are usually clearly superior and more informative. For example, the newspaper title "Irish Writers Ought to Take Irish Subjects – *A Sicilian Idyll*" seems superior to the book version's "Ireland's Heroic Age" in both accuracy and extent of information. In other cases, the newspaper title consists of a full list of subjects of the contribution, whereas the book title simply selects the first one or two. Particularly misleading are the dates in the book version, which refer to the day of first publication, whereas the newspaper texts usually include instead the date of dispatch. We have restored the newspaper title and, where present, date of dispatch for each item, while a footnote printed on the same page gives the title and date printed by Reynolds, for those who are more familiar with them. At various times, the compositors for the two journals separated different parts of the title by spaced hyphens, periods, or a line set partially across a column; in the interest of consistency, we have standardized these divisions as spaced hyphens except in two instances where colons were more appropriate to the sense. The copy-text contains a number of corrections to the quotations given in each item, particularly for long indented quotations, and we have followed those while noting remaining errors in the Notes. The Notes also provide information about names, places, historical events, titles, quotations, and allusions that are not identifiable from their immediate contexts.

The following typographical and format conventions have been silently adopted for Yeats's texts, in accord with the general policy for the prose volumes of *The Collected Edition of the Works of W. B. Yeats.*

1 The titles of each item have been set in upper- and lower-case letters (upper-case for the first letter of main words). The same policy governs column headings and Reynolds titles cited in notes. All displayed headings are centered and end without a full point.

2 The opening line of each new paragraph is indented, except following a displayed heading or section break.

3 All sentences open with a capital letter followed by lower-case letters.

4 A colon that introduces a quotation does not have a dash following the colon.

5 Quotations that are set off from the text and indented have not been placed within quotation marks.

6 Titles of stories, essays, and poems have been placed within quotation marks; titles of books, plays, long poems, periodicals, operas, paintings, statues, and drawings have been set in italics.

7 Abbreviations such as "i.e." have been set in roman type.

8 A dash, regardless of its length in the copy-text, has been set as a spaced en rule when used as punctuation. When a dash indicates an omission, as in "Miss S——," a two-em rule is used.

9 Ampersands have been expanded to "and."

10 When present, the author's signature is indented from the left margin, set in upper- and lower-case letters, and ends without punctuation (except where the signature appears as initials followed by points).

11 When present, the place and date are indented from the left margin, set in italics in upper- and lower-case letters, and end without punctuation.

Our edition follows American typographical conventions for quotation marks and the placing of associated punctuation because all extant forms of the text do so, because the only existent manuscript (the typescript of the Preface prepared by George Yeats and corrected by W. B. Yeats) does so, and because the text was explicitly intended for publication in the United States in both periodical and book form. For the same reasons, we have also retained the American conventions of spelling, capitalization of main words in titles of literary works, and punctuation of contractions in personal titles (e.g. "Mr.") that are employed in the copy-text. These conventions here carry semantic value as a reminder of the primacy of American publication and audiences in Yeats's mind at the time of composition. For the sake of consistency, our editorial apparatus follows the same conventions. However, where British spellings occur in the copy-text and in passages quoted in the editorial apparatus, we have not emended them.

Appendix II differs in its styling from the rest of the edition. For reasons explained in the headnote, Appendix II follows the format of the 1934 Harvard University Press edition of *Letters to the New Island*. It thus shows how the copy-text of the present edition was originally styled.

A work of this kind involves assistance from a wide spectrum of the scholarly community. The editors are gratified by the generous help we received at every stage of our labors. In particular we would like to thank the following individuals: Jonathan Allison, Richard Badenhausen, Pamela M. Baker, Eileen Black, Heather Bryant, Donald Callard, Thomas J. Collins, Paul Cunniffe, Alan Denson, Joseph Donohue, Linda C. Dowling, Peter Faulkner, C. Fahy, Mary FitzGerald, Richard J. Finneran, Roy Foster, Russell Fraser, Joseph T. Freeman, Warwick Gould, Spencer Hall, Maurice Harmon, George Mills Harper, Marjorie Howes, A. Norman Jeffares, K. P. S. Jochum, Colton Johnson, David R. Jones, John Kelly, Peter Kuch, James MacKillop, Christina Hunt Mahony, Phillip L. Marcus, John Maynard, Philippe Mikriammos, William M. Murphy, E. B. Murray, Ingeborg Nixon, William H. O'Donnell, Dáithí O hOgáin, Jan Piggott, Donald H. Reiman, Anthony W. Shipps, Edgar Slotkin, Peter Alderson Smith, Colin Smythe, John Stokes, Mary Helen Thuente, Dorothy Wonsmos, and H. M. Young. For support of our research, Professor Bornstein wishes to thank the John Simon Guggenheim Memorial Foundation and both the Research Partnership Program and the College of Literature, Science, and the Arts at the University of Michigan; Professor Witemeyer wishes to thank the College of Arts and Sciences at the University of New Mexico.

We are also grateful to Anne and Michael Yeats and to Linda Shaughnessy of A. P. Watt Ltd, for permission to use material from the Yeats estate; to John Kelly and the Oxford University Press for permission to quote from *The Collected Letters of W. B. Yeats*, volume 1; to Miss Riette Sturge Moore and the University of London Library for permission to quote from the unpublished correspondence of T. Sturge Moore and to reproduce his cover design for *Letters to the New Island* (1934); to the Ulster Museum, Belfast, for permission to reproduce H. M. Paget's portrait of Yeats; and to the Houghton Library, Harvard University, for permission to quote from the unpublished papers of Horace Reynolds. Harvard University Press kindly granted permission to reprint the extracts from Yeats's *Letters to the New Island*, edited by Horace Reynolds (Cambridge, Mass.: Harvard University Press, 1934), © 1934 by the President and Fellows of Harvard College; copyright renewed 1962 by Horace Reynolds.

Finally, we would like to dedicate our work on this edition to our children – Hazen, Rebecca, and Ben.

G.B.
H.W.

LIST OF ABBREVIATIONS

Au   W. B. Yeats, *Autobiographies* (London: Macmillan, 1966)

BP   Boston *Pilot* (newspaper)

BIV   *A Book of Irish Verse Selected from Modern Writers*, ed. W. B. Yeats (London: Methuen, 1895)

CL1   *The Collected Letters of W. B. Yeats*, vol. I: *1865–1895*, ed. John Kelly, associate ed. Eric Domville (Oxford: Clarendon Press; New York: Oxford University Press, 1986)

CT   W. B. Yeats, *The Celtic Twilight* (London: Lawrence and Bullen, 1893)

E&I   W. B. Yeats, *Essays and Introductions* (London and New York: Macmillan, 1961)

FFT   *Fairy and Folk Tales of the Irish Peasantry*, ed. W. B. Yeats, Camelot Classics series, no. 32 (London: Walter Scott, 1888)

HR   W. B. Yeats, *Letters to the New Island*, ed. Horace Reynolds (Cambridge, Mass.: Harvard University Press, 1934)

IFT   *Irish Fairy Tales*, ed. W. B. Yeats (London: T. Fisher Unwin, 1892)

PBYI   *Poems and Ballads of Young Ireland* (Dublin: M. H. Gill and Son, 1888)

PNE   *W. B. Yeats: The Poems, A New Edition*, ed. Richard J. Finneran (New York: Macmillan, 1983; London: Macmillan, 1984)

PSJ   *Providence Sunday Journal* (newspaper)

UP1   *Uncollected Prose by W. B. Yeats*, vol. 1, ed. John P. Frayne (London: Macmillan; New York: Columbia University Press, 1970)

UP2   *Uncollected Prose by W. B. Yeats*, vol. 2, ed. John P. Frayne and Colton Johnson (London: Macmillan, 1975; New York: Columbia University Press, 1976)

VP   *The Variorum Edition of the Poems of W. B. Yeats*, ed. Peter Allt and Russell K. Alspach, corrected 3rd printing (New York: Macmillan, 1966)

EDITORS' INTRODUCTION

"Is there any news from John Boyle O'Reilly," wrote W. B. Yeats to John O'Leary on 13 June 1887. "I hope the poems did not go astray" (*CL1* 20). That letter contains the earliest surviving evidence of Yeats's contact with either of two major American outlets for his early work, the Boston *Pilot* edited by O'Reilly and the *Providence Sunday Journal* edited by Alfred M. Williams. Although Yeats first published a single poem in each journal ("How Ferencz Renyi Kept Silent" in the *Pilot* for 6 August 1887 and "A Legend of the Phantom Ship" in the *Sunday Journal* for 27 May 1888), both papers became major publishers of his prose journalism rather than his poetry. With the exception of his retrospective Preface, all of the twenty-two items reprinted in the present volume first appeared there.

The *Providence Sunday Journal* published the first articles. Its editor was Alfred M. Williams (1840–96), an American reporter who joined the *Providence Journal* as a reporter in 1875 and became in turn associate editor, managing editor, and finally editor by 1885.[1] Williams's interest in Ireland dated from 1865, when Horace Greeley sent him to investigate the Fenian question; Williams was arrested as a suspect by the British authorities and released through intervention of the American ambassador, Charles Francis Adams.[2] In 1881 Williams edited the anthology *Poets and Poetry of Ireland*, and in 1887 he visited the country again, partly to enlist Irish contributors for the new *Sunday Journal* begun two years previously. There he met Yeats's friend Katharine Tynan, who had the odd impression that he was originally English (Williams was born on a farm near Taunton, Massachusetts). She recalled,

It must have been in 1887 that Mr. Alfred Williams of the *Providence Journal* came to Dublin, and asked me to write for his *Sunday Journal*. . . . In the *Providence Sunday Journal*, a very wilderness of a paper, one discovered the stars in the English literary sky while they were yet only on the horizon. I remember the delight with which I first read "Danny Deever" there, and Meredith's short stories, and other delectable things.

Mr. Williams was visiting in Ireland Mrs. Banim, the widow of Michael Banim, the Irish novelist ... with her two daughters, Mary and Matilda. The Banim sisters contributed constantly to the *Providence Sunday Journal*. . . . Mr. Williams made me begin seriously to write prose. My diary for 1888 is studded with cheques from the *Providence Journal*.[3]

Apparently, Tynan put Yeats in contact with Williams. On 14 March 1888 Yeats wrote to her, "I have a couple of poems that may suit the Providence Journal, one being the Phantom Ship. Would you kindly send me the Editors address?" (*CL1* 55). Besides that poem, the *Sunday Journal* published seven items by Yeats between 2 September 1888 and 26 July 1891. They include, in order, reviews of William Allingham's *Irish Songs and Poems*, John Todhunter's *The Banshee and Other Poems*, D. R. McAnally's *Irish Wonders*, Todhunter's play *A Sicilian Idyll*, William Watson's *Wordsworth's Grave and Other Poems*, an Arts and Crafts exhibition, and Todhunter's play *The Poison Flower*.

With Williams's retirement in July 1891, Yeats's association with the newspaper came to an end. The new editor did not share Williams's enthusiasm for Irish culture. In asking John O'Leary for a loan of a pound during November 1891, Yeats explained, "my only regular & certain paymaster 'the Providence Journal' has either not taken or has postponed my article sent last month. The late editor Williams is now doing most of the literary work himself – Hence the rest of us are elbowed out to some extent" (*CL1* 272). But Yeats's other American outlet would continue to publish him for another year.

Yeats ascribed his contact with the Boston *Pilot* to his mentor John O'Leary (HR 5), who knew the colorful Irish editor and author John Boyle O'Reilly (1844–90). Trained as a journalist, O'Reilly became a Fenian, enlisted in the 10th Hussars in 1863 to recruit revolutionaries from the Irishmen in the unit, was court-martialed and transported to Australia, escaped, and traveled on American ships to Philadelphia, where he landed in

November 1869. The next year he joined the staff of the *Pilot*, the best-known Irish Catholic weekly newspaper in the United States. Founded in 1829 as the *Jesuit*, that paper underwent several changes in name before 1835, when it became the *Boston Pilot* in sympathy with the Irish O'Connellite newspaper the *Pilot*, which had been suppressed the previous year; in 1858 the American journal enlarged its format and became simply the *Pilot*, although it was still published in Boston and often referred to by its earlier name.[4] The resourceful O'Reilly soon became editor and, in 1876, part-owner. By the summer of 1887 Yeats was writing about the possibilities of publication in the *Pilot* to O'Leary, who in turn let him read a letter from O'Reilly about the matter (*CL1* 20, 31).

As with the *Providence Sunday Journal*, Yeats's contributions to the *Pilot* quickly shifted from poetry to prose. Between 3 August 1889 and 19 November 1892 the *Pilot* published fourteen articles by Yeats, most of them in a column headed "The Celt in London." Besides overlapping with those on Allingham and Todhunter for the *Sunday Journal*, they included among their subjects Irish poets such as Rose Kavanagh and Ellen O'Leary, folklorists such as Douglas Hyde and Lady Wilde, nationalists such as the O'Learys and Maud Gonne, and a number of English writers, including Browning and some of the Rhymers' Club members. Throughout, the relation of literature and nationality preoccupied the young Yeats.

Again like the *Sunday Journal*, the *Pilot* provided an important source of income for the ever hard-pressed young Irishman. On 1 July 1890 he wrote to fellow contributor Katharine Tynan,

> Can you tell me what the Pilot gives you for a column or for an article of average length. They give me one pound for my Celt in London letter. I am thinking of asking for more – I fixed a pound myself, I think, in the beginning. I dont want to write to Pilot on the matter until I know what their usual pay is. (*CL1* 223)

As John Kelly notes, the figure of £1 was probably per column, since the diary of Yeats's sister Lolly lists payments varying between £1 3s. and £3 from the *Pilot*; the month after the letter the payment jumped to £4. Payments continued through 1892, when Yeats's connection with the paper ceased. So, too, did the first phase of the history of these important early works.

That history resumed in the summer of 1927, when the young American Horace Mason Reynolds (1896–1965) visited Ireland and met Yeats. After graduating from Harvard in 1919 and taking his AM there in 1923, Reynolds served as instructor in English at Brown University (1923–6) and had just been promoted to assistant professor. He would later teach at the College of William and Mary, Harvard University, and Emerson College, but he came to think of himself less as an academic than as a "journalist."[5] Reynolds specialized in Anglo-Irish literature, and on his 1927 trip met many leading figures of the Irish revival, including Oliver St. John Gogarty, George Russell (AE), Maud Gonne, and Yeats himself. One evening Yeats innocently asked Reynolds, who lived in Providence while teaching at Brown, "Is a paper I used to write for years ago called The Providence Journal still in existence?"[6]

After his return to the United States, Reynolds continued to think of Yeats's connection with the *Providence Sunday Journal*, to which he himself was a contributor (as were several other members of the Brown University faculty). He collected Yeats's articles in both the *Sunday Journal* and the *Pilot* and showed photographic copies of them to Yeats in early December 1932, during the author's last American lecture tour, with a view toward publishing them.[7] By that time Reynolds had moved from Brown to William and Mary and then back to Harvard. He naturally approached the press of his own university, and the resultant *Letters to the New Island* was published by Harvard University Press in 1934.

Yeats took a more active role in publication of the volume than simply giving Reynolds leave to prepare it. He consulted with Reynolds about the contents, reviewed Reynolds's introduction, suggested the portrait of himself that became the frontispiece and even arranged for a photograph of it to be sent to Reynolds, wrote a retrospective preface for the book, and nominated his friend T. Sturge Moore to design the symbolic cover. His chief concern about content was the omission of the two poems he had published in the American papers. As he told Reynolds in a postscript to a letter of 24 December 1932, "If you could find it in your heart not to print the poems I shall be glad: they were in my first book and have never been reprinted by me. If you give the signal by printing them, some anthologist or ghastly musician will appropriate them."[8] Yeats did not remark that Reynolds had inadvertently omitted two essays originally published in the *Providence Sunday Journal* on 5 May and 26 October 1890.

The main body of the letter of 24 December gave Yeats's views of the essays and their forthcoming republication:

Dear Mr. Reynolds,

I have read your admirable essay and the photographic reproductions of my various essays. I am greatly interested, and on thinking over things have made the joyous discovery that, as I have no copyright, I have no responsability [*sic*] – at least so I imagine. I therefore give you leave to do what you can do, and doubtless would do in any case. I have made one or two slight corrections in pencil on your essay, and there is another which I should have made but did not. You say Florence Farr spent her latter years teaching blacks. The people of Ceylon are not blacks. I remember Lord Salisbury getting into no end of a mess through calling some Indian a black man. I am glad to have read those essays of mine after so many years. I find that I am still in agreement with all the generalisations, but not with the examples chosen. I praise Todhunter and others out of measure because they were symbols of generalisations and good friends to my father and myself. The articles are much better than my memory of them, but I knew better than I wrote. I was a propagandist and hated being one. It seems to me that I remember almost the day and hour when revising for some reprint my essay upon the Celtic movement (in "Ideas of Good and Evil") I saw clearly the unrealities and half-truths propaganda had involved me in, and the way out. All one's life one struggles towards reality, finding always but new veils. One knows everything in one's mind. It is the words, children of the occasion, that betray.

I thank you for a pleasure received and wish you good luck.

Yeats was obviously pleased at the prospect of republication and surprised to discover how intimately the essays anticipated his later thought. He seems to have exercised no further control over the texts, beyond getting the poems removed. But he did suggest the frontispiece by the painter H. M. Paget, reproduced in the present volume. On 9 June 1933 he wrote to Reynolds from his house at Riversdale, Rathfarnham, that "the Belfast municipal gallery has got a painting of me, done at the time when I was writing these articles, by a competent but not very origonal [*sic*] painter. I can send you a reproduction." In the event, Yeats did not procure the photograph himself but got the painter Sarah Purser, an old friend of the Yeats family, to do so.[9]

During the early summer of 1933 Yeats produced a preface for the book as well. On 27 July 1933 he wrote to Reynolds, "I have finished & will send you when typed a preface for your book, rather a good preface I think." The "rather good" Preface, reprinted as item 1 in the current volume, sets forth the mature Yeats's views on his early work. Meanwhile, Reynolds recorded his account of the same work and of his dealings with Yeats in a substantial introduction, reproduced here as Appendix II.

The title of the volume was apparently suggested by Reynolds and approved by Yeats. At one stage, it was to be *Letters to the Other Island*, but Reynolds altered that wording after receiving Yeats's letter of 27 July, in which the poet observed that "the words 'other island' applied to America is unknown to me." By 23 September the Harvard University Press, in its correspondence with Sturge Moore, was calling the projected volume *Letters to the New Island*.[10]

Thomas Sturge Moore (1870–1944) was in contact with Harvard because he had been nominated by his friend Yeats to design the cover of the new book. "Now that Charles Ricketts is dead I know no better" designer than Moore, Yeats told Reynolds in his letter of 27 July 1933. Ricketts (1866–1931) had designed the cover of the six-volume *Collected Edition of the Works* of Yeats published by Macmillan in 1922–6. Harvard wished to follow closely the Macmillan format of decorated, light-green cloth binding and $7\frac{1}{2} \times 5\frac{1}{8}$ inch pages to encourage prospective customers to purchase *Letters to the New Island* as a supplement and companion to the Macmillan set. Moore undertook the Harvard commission for a fee of $25 or £5 0s. 8d.[11]

Yeats had already ruled out "harp & shamrock" for the cover on the grounds that they "are disliked by most of us today."[12] Reynolds therefore suggested other themes in his initial letter to Moore of 8 August 1933:

I should like a design developed from some symbol or motif expressive of the ideas that were in Mr. Yeats's mind at the time he wrote these articles. In these papers Mr. Yeats wrote much of Todhunter's plays and poems, including the Children of Lir. Because of that and also because of the Irish reverence and fondness for the swan I have thought that might be an appropriate figure. As of course you know, the swan children of Lir were three.[13] Perhaps you who know Mr. Yeats's work so well can think of some more appropriate symbol than the swan. Mr. Yeats was dreaming much of a revival of the poetic drama at that time, as these articles prove, but I can think of no appropriate pictorial symbol to figure forth that dream.

Moore replied that "It is essential that the motive should not be hackneyed and the Swan is perhaps already that," but in the end he based his design almost entirely upon Reynolds's suggestions. The essays themselves, Moore admitted, "I have never read."[14]

Moore combined the motifs of Irish lore and poetic drama in an emblematic design (reproduced in the present volume) that shows the swan children of Lir swimming under a theatrical curtain toward a row of footlights.[15] Above and below the swans are envelopes, presumably symbolizing letters, sealed with masks of comedy and tragedy. The idea of poetic drama is followed out in the laurel wreaths on the spine. The design does not appear to have been submitted to Yeats for his approval.

Reynolds's edition of *Letters to the New Island* was first published in 1934 and reprinted by Harvard University Press in 1970. Both printings were distributed in the United Kingdom by Oxford University Press. Of the two missing essays from the *Providence Sunday Journal*, one ("The Arts and Crafts: An Exhibition at William Morris's") was reprinted in the first volume of John P. Frayne's edition of *Uncollected Prose by W. B. Yeats* (1970). The present edition of *Letters to the New Island* thus gathers for the first time in one volume all twenty-one of these important early essays, together with Yeats's retrospective Preface.

NOTES

1. Henry R. Davis, *Half a Century with the Providence Journal* (Providence: Journal Company, 1904, for private distribution) pp. xii, 36, and *passim*; George W. Potter, Foreword to *An Irish Pilgrimage* (Providence: Providence

Journal Company, 1950); and Garrett D. Byrnes and Charles H. Spilman, *The Providence Journal: 150 Years* (Providence: Providence Journal Company, 1980) pp. 197–217.

2. Davis, *Half a Century*, pp. 36–7; cf. Horace Reynolds, *A Providence Episode in the Irish Literary Renaissance* (Providence: Study Hill Club, 1929) p. 4.

3. Katharine Tynan, *Twenty-five Years: Reminiscences* (London: John Murray, 1913) pp. 279–80. Elsewhere, she described the paper as "a huge ten-sheet American daily" (*CLI* 67).

4. For the early history of the paper, see Patrick F. Scanlan, "The Boston Pilot," *Commonweal*, 21 May 1930, pp. 76–8; and Arthur J. Riley, "Notes on Serial Publications," *Catholic Library World*, 2 (Mar 1931) 39–40.

5. The best sources of information on Reynolds are the *Harvard Class of 1919* reports, issued at regular intervals of five or ten years; a complete set is available in the Harvard University Archives. Throughout this edition we have drawn on Reynolds's unpublished papers, which are housed in the Houghton Library, Harvard University. They are identified below as "Houghton" followed by the manuscript number in the typed list "PAPERS OF HORACE REYNOLDS"; the call number for the list is 65M-211.

6. HR 3; cf. Houghton 580.

7. See Yeats's Preface (item 1 in the present volume) and the accompanying note 1.1.

8. The four surviving letters from Yeats to Reynolds in Houghton Library are catalogued separately from the other items on the list cited above in note 5. Their call number is 58M-62/338.10, and they will henceforth be identified simply by date.

9. Letter of 27 July 1933.

10. For Moore's letters to Reynolds, see Houghton 276. The letters Moore received from Reynolds and David T. Pottinger, head of the Harvard University Press, are among the Sturge Moore papers in the University of London Library, box 9, items 52–61. On the backs of some of these letters are pencilled drafts of Moore's replies. The letters received by Moore are identified below as "ULL" followed by box and item numbers. Reynolds uses the title *Letters to the Other Island* in ULL 9/52 (8 Aug 1933). Pottinger uses the title *Letters to the New Island* in ULL 9/54.

11. ULL 9/53, 9/54, and 9/59.

12. Letter to Reynolds, 27 July 1933.

13. ULL 9/52. Reynolds later apologized to Moore (ULL 9/60) for misleading him as to the number of swan children, which should be four. Moore replied that it was "too late for the alteration in the number of Swans to be made. So that it is necessary to suppose Fianoula is hidden behind her brothers which in those times might have been supposed her proper place" (Houghton 276, 31 Mar 1934).

14. Houghton 276, undated (probably Aug 1933).

15. ULL 65/64, i–ii. Design in black paint and white ink on white card.

T. Sturge Moore, Cover-design for *Letters to the New Island*, 1934 (University of London Library)

H. M. Paget, *Portrait of W. B. Yeats*, 1889 (Ulster Museum Collection, Belfast)

LETTERS TO THE NEW ISLAND

*"Was man in der Jugend wünscht,
hat man im Alter die Fülle."*
Old German Proverb

1 Preface

While I was lecturing somewhere in the Eastern States Mr. Reynolds sent me a bundle of photographic copies of articles of mine published in American newspapers when I was a very young man, said they would interest students of the Irish intellectual movement and asked leave to publish them.[1] I thought his letter generous, for all but two or three had been published before the Copyright Act of 1891.[2] I read what was not too blurred or in too small print for my sight, and noticed that I had in later life worked out with the excitement of discovery things known in my youth as though one forgot and rediscovered oneself. I had forgotten my early preoccupation with the theatre, with an attempt to free it from commercialism with a handsome little stage in a Bedford Park Clubhouse.[3] As I read, Florence Farr's acting in Todhunter's *Sicilian Idyll* came into my mind, her beautiful speaking, the beautiful speaking of Heron Allen, cheiromantist and authority upon old violins, the poor acting and worse speaking of some woman engaged from some London theatre.[4] Two or three times in later life I made, as I thought for the first time, the discovery made in that little theatre that the highly cultivated man or woman can in certain kinds of drama surpass an actor who is in all things save culture their superior. Since then my friends and I have created a theatre famous for its "folk art," for its realistic studies of life, but done little for an other art that was to come, as I hoped, out of modern culture where it is most sensitive, profound and learned. In these articles I overrated Dr. Todhunter's poetical importance, not because he was a friendly neighbour with a charming house, a Morris carpet on the drawing-room floor, upon the walls early pictures by my father painted under the influence of Rossetti, but because a single play of his, the *Sicilian Idyll* – I did not overrate the rest of his work – and still more its success confirmed a passion for that other art.[5] When Shelley wrote *The Cenci* – it had just been played for the first time – when Tennyson wrote *Becket*†, they were, I argued with Todhunter, deliberately oratorical; instead of creating drama in the mood of "The Lotos-Eaters"† or of *Epipsychidion* they had tried to escape their characteristics, had thought of the theatre as outside the general movement of literature.[6] That he might keep within it I had urged upon Todhunter a pastoral theme, and had myself begun *The Countess Cathleen*, avoiding every oratorical phrase or† cadence.[7] A few months before I had seen George Macdonald and his family play in the Bedford Park Clubhouse a dramatised version of the *Pilgrim's Progress* before hangings of rough calico embroidered in crewel work, and thought that some like method might keep the scenery from realism.[8] I should have added that to avoid the suggestions of the press that bring all things down to the same level, we should play before an audience vowed to secrecy. I spent my life among painters who hated the Royal Academy, popular art, fashionable life.[9] I could remember some painter saying in my childhood, "Holman Hunt will never come to anything, I have just heard that he gets his dress clothes at Poole's" – Poole was the most fashionable of all tailors.[10] When I had founded the Irish Literary Society and gone to Ireland to found a similar society there I had all the fanaticism of the studios.[11] The article that interests me most is that written in the Dublin National Library, where everybody was working for some examination, nobody, as I thought, for his own mind's sake or to discover happiness.[12] New rules have compelled the students to go elsewhere for their school books, but Irish education is still commercialised. I can remember myself sitting there at the age of twenty-six or twenty-seven looking with scorn at those bowed heads and busy eyes, or in futile revery listening to my own mind as if to the sounds in a sea shell. I remember some old man, a stranger to me, saying, "I have watched you for the past half hour and you have neither made a note nor read a word." He had mistaken the proof sheets of *The Works of William Blake, edited and interpreted by Edwin Ellis and William Butler Yeats*, for some school or university text book, me for some ne'er-do-weel student.[13] I am certain that everybody outside my own little circle who knew anything about me thought as did that cross old man, for I was arrogant, indolent, excitable. To-day, knowing how great were the odds, I watch over my son, a boy at the preparatory school, fearing that he may grow up in my likeness.[14]

I knew Blake thoroughly, I had read much Swedenborg, had only ceased my study of Boehme for fear I might do nothing else, had added a second fanaticism to my first.[15] My isolation from ordinary men and women was increased by an asceticism destructive of mind and body, combined with an adoration of physical beauty that made it meaningless. Sometimes the barrier between myself and other people filled me with terror; an unfinished poem, and the first and never-finished version of *The Shadowy Waters* had this terror for their theme.[16] I had in an extreme degree the shyness – I know no better word – that keeps a man from speaking his own thought. Burning with adoration and hatred I wrote verse that expressed emotions common to every sentimental boy and girl, and that may be the reason why the poems upon which my popularity has depended until a few years ago were written before I was twenty-seven. Gradually I overcame my shyness a little, though I am still struggling with it and cannot free myself from the belief that it comes from lack of courage, that the problem is not artistic but moral. I remember saying as a boy to some fellow student in the Dublin art schools, "The difference between a good draftsman and a bad is one of courage."[17] I wrote prose badly, *The Celtic Twilight*,[18] written before I had finished the last of the articles in this book, excepted, and that more for its matter than its form; prose, unlike verse, had not those simple forms that like a masquer's mask protect us with their anonymity. Perhaps if he had not been to so much trouble and expense I should have asked Mr. Reynolds to give up his project and yet been sorry afterwards, for these essays, which I have not seen for years, fill me with curiosity.

W. B. Yeats
†
August 1, 1933

FROM THE BOSTON *PILOT*

2   Irish Writers Who Are Winning Fame*

London, July 10

England is an old nation, the dramatic fervor has perhaps ebbed out of her. However that may be, most of the best dramas on the English stage from the times of Congreve and Sheridan and Goldsmith to our own day have been the work of Irishmen.[1] The most prominent London dramatist at the present time is certainly the Irishman, Mr. W. Wills; his much more renowned countryman, Mr. Dion Boucicault, can hardly any longer be called a London dramatist.[2] The revival of Mr. Wills' *Claudian* at the Princess, previous to its departure for America, has brought up again the old gossip as to the disputed authorship of the famous earthquake incident which concludes the piece.[3] As a matter of fact the whole merit of the originality belongs to Mr. Wills, and dates as far back as the year following the catastrophe at Ischia, when Mr. Wills, being in Rome, wrote the piece in communication with eye witnesses of the kind of incident he was venturing for the first time to introduce into a drama.[4] But rumor would have it that he was a mere poet and incapable of so scenic a conception. His collaborator was also a man of literature and not equal to so great a stage climax.[5] The manager had a brief period of glory, but then it was decided that he was not enough of a machinist. So the carpenter would have ended by keeping all the laurels, but that he was deprived of them in a most unexpected way. A well known dramatist[6] taking his seat in the stalls the other night remarked to the spruce young female attendant who distributed the programmes, "That earthquake idea was a very fine one of ——" he was not able to finish his sentence. "Oh, thank you, sir," she exclaimed with effusion, and retired blushing and triumphant.

* This letter appeared in *BP* for 3 Aug 1889 under the column heading "The Celt in London." HR title: "Mr. William Wills."

A play on King Arthur and his Round Table by Mr. Wills is announced to follow *Macbeth* at the Lyceum, with Ellen Terry as Guinevere.[7] There was a rumor going the rounds some time ago that he had written a *Robert Emmet* for Irving, and that the censor interfered. It is probably a canard.

One day Mr. Burnand, the editor of *Punch* and general critic and wit, was sitting reading a newspaper in the Savile Club, a place of general resort for men of letters, Messrs. Austin Dobson, Edmund Gosse and Herbert Spencer being among its more constant frequenters.[8] Mr. Wills came in. Now Mr. Burnand had just damned a play of his and so was careful to bury his head in the paper. "I have something to say that very much concerns Mr. Burnand," said the dramatist, leaning his back against the fire. The editor of *Punch* looked up. Mr. Wills† went on: "You will remember Dutton Cook, and how he was always damning my plays and Miss S——'s acting?[9] [Mr. Burnand remembered.] One day I said to Miss S——, 'Let us make a little wax image of Dutton Cook'; we made it. 'Now, let us melt it before the fire and stick pins in it'; we did so. Next day I met a friend, and he said to me, 'Have you heard the news – Dutton Cook is dead?'" Having finished his story, Mr. Wills went out, and since that day Mr. Burnand, who is no less superstitious than witty, is said to have only abused Mr. Wills' plays in reason.

I wonder are all the cheap reprints of good books read as well as bought. A very distinguished poet who has always issued his own poems at very high prices said in my hearing the other day that he believed the cheap books were only bought for their cheapness.[10] A friend of his once purchased, he said, a London Directory twenty years old because he could get it for threepence: it was such a large book for the money. I hope the threepenny reprint of Aubrey de Vere's beautiful *Legends of St. Patrick*, just issued by Cassell, Petter and Galpin, will have a kinder fate and be read as well as bought.[11] It will probably sell by tens of thousands, if one can at all judge by the immense sale of the same publishers' threepenny editions of such poems as Coventry Patmore's *Angel in the House*, and the sculptor Woolner's *Beautiful Lady*. Its being reprinted at all is a sign of the times. A few years ago no Englishman would look at any Irish book unless to revile it. *Ça ira.*[12]

Apropos of poets, the peasant poet is less common in England than with us in Ireland, but I did meet the other day an Englishman who was a true specimen of the tribe. He is a Mr. Skipsey.[13] He is from the coal country – a strange nursing mother for a poet – and taught himself to write by scribbling with a piece of white chalk on the sides of coal shafts and galleries. In the depth of a mine hundreds of feet under the earth he has written many† sweetest and tenderest songs. He has not been left to sing his songs to the dull ear of the mine, however. The most sensitive ears of our time have heard them. Rossetti, a little before his death, read and praised these simple poems.[14] The last few months Walter Scott's collection of Mr. Skipsey's mining poems has made new admirers for their author. He is more like a sailor than a miner, but like a sailor who is almost painfully sensitive and refined. He talked to me about Clarence Mangan a good deal.[15] Mangan is a great favorite of his. He recited, for the benefit of a Saxon who stood by, Mangan's "Dark Rosaleen." Himself a peasant, he turned for the moment's inspiration to the country where poetry has been a living voice among the people.

There has been some talk lately in the Parnell Commission about the Clondalkin Branch of the National League.[16] Archbishop Walsh in his evidence mentioned it as the only branch whose action he had been compelled to condemn.[17] They had written up a black list of people they did not approve of. When I was last in Ireland I saw a good deal of the main mover in the matter. Not at all a firebrand, one would think, but a quiet shoemaker, who had read and thought a great deal.[18] I used often to stray into his shop to have a chat about books, among the leather clippings. Since then I have seen at odd times in Irish papers sketches and stories of peasant character by him, all full of keen observation. Carlyle, Emerson and Miss Laffan are his favorite authors.[19] When I saw him last he was struggling with Emerson's Over-Soul, but told me that he always read Carlyle when "wild with the neighbors." Perhaps his black list was only a piece of Carlylese. The biographer of Frederick did so love the strong hand! Though, indeed, most men of letters seem to have a tendency towards an amateurish love of mere strength. They grow impatient of the slow progress of thought perhaps, and long to touch the hilt of the sword.

I have some literary news from Ireland. Mr. T. W. Rolleston, who has just translated Walt Whitman into German, is now busy on a life of Lessing for Mr. Walter Scott, who published

last autumn the shilling reprint of his translation from Epictetus.[20]
Mr. Rolleston has just removed to Dublin from his pretty
Wicklow house, where for years now he has been busy with his
beehives and Walt Whitman.[21] He is a fine Greek scholar and
quite the handsomest man in Ireland, but I wish he would
devote his imagination to some national purpose. Cosmopolitan
literature is, at best, but a poor bubble, though a big one.
Creative work has always a fatherland.

   Miss O'Leary is preparing for the press a collection of her
poems.[22] Her friends, who have undertaken all business matters
concerning the book, have decided to have for frontispieces
photographs of Miss O'Leary and Mr. John O'Leary.[23] There
will be an introduction describing their life and connection with
the old Fenian movement, and, by way of appendix, Sir Charles
Gavan Duffy's article on Miss O'Leary's poems.[24] They are,
indeed, tender and beautiful verses – Irish alike in manner and
matter. One of the most, if not the most, distinguished of critics
now writing in the English tongue once said to me, though he
did not in the least sympathize with her national aspirations,
"Miss O'Leary's poems, like Wordsworth's, have the rarest of
all gifts – a true simplicity."[25] Nothing quite like them has been
printed anywhere since Kickham wrote, "She lived beside the
Anner."[26] They are the last notes of that movement of song, now
giving place to something new, that came into existence when
Davis, singing, rocked the cradle of a new Ireland.[27] We of the
younger generation owe a great deal to Mr. John O'Leary and
his sister. What nationality is in the present literary movement
in Ireland is largely owing to their influence – an influence all
feel who come across them. The material for many a song and
ballad has come from Mr. John O'Leary's fine collection of Irish
books – the best I know. The whole house is full of them. One
expects to find them bulging out of the windows. He, more
clearly than any one, has seen that there is no fine nationality
without literature, and seen the converse also, that there is no
fine literature without nationality.

   W. B. Y.

3   Some Forthcoming Irish Books*

London, Sept. 7

London has been empty a long while now, all folk who could
having fled to the continent or Brighton or elsewhither in search
of green fields and sea winds.[1] They will soon be on their way
home, with much secret satisfaction, for your Londoner, in spite
of all he may say, does not much care for the country. He is not
used to be alone, and considers the joys of country solitude a
fiction of the poets, all the pleasanter to read about because it is
only fiction and no reality questioning his own noisy and talkative
existence.

Lady Wilde[2] still keeps up, in spite of London's emptiness,
her Saturday afternoon receptions, though the handful of callers
contrasts mournfully with the roomful of clever people one meets
there in the season. There is no better time, however, to hear
her talk than now, when she is unburdened by weary guests,
and London has few better talkers. When one listens to her and
remembers that Sir William Wilde was in his day a famous
raconteur, one finds it no way wonderful that Oscar Wilde should
be the most finished talker of our time.[3] Lady Wilde has known
most of our '48 poets and novelists – Carleton, Lover, Lever and
the rest, and can say something vital and witty of them all.[4] She
has a pile of Carleton's letters and can tell many things of our
great humorist whose heart was so full of tears. She never saw
Davis,[5] but some one described to me how his funeral gave her
a first impulse toward nationalism. She was walking through
Grafton Street (I think it was), when a great crowd came by
following a hearse.[6] It seemed as though the crowd would never
end. She stepped inside a bookshop to let it pass. The crowds
still streamed by. "Whose funeral is this?" she asked the shop-
boy. "The funeral of Thomas Davis," was the answer. "Who

* This letter appeared in *BP* for 28 Sep 1889 under the column heading
"The Celt in London." HR title: "Lady Wilde."

was Thomas Davis?" "A poet," was the reply. It seemed to her there must be something great and imaginative in a country where so many followed a poet to the grave. Thenceforth she began to think deeply on these matters; the result soon came in the poems of "Speranza." This story has never been printed before.

Lady Wilde would do good service if she would write her memoirs, the appearance and ways of our '48 men are often so scantily known to us. Many a writer of incomparable song and ballad has no more record than his voice. We do not know even whether he was witty or wearisome, dark or fair. A hundred years hence men will peer about in vain for any history of Keegan, the farm laborer; and concerning Edward Walsh they will find no more, or little more, than that he used to wander about the roads near Dublin, a little harp on his left arm.[7]

Lady Wilde could fill many blank spaces. Meanwhile, she is doing good work in setting down in good English Sir William Wilde's great collection of folk-lore and legend. Sir William Wilde employed peasants in all parts of Ireland to gather together everything in the way of charm or fairy tale. Old men and women, too, when going away cured from his hospital, would ask leave to send him eggs or fowl, or some such country gift, and he would bargain for a fairy tale instead. Lady Wilde is now preparing for the press a new volume taken from this great collection. It will be of some size, and deal mainly with charms and spells.

Two other writers are about to publish with David Nutt books on Irish folk and fairy lore – David Fitzgerald and Douglas Hyde.[8] Fitzgerald's articles in *La Revue Celtique* promise well for his volume, some of the stories being most curious and weird, though spoiled a good deal by the absence of any attempt to give the native idiom they were told in. They are written more from the side of science than literature. Douglas Hyde's, on the other hand, will be, I feel sure, the most Irish of all folk-lore. He understands perfectly the language of the people and writes it naturally, as others do book-English. Most of the stories in his forthcoming book have already appeared in the original Gaelic in his *Leabhar Sgéulaigheachta* (Gill, Dublin). The† three stories he translated for *Fairy and Folk Tales of the Irish Peasantry* show what a master he is of dialect. He is surely the most imaginative of all Irish scholars, and I believe these wild and sombre stories of his will make some noise in the world.

Douglas Hyde also has on hand a little Gaelic book on the famous musician and poet, Carolan.[9] He will give therein a number of anecdotes and unpublished verses gathered among the old men of Connaught.[10] I hope he will take pity on us poor folk who have no Gaelic and translate it some day. He owes us also a volume of his own ballads. His contributions to *Poems and Ballads of Young Ireland*, 1888, and the new and very unequal *Lays and Lyrics of the Pan-Celtic Society* (a book that has lain too short a time on my table for any more detailed verdict now) are full of true Gaelic flavor.[11]

The new publishing season, however, will bring forth much more than goblin, witch and fairy legends. Sir Charles Gavan Duffy's long expected life of Thomas Davis alone would make it a red letter season for us.[12] Its author is now working away in a house near Park Lane at the last two chapters, and the whole will be in Kegan Paul's hands in a week or two.

Kegan Paul will publish also a work on the treatment of Irish political prisoners by Dr. Sigerson of Dublin, well known in Ireland and elsewhere as a physician, publicist and historian.[13] A great portion of the book appeared piecemeal in the Dublin *Freeman's Journal*,[14] but well deserves preservation in the more permanent book form. Dr. Sigerson was a member of the last commission of inquiry into prisons and prison discipline, and is necessarily thoroughly acquainted with his subject. He has, besides, a very large knowledge of Irish history, statistics and the like, and that shaping brain which knows how to use its materials.

So much for forthcoming books. Among those just published are two of some importance on the same subject as Dr. Sigerson's. The first is issued from the office of *The Freeman's Journal*, and edited by Mr. E. Dwyer Gray, and has a preface by Sir C. G. Duffy,[15] who, however, in no way vouches for the contents of the book, which he has apparently not read, but simply expresses his views on the general question. The book is mostly made up of a reprint of the various letters on the subject addressed to *The Freeman* by foreign, colonial and other gentlemen of more or less importance in their respective countries. It would, however, be very much the better for a good deal of boiling down, for while some of the letters are of very great importance and some of less, a great many are simply of no importance whatever.

The second book is from the hands of an ex-Cabinet Minister, Mr. Shaw Lefevre, and is chockful of facts and figures somewhat Dryasdustically† arranged, like all Mr. Shaw Lefevre writes.[16] This may be said to be good work but bad workmanship. It is, however, useful, as all his books are, and valuable as an admission from the English Radical standpoint of iniquitous treatment of political prisoners by England, both in the past and the present.[17]

This letter has been somewhat bookish, but then, as I explained, the season is over and every one has fled from town and left me no gossip of men and things any way up-to-date. Also the book time is near at hand – another season than that of London has come to an end – the season of swifts and swallows. They are now all flying southward, piercing the dew by the Pillars of Hercules[18] or gathering together on house tops preparing for their journey. The trees are turning gold and red and yellow, and the whole appearance of the outer world makes one grow mindful of the fireside. And thither this coming winter all reading Irishmen will certainly take *The Life of Thomas Davis*, and when the witching hour has come and ghosts are creeping about, if they be wise, they will open Hyde's translated *Leabhar Sgéulaigheachta*†. These two volumes, one of the old generation, the other of the new, will, I imagine, be the events of the season for us.

W. B. Yeats

4　What the Writers and Thinkers Are Doing*

London, Oct. 31

We have all been saddened by Miss O'Leary's sudden death on
the fifteenth of this month. The death of this heroic woman who
lived ever, in the words of her own song, written of another, "to
God and Ireland true," has left a sore place in numerous hearts.
Everywhere sympathy is felt for her brother, Mr. John O'Leary,
whose lifelong friend and ally she was.[1]

This is Hallow Eve night,[2] the night of fairies, and opportune
to the occasion a paper comes to hand with a report of Colonel
Olcott's lectures, last week in Dublin, on our Irish goblins.[3] He
asserted that such things really exist, and so strangely has our
modern world swung back on its old belief, so far has the reaction
from modern materialism gone, that his audience seemed rather
to agree with him. He returns to London at once, where the
faithful of his creed are busy with many strange schemes – among
the rest the establishing of an occult monastery in Switzerland,
where all devout students of the arcane sciences may bury
themselves from the world for a time or forever.

H. P. Blavatsky, the pythoness of the Movement, holds
nightly levees at Lansdowne Road.[4] She is certainly a woman of
great learning and character. A London wit once described her
as the low comedian of the world to come.[5] This unkind phrase,
anything but an accurate account of this strange woman, had
this much truth, that she can always enjoy a joke even against
herself. The other day she was returning from Jersey, whither
she had gone for her health. A young man from Birmingham
began talking to her.[6] "They are a rum lot, them theosophists,"
he said. "Yes, a rum lot," she replied. "And that rum old woman
at the head of them," he went on. "That rum old woman, H. P.
Blavatsky, has now the honor of speaking to you." "Ah! I do

* This letter appeared in *BP* for 23 Nov 1889 under the column heading
"The Celt in London." HR title: "The Three O'Byrnes."

not mean that old woman," he stammered out, "but another old woman."

Apropos of the fairies, a friend brings me a strange story from Donegal.[7] It has nearly made him a believer in the actual existence of the creatures, like Colonel Olcott, whom Andrew Lang called the other day "the Fairies' Friend."[8] He was poking about in a rath at the foot of Slieve League, in Donegal, and seeing a large hole, asked what made it.[9] "That is where the three O'Byrnes dig for treasure," a countryman told him. Presently a shoeless man, with ragged hair and ragged clothes, came up and began working at the hole with a crowbar. He asked who it was. "The third O'Byrne," was the answer. He spoke to the man, who only shook his head – he only knew† Gaelic. The people about told my friend, who was staying in their village, the story of the treasure. It was buried long ago under a ban. Three O'Byrnes had in succession to seek it and die just at the moment of its discovery, but when the last had died it would be the possession of their heirs forever. Two had already died, the first torn to pieces by a phantom dog that came rushing down the mountain; the second saw the treasure and was driven mad by some terrible apparition and died. Now the third sought all day long, time after time; my friend saw him at work. He would die, he knew, but the O'Byrnes would be enriched.

A German translation of Miss Katharine Tynan's poems has just appeared. The translator's name is Fräulein Clara Commer of Breslau, and the volume is dedicated by special permission to the Empress's mother, Augusta.[10] The translation is, I hear, a very good one. Miss Tynan herself has just returned to Ireland after a long stay in London, and the stream of callers will have commenced again, on Sunday afternoons, to pour into the pretty thatched Clondalkin farmhouse.

I announced in my last letter the forthcoming life of Davis.[11] It will be preceded a week or two by the Camelot edition of his essays, which will be published on December first. The editor is Mr. T. W. Rolleston, who has had all through the assistance of Sir Charles Gavan Duffy.[12]

A short while since, literary London was deeply moved by the suicide of the young Jewish novelist and verse writer, Miss Amy Levy.[13] Many will take up with sad interest the posthumous volume, *A London Plane-Tree*, now in the press. She and her works are so typical of our day. Social problems have made us melancholy, and the old resting places for the mind have been swept away. Any poor heart otherwise overladen has a hard time of it. Miss Levy had much in her own life to make her unhappy, and all the fretfulness of our age bore in upon her as well. One day she could stand it no longer, and so shut to her door and her window, and lighted a pan of charcoal and died. Fame that so long had turned from her awoke round her grave. *Reuben Sachs*, her sad Jewish novel, has found its meed of notability now. Man will turn anywhere where life is, anywhere rather than the dull round of meals and newspapers, even towards a heart so strewn with salt and bitterness that Lethe[14] and its darkness seemed sweeter far than youth and all its possibilities. Miss Levy's poems many times dwell on the thought of suicide, dwell on it in a simple matter-of-fact way, without sentimentality. Here is a little poem, published six years ago, and called "A Cross-Road† Epitaph":

> When first the world grew dark to me,
> I call'd on God, yet came not He.
> Whereon, as wearier waxed my lot,
> On Love I call'd, but Love came not;
> When a worse evil did befall,
> Death, on thee only I did call.[15]

The burthen of her poetry is ever much the same, and yet she never seems to assume wretchedness for effect. One verse struck me as having an unusual force:

> Of warmth and sun and sweetness,
>   All nature takes a part;
> The ice of all the ages
>   Weighs down upon my heart.[16]

The immediate cause, if any, of her suicide we may never know. The veil will cover it. I saw her no long while before her death. She was talkative, good-looking in a way and full of the restlessness of the unhappy. Had she cared to live, a future of some note awaited her. Her poetry (her prose I have but glanced at) showed a strong literary faculty, not so much poetic as tending to the precise, definite thoughts that make good prose, and sometimes rising by sheer intensity to the region of poetry.

Two other books full of present day world sadness have just reached me, and both by Irish ladies. The first is Miss Ryan's poems, *Songs of Remembrance* (Gill and Sons, Dublin),† the second an advance copy of Miss Keeling's prose sketches *In Thoughtland and in Dreamland*.†[17] Miss Keeling seems to have picked up her world sadness, like the swallow in Mrs. Carlyle's poem, "under German eaves,"† and Miss Ryan hers maybe on the benches of her own village chapel; yet both are alike in being a little sentimental. Indeed Miss Keeling is not a little sentimental, but very much so. There is scarcely anything in the world she would not drop a tear on. Miss Ryan can write very prettily sometimes, as thus:

> On earth and sky and far-off sea,
> It is a lovely tender hour:
> A sweet virgin crowned with gracious power.
> To-night in heaven what must it be![18]

The notion of heaven sharing somehow the more gentle changes of earth receives a new thought and a pleasant one. Miss Ryan is one of the little group of poets who surround *The Irish Monthly*, one of the same school with Miss Tynan, Miss Mulholland, the late Attie O'Brien and others who have made religion their most common inspiration.[19] She is too sad by a great deal. Most good poets have much sadness in them, but then they keep it more implicit than explicit. It comes in spite of them; they do not fondle it and pet it.

In this matter Miss Keeling's sins are even greater. She seems to have read second-rate German romances without end. Her whole book is simply a huge, iridescent tear; but it is really iridescent. The style always glitters. It glitters too much, indeed. It has more of the gleam of drawing-room candelabra than the soft lustre of nature. She has genuine wit, though, and power of description. Old ladies at lodging-houses, old maids, children, door-step cleaners, maids-of-all-work, lady artists in reduced circumstances, sentimental Germans, the whole squalid rabble of the lodging house, pass by, drawn with much real vigor. Miss Keeling has been everywhere and seen everything and may yet write good novels – though, indeed, I am told she has already done this in *Two Sisters*.[20] She is young and ardently Irish – witness the very pretty chapters on Ireland in the present volume.

One must be on the watch to see what may come out of this glittering faculty of hers. She must, though, give up the iridescent tear. It is not her own, it is stolen goods. Meanwhile she should go over to Ireland and see what she can find there to write about. After all, Ireland is the true subject for the Irish.

W. B. Y.

5 Chevalier Burke – "Shule Aroon" – Carleton and the Banims'† Novels – An Autograph Sale at Sotheby's† – William Allingham – Miss Ellen O'Leary*

London, Dec. 5

I have just been reading Mr. R. L. Stevenson's *Master of Ballantrae.*[1] We Irish people have a bone to pick with him for his sketch of the blackguard adventurer, Chevalier Burke. I do not feel sure that the Chevalier is not a true type enough, but Mr. Stevenson is certainly wrong in displaying him for a typical Irishman. He is really a broken-down Norman gentleman, a type found only among the gentry who make up what is called "the English garrison."[2] He is from the same source as the Hell Fire Club and all the reckless braggadocio of the eighteenth century in Ireland; one of that class who, feeling the uncertainty of their tenures, as Froude explains it, lived the most devil-may-care existence.[3] One sometimes meets even at this day vulgar, plausible, swaggering "Irishmen," who are its much decayed survivals, and who give Mr. Stevenson his justification. They are bad, but none of our making; English settlers bore them, English laws moulded them. No one who knows the serious, reserved and suspicious Irish peasant ever held them in any way representative of the national type. It is clear that Mr. Stevenson has no first hand knowledge of Ireland, and when a member of the English garrison, private or subaltern, comes to England and chooses to masquerade as a genuine Irishman, he too often, through some perversion of moral judgment, affects to be some such Irishman as this rogue and charlatan and mountebank "gentleman," Chevalier Burke. I do not, of course, assert more

---

* This letter appeared in *BP* for 28 Dec 1889 under the column heading "The Celt [in] London." HR title: "Chevalier Burke and Shule Aroon."

than that there is a bad tradition amongst the English garrison of which the mean and reckless nature takes advantage.

Mr. Stevenson puts into the mouth of the Chevalier a curious version of "Shule Aroon," which he seems to suppose the correct one.[4] Before the publication of *The Master* I heard from a common friend that he would use this version, and wrote at once to a well known authority on Irish songs about it and got the answer I expected, that it was a Scotch or North of Ireland variation, and certainly much later than the words given by Gavan Duffy.[5] It is a corruption, but a pretty one. I have the whole somewhere, but have mislaid it. Here is the verse quoted in *The Master*:

> O, I will dye my petticoat red,
> With my dear boy I'll beg my bread,
> Though all my friends should wish me dead,
> For Willie among the rushes, O!

The same verse in the old version goes thus:

> I'll dye my petticoats, I'll dye them red,
> And round the world I'll beg my bread,
> Until my parents shall wish me dead,
> Is go d-teidh tu, a mhuirnin, slan![6]

"For Willie among the rushes, O!" is beautiful. I wish we could claim it.

Apropos of novels, a publisher told me the other day that he constantly had orders for complete editions of the *Tales by the O'Hara Family*, but finds that the best novels of the brothers Banim are out of print, while some of the worst are still selling merrily.[7] The same is true of Carleton, as far at least as Ireland is concerned.[8] I have made some inquiries and find that some of the worst books he wrote, books written to raise the wind in his time of decadence, are still in print and selling steadily, while his greatest novels, *Fardorougha* and *The Black Prophet*, the two greatest of all Irish stories, can only be found on the second-hand bookstalls. The ways of publishers are mysterious. You are more lucky in America. I saw both novels in a book list in *The Pilot* the other day. But why do you miscall *Fardorougha*, "Farah"?[9]

There was a great autograph sale at Sotheby's last week.[10] Letters of Sheridan's, Burke's, Goldsmith's, Beaconsfield's,

Shelley's, Lamb's and Blake's were put to the hammer.[11] One heard the market value of many a great name. The old man at the high desk has seen the rise and fall of many reputations. His little wooden hammer has registered the degrees of many a decadence. When he was young, Bulwer Lytton must have been at his zenith, his name in all men's mouths, but

> The secret worm ne'er ceases,
> Nor the mouse behind the wall.[12]

The other day his black hammer knocked down an unpublished history of the Lytton family, thirty-one pages long, written by the late Lord Lytton himself, for no more than three pounds, ten shillings, not half what a single letter of Blake's fetched; yet Blake, when he was alive, had no fame at all, and lived constantly close down to the zero, starvation. He and his wife had for some time no more than ten shillings a week between them. For a copy of his poem, *America*, illustrated with what we know to be the most beautiful of his designs, and all colored by hand, he could then get no more than half – it would fetch fifty times the price now – the eight pounds, ten shillings paid for this letter written in shaking strokes by his dying hand.[13] Other letters of his fetched good prices, but this was the most beautiful of all the letters, his own and other people's.

"I have been very near the gates of death," it goes, "and have returned very weak, and an old man feeble and tottering, but not in spirits and life, not in the real man, the imagination which liveth forever. In that I am stronger and stronger as this foolish body decays. . . . Flaxman is gone, and we must all soon follow, everyone to his own eternal house."[14] A letter of George Meredith's was put up and sold for five pounds.[15] A dealer who had bid five shillings seemed greatly surprised. Meredith was a new star. "Who is he?" he muttered. "He must be bidding himself." Among the letters were several from kings and princes. On the whole, potentates went dirt cheap. As I came into the room the auctioneer was crying out, "Any advance on eight shillings for Joseph Bonaparte?"[16]

We have lost an Irish writer whose eminence will be more visible a hundred years hence than it is to-day. The papers have just chronicled the death of the poet Allingham.[17] Shortly before his death he published the last volume of a complete edition of his poems in, I think, four volumes: one volume of short Irish poems and two of miscellaneous lyrics, and one containing *Laurence Bloomfield*, the long agrarian poem Gladstone so much liked. They were brought out by Reeves and Turner.[18] It is not by his long poems he will live. He was the Herrick of the century.[19] Time will take but little toll from his best lyrics; they are a possession for Ireland for ever. His native Ballyshannon will some day be very fond indeed of this child of hers, and may even be a place of literary pilgrimage some day. He will make the little town he loved very familiar to the twentieth century, the little town he sang of so wistfully:

> A wild west Coast, a little Town,
> Where little Folk go up and down,
> Tides flow and winds blow:
> Night and Tempest and the Sea,
> Human Will and Human Fate:
> What is little, what is great?
> Howsoe'er the answer be,
> Let me sing of what I know.[20]

Time has taken a great deal from us this autumn. William Allingham was to most of us merely a distant celebrity, a literary influence. So far as his being alive affected us personally it was merely with irritation at the constant changes for the worse he made in his poems; but Miss O'Leary's austere and sweet face was very near to the heart of most of us Irish scribbling folk.[21] It will be a good while before Dublin seems the same again to the writer of this note. All that was most noble and upright in Irish things was dear to her. The good of Ireland was her constant thought. As a friend she ever drew from one the best one had. She, like her brother, was of the old heroic generation now passing away, the generation whose efforts for Ireland made the present movement possible. Our movement may surpass theirs in success; it will never equal it in self-sacrifice. She had the manner of one who had seen something of great affairs and shared in them, yet under all was a heart ever delighted with simple things, a heart from which rose a little wellspring of song. Her poetry had in its mingled austerity and tenderness a very Celtic quality. It was like a rivulet flowing from mountain snows. She was her brother's lifelong friend and fellow-worker. One thinks of him now sitting among his books in the house at Drumcondra.

W. B. Y.

6 Browning – A New School – Edward Carpenter – Mr. Curtin's *Irish Myths and Folklore†* – Lady Wilde's *Ancient Cures* – Allingham*

London, Eng., Jan. 23

The one literary topic of these latter weeks is, of course, Browning.[1] A great deal – wise and foolish – has been written about him in all the papers, and a great many anecdotes hunted out of the obscure places of people's memories and well dusted and set upon their legs again. Our newspapers and popular preachers seem all to have fastened on Browning's optimism as the one thing about him specially to be commended, and to have magnified it into a central mood. I was talking recently with a great friend of Browning's,[2] who insisted that this way of taking him as a kind of sermon-maker was quite false, that he was only an optimist because he was an artist who chose hopefulness as his method of expression, and that he could be pessimistic when the mood seized him. I think, though going rather too far, there is a good deal of truth in this: thought and speculation were to Browning means of dramatic expression much more than aims in themselves. He did speak out his own thoughts sometimes though – dramatized Robert Browning. I like to think of the great reverie of the Pope in *The Ring and the Book*, with all its serenity and quietism, as something that came straight from Browning's own mind, and gave his own final judgment on many things.[3] But nearly always he evades giving a direct statement by what he called his dramatic method.[4] It is hard to know when he is speaking or when it is only one of his *dramatis personae*. An

* This letter appeared in *BP* for 22 Feb 1890 under the column heading "The Celt in London." HR title: "Browning."

acquaintance of mine said once to him, "Mr. Browning, you are a mystic." "Yes," he answered, "but how did you find it out?"[5]

To Browning thought was mainly interesting as an expression of life. In life in all its phases he seems to have had the most absorbing interest; no man of our day has perhaps approached him there. In a thinker like Herbert Spencer one finds, I imagine, Browning's opposite.[6] Spencer probably cares little for life, except as an expression of thought. He lives in boarding houses surrounded by endless clatter and chatter, but has proved himself equal to the occasion. He has had two buttons, or things like buttons, designed by an aurist† and made exactly to fit his ears. When the clatter and chatter grows too great, he simply thrusts in the buttons and is at once deaf as a post. Eager lion hunters may gather round in vain; he smiles and says, "Yes, yes," but all the time his mind is far off, thinking those abstract generalizations of his. To Robert Browning the world was simply a great boarding house in which people come and go in a confused kind of way. The clatter and chatter to him was life, was joy itself. Sometimes the noise and restlessness got too much into his poetry, and the expression became confused and the verse splintered and broken.

Somewhere in *Wilhelm Meister's Apprenticement* it is told how a father went to see his son, who was being taught at a kind of ideal Goethean school.[7] The master pointed out to him a cloud on the horizon; when it came nearer he saw that it was dust raised by his son who was training horses. The master explained that the boy had proved most fitted to be a groom, and so a groom he was made. A school has just been started in the Peak District of Derbyshire where such a thing might really happen.[8] The prospectus, artistically bound in brown paper and stamped with the five-pointed star of the occultists, is now lying before me. The pupils are to be brought up according to socialistic ideas, taught manual work as well as book learning, and be made accustomed to do everything for themselves. Each boy will be educated, not according to any hard and fast rule or system forced on all as in other schools, but according to the tendencies he shows, whether they be to follow the plow or paint pictures, to train horses or write histories.

Edward Carpenter, the founder, is one of the most picturesque thinkers of the day.[9] He was a fellow of Oxford, with good prospects of all kinds, but found himself getting sadder and sadder. Stepniak met him and turned to a bystander, and said, "That young man is like one of our young Russian anarchists who have a great deal on their minds."[10] Carpenter has turned out a teacher of what must seem to many strangely anarchic notions. Some time after Stepniak saw him he got ill. Some one gave him a copy of Walt Whitman's *Leaves of Grass*.[11] It changed his whole life. When he got well he gave up his fellowship and bought a little patch of land in Derbyshire, where he grew vegetables and sold them on his own hand cart with his own hands for a living. He built a small cottage for himself, and there he and his wife lived. They have found, he believes, the true basis of happiness in simplicity of life, and a proper mingling of manual and mental labor. From time to time this English Thoreau preaches his opinions in essays printed in various more or less socialistic magazines.[12] The last one, "Civilization: Its Cause and Cure," has made some small stir.[13]

Messrs. Little, Brown and Company of Boston have kindly sent me some advance sheets of a book to be called *Irish Myths and Folklore*†.[14] The author is Mr. Jeremiah Curtin. When the completed book comes I will review it at length, for it promises to be the most careful and scientific work on Irish folk-lore yet published. The introduction is most interesting, and contrasts strikingly with the introduction to Campbell's *Tales of the West*† *Highlands*, the great Scotch folk-lore book.[15] Campbell was an imaginative man and a good writer, but his long introduction leaves me at any rate rather bored. Mr. Curtin is not less scientific, but the whole science of folk-lore has grown more imaginative these last twenty years. To the old folk-lorists, fables and fairy tales were a haystack of dead follies, wherein the virtuous might find one little needle of historical truth. Since then Joubainville and Rhys[16] and many more have made us see in all these things old beautiful mythologies wherein ancient man said symbolically all he knew about God and man's soul, once famous religions fallen into ruin and turned into old wives' tales, but still luminous from the rosy dawn of human reverie.

Another folk-lore book I have just been dipping into is Lady Wilde's just published *Ancient Cures, Charms, and Usages of Ireland*.[17] I have had no time to do more at present than read the chapter on Irish proverbs at the end. They are full of a kind of half-Oriental tenderness and fancifulness. A proverb like the following might have come from Saadi: "The lake is not encumbered by its swan; nor the steed by its bridle; nor the sheep by its wool; nor the man by the soul that is in him." This, too, is quite as fine: "God is nigher to us even than the door. God stays long, but He strikes at last."[18] It seems less Oriental because it makes us think of an Irish peasant's cabin where the door is very near. I will return to this book. I want to remind Irish–American readers of the books of folk-lore that are just out or coming. The newly awakened interest in all things Irish is serving our folk-lore well. We have now these *Ancient Cures*, published this week; a little later will come Mr. Curtin's book; then Mr. Nutt of London will bring out Mr. David Fitzgerald's long expected volume, and Dr. Douglas Hyde's English and enlarged edition of his Gaelic *Leabhar Sgéulaigheachta*†.[19] Dr. Hyde, if he comes up to my expectations, will give us the most completely Irish folk-lore book, both in manner and matter, that has yet come from any press. He has already given us in "Teig O'Kane" the best told folk-tale in our literature.[20]

A friend of mine was at Trinity College, Dublin, with a brother of the late William Allingham's, and tells me that Allingham's literary sensitiveness was then greatly troubled by a custom his brother had of writing poems and publishing them in the Ballyshannon papers by way of joke with the name William Allingham at the foot.[21] When one remembers his fastidiousness and his constant habit of polishing and polishing† all he wrote, one can well imagine his indignation. Another brother is now a doctor in Belfast and wrote a capital letter to *The Freeman* the other day, saying that William Allingham's best work was Irish and that he would have written far more effectively in every sense had he remained in Ireland in touch with the people; and that had he done so his political sympathies would certainly have widened instead of remaining ever at the *Laurence Bloomfield* stage.[22] This letter is the truest thing yet written about this most delicate of our poets. Allingham had the making of a great writer in him, but lacked impulse and momentum, the very things national feeling could have supplied. Whenever an Irish writer has strayed away from Irish themes and Irish feeling, in almost all cases he has done no more than make alms for oblivion. There is no great literature without nationality, no great nationality without literature.

W. B. Y.

7 Irish Writers Ought to Take Irish Subjects – *A Sicilian Idyll*†*

London, April 21

Dr. Todhunter of Trinity College, Dublin, has written a charming little pastoral drama, called *A Sicilian Idyll*, and founded on a story in Theocritus.[1] He is bringing it out early in May at the little club theatre here, in this red-bricked and red-tiled suburb, Bedford Park, where so many of us writing people have gathered.[2] It is certainly one of the best things he has written, and has had the good fortune to fall into the hands of a decidedly strong company of mingled amateurs and professionals. I have never heard verse better spoken than by the lady who takes the part of the shepherdess heroine, Amaryllis, and the singing of the chorus of shepherds and shepherdesses – so far as my untechnical ear can judge – rings out finely.[3] The music is being written and superintended through the rehearsal by Mr. Luard-Selby, the author of a number of well known songs and the beautiful church service used in Salisbury Cathedral.[4] The whole play, with its graceful and many-colored Greek costumes, will make a charming unity with the quaint little theatre, with its black panels covered with gilt cupids. If successful, and there is every likelihood of its rousing even more interest than Professor Herkomer's yearly play at Bushey, there is some talk of getting up an annual venture of this same kind, a sort of May Day festival of dramatic poetry.[5] What the play next year will be I cannot say; at present all concerned are deep in Arcadia.[6] In every corner of Dr. Todhunter's study are shepherd crooks and long sticks topped with pine cones to serve as wands for the shepherd priests of Bacchus,[7] who in the first scene enter in slow procession carrying the image of the god and singing his praises, and on the chairs are colored silks to be made into stately costumes.

* This letter appeared in *BP* for 17 May 1890 under the column heading "The Celt in London." HR title: "Ireland's Heroic Age."

The play seems to me much more interesting than his previous drama, *Helena in Troas*, and *Helena* was very successful, its eloquent verse and incomparable staging having made it the feature of its season.[8] The present poem, one need hardly say, is being got up in nothing like so elaborate a manner. Its fine verse will, I believe, quite make amends, and Dr. Todhunter will have as many requests for leave to revive it as in the case of the larger work, and will feel readier to consent. He has several times refused leave to ambitious amateurs who wished to perform *Helena*, in the belief that their resources would be only equal to making it absurd. In one case he consented. It was acted at Exeter in connection with the University Extension Lectures.[9] There is now more talk of its revival in America at a regular theatre and on a proper scale.

Anything that brings, even for a moment, good verse onto the stage is certainly a desirable thing, and yet these Greek plays do not seem to me quite the most valuable work Dr. Todhunter might do just now. They have at best but a reflected glory – modern imitation of the antique. Mr. Justin McCarthy, in an article last week, said that Irishmen leave little impression on contemporary literature – they are absorbed into journalism and politics.[10] This is true, unhappily, though he did not mention all the things that absorb us. Cosmopolitanism is one of the worst. We are not content to dig our own potato patch in peace. We peer over the wall at our neighbor's instead of making our own garden green and beautiful. And yet it is a good garden and there have been great transactions within it, from the death of Cuchulain down to the flight of Michael Dwyer from the burning cabin.[11] Dr. Todhunter could easily have found some pastoral incident among its stories more new† and not less beautiful than anything in Tempe's fabled vales.[12]

The first thing needful if an Irish literature more elaborate and intense than our fine but primitive ballads and novels is to come into being is that readers and writers alike should really know the imaginative periods of Irish history. It is not needful that they should understand them with scholars' accuracy, but they should know them with the heart, so as not to be repelled by what is strange and *outré* in poems or plays or stories taken therefrom. The most imaginative of all our periods was the heroic age and the few centuries that followed it and preceded the Norman Invasion – a time of vast and mysterious shadows,

like the clouds heaped round a sun rising from the sea.[13] Anyone
who knew Standish O'Grady's *History of Ireland: The Heroic Period*,
and Lady Ferguson's *Ireland Before the Conquest*, and perhaps Mrs.
Bryant's *Celtic Ireland* (taking care to forget her prosaic and
baseless notions about the early races) would have a very fair
knowledge of the time.[14] I am glad to see that George Bell and
Sons have just issued a new edition of Lady Ferguson's book. It
should be on the shelves of every Irish student. It is quite
indispensable for reference, going as it does, king by king, saint
by saint, and battle by battle, through the ten or twelve centuries
from early pagan times to the Strongbow invasion.[15] It is a
complete contrast to Mrs. Bryant's volume, published last year.
Mrs. Bryant picks out various matters that interest her, the
Brehon laws, the coming of Patrick, the bards, and so forth, and
writes a chapter upon each.[16] Anyone who really knew these
books would soon begin to look about for a chance of reading
the great old poems and stories themselves. He would find it a
hard thing to do. No publisher has yet ventured to gather into
one volume a few of the best translations of the most famous old
stories – the children† of Lir, Deirdre and the rest.[17] Even then
the best of all would remain hidden – *The Táin Bó*† lies translated
and unpublished on the shelves of the Royal Irish Academy.[18]
There is some demon especially told off to keep from the Irish
reading public the most poetic part of their literature. Even Sir
Samuel Ferguson's great poem, "Conary," not to be confused
with *Congal* – a fine but heavy work – cannot be got for less than
seven shillings and sixpence, though his poetically unimportant
Patrician Papers is buyable for a shilling.[19] Yet, to my mind,
"Conary" is the best poem in modern Irish literature, and
Aubrey de Vere† has said just the same.[20]

Mr. O'Grady, in his Dublin letter to *The Daily Graphic*, has
been criticizing the Irish wolf hounds at the Royal Dublin
Societies' show, from the standpoint of a specialist in the bardic
literature.[21] The breeders, he says, are wholly on a false track.
The ancient wolf hound was, he believes, certainly parti-colored
and probably smooth coated. He quotes the following description
of the favorite hound of Finn:

> Yellow feet had Bran, and red ears;
> She had a white spot on her breast;
> The rest of her body was black with this exception,

She was sprinkled with white over the loins.[22]

By the by, the general tone of these *Daily Graphic* letters makes
it pretty plain that Mr. O'Grady is seeing the error of his ways
and growing into a good Nationalist after all. He was always
out of place – with his enthusiasm for Irish history – among the
West British minority with their would-be cosmopolitanism and
actual provincialism.[23] O'Grady's political vagaries have all
sprung, it seems to me, from that love of force common among
a certain type of literary men. The impatience of minds trained
to see further than they can go, to discover far-off ideals before
the road that leads to them, are responsible for much of it, and
Carlyle for the rest perhaps.[24] It is the fault of a quality†, but
none the less irritating at times, as when, for instance, Mr.
Standish O'Grady in his incomparable monograph, *Red Hugh*,
writes many pages to glorify extremely murderous Sir John
Perrot.[25]

A bundle of about fifty letters written by the peasant poet,
John Keegan, author of "Caoch O'Leary," has just been placed
in my hands.[26] None have ever been published. They are full of
gloomy interest, biographical and other, and as time goes on I
dare say *The Pilot* will hear more from me on this matter. At
present I have but skimmed through their time dimmed pages.
He seems to have had scarcely less wretched a life than Mangan.[27]
The letters are full of lamentations, now for himself, now for
Ireland. He will not hear of hope. "Believe me," he writes (this
was in 1847), "the old leaven of Orangeism and anti-Irishism
will start up from their graves. . . . England is England still; the
Saxon is unchanged – as indomitable as the hyena. Britain is
strong, Ireland is prostrate, fallen, nearly annihilated." "If the
country does not rise," he writes, "we will be trampled into the
unblessed graves of those who have already sunk victims of
hunger and disease," and if on the other hand they shake off
this "vile torpor of slavery and contented beggary" and take to
arms, still he has small hope, but then at any rate they will be
"going like their fathers of old . . . to die nobly rather than live
as paupers, whining and cringing slaves"; and he adds, "should
such things happen may I share this glorious privilege." This
letter, one is not surprised to find by the postscript, was sent to
his correspondent by some little peasant girl whom he could

trust, and not by the post office, a somewhat dangerous place
for such unwatered treason.

I am always especially pleased to come across anything that
throws light on the personal side of Irish history or literature in
the way these Keegan letters do. We have paid far too little
attention to it. How many of the men whose poems delight us
in the ballad books are merely names?†

The Fenian period at any rate is now to find authentic record.
We shall learn what manner of men Stephens and Luby and
Kickham and the others were in the ordinary and extraordinary
affairs of life – and learn it, too, from one of the most polished
writers of our time.[28] Mr. O'Leary is writing his reminiscences,
and his friends are collecting subscribers' names.[29] I have just
been looking through the printed list and find very different
shades of politics. Interlined with names like Sir Charles Gavan
Duffy, Michael Davitt, William O'Brien, Sir Charles Russell
and Professor Galbraith are high Tories like Professor Armstrong,
author of the *Stories of Wicklow*, Dean Gwynn and so forth.[30] I
see by the evening papers that Mr. Parnell has just added his
name. It will be a remarkable list when completed. Seldom have
such diverse opinions been represented on the subscription list
of a political memoir. Mr. O'Leary's powerful personality has
impressed everyone he has come across, and it is now likely that
future generations may receive from his written word something
of the stimulus his personal presence has been to us.

W. B. Y.

8 Dr. Todhunter's *Sicilian Idyll**

London, May 13

William Blake, in one of his little read, or altogether unread, Prophetic Books, has this description of the playgoer at "a tragic scene"†: "The soul drinks murder and revenge, and applauds its own holiness" – a description that applies, and was surely only meant to apply, to melodrama and its easy victory over our susceptibilities.[1] When we look on at the common drama of murder and sentiment, there is something about it that flatters us. We identify ourselves with the hero, and triumph with him in his soon gained conquest over evil. We hate the villain, and remember that we are not as he is. A fine poetic drama, on the other hand, affects us quite differently. It lifts us into a world of knowledge and beauty and serenity. As the Mohammedan leaves his shoes outside the mosque, so we leave our selfhood behind before we enter the impersonal temple of art. We come from it with renewed insight, and with our ideals and our belief in happiness and goodness stronger than before. Melodrama can make us weep more; farce can make us laugh more; but when the curtain has fallen, they leave nothing behind. They bring us nothing, because they demand nothing from us. They are excitements, not influences. The poetic drama, on the other hand, demands so much love of beauty and austere emotion that it finds uncertain footing on the stage at best.

Dr. Todhunter is one of the few moderns who has succeeded in bringing it there even for a moment. His *Helena in Troas*, a few years since, was the talk of a London season.[2] Its sonorous verse, united to the rhythmical motions of the white-robed chorus, and the solemnity of burning incense, produced a semi-religious effect new to the modern stage. He has now come again

---

* This letter appeared in *BP* for 14 June 1890 under the column heading "The Celt in London." HR title: "A Sicilian Idyll."

before that circle of cultivated people who remain faithful to the
rightful Muses, and have not bowed the knee to those two
slatterns, farce and melodrama, with a little verse play of
shepherds and shepherdesses, founded on a story in Theocritus,
and called *A Sicilian Idyll*.[3] It has been acted three times –
Monday, Wednesday and Friday last – at the little club theatre
in Bedford Park, and will be again next Saturday, preliminary
to its probable revival elsewhere. The long room with its black
panels and gilt Cupids has been crowded with really distinguished
audiences.

On Friday I noticed Miss Alma Murray, the creator of the
part of Beatrice in the Shelley Society's performance of *Cenci*;[4]
Miss Winifred Emery, now performing in Buchanan's *Tomboy*†;
Mr. Cyril Maude; Mr. Terriss, just returned for a time to the
Lyceum fold; and Lady Archibald Campbell, of pastoral drama
celebrity;[5] and among social and literary notables, Mrs. Jopling
Rowe; Miss Mathilde Blind, whose translation of Marie
Bashkirtseff's Diary is making a stir just now; Mrs. Charles
Hancock, of the Woman's Liberal Association; Mr. Theodore
Watts, the critic; and Miss May Morris, daughter of the poet
of *The Earthly Paradise*, and herself well known for her
embroideries.[6]

The story proved to be a very simple one – the play had just
enough action to sustain the verse without letting it seem
monotonous, and no more. A proud shepherdess, Amaryllis, is
kissed by a shepherd, Alcander†, against her will, and before
her anger is cool, sees him as she supposes making love to her
friend, Thestylis†. Believing that he kissed her in mockery, she
tries to kill him with an incantation before "it becomes a
shepherd's tale." He is brought in dying to her feet. She is at
once stricken with remorse. There is only one thing that can
save him now, he cries – her love. But did he not woo her friend,
Thestylis?† "It was but in pretty sport," he answers. Thestylis†
bid him do so "to move her amorous Daphnis, who stood by."
The lovers are reconciled and all goes well. There is also a
secondary story that crosses and recrosses the main theme, the
story of the love of Thestylis† and Daphnis. This meagre plot
was made fascinating and absorbing by fine verse, beautiful
scenery and picturesque costumes, the shepherds in their leopard
skins, and the shepherdesses in their many colored robes, and
the scene with its far glimpse of the blue Mediterranean, and its

festoons of grape and vine leaves, being a sight to dream of. The play itself was full of human interest and fine poetic passages. It made the Golden Age seem very near. The main impression was one of a divine innocence and youthfulness, the freshness of a world still shining with the dew of dawn. There was one place where the chorus of shepherd youths and maidens, who sing hymns to Bacchus, seemed to strike the keynote of the whole play. They bid Bacchus come crowned "with purple clusters," and they will greet him "with seasonable mirth":[7]

> But come not, as to those who love thee not,
> Thy panther Moenads with their panther kin
> Furiously leaping to the frantic din
> Of clashing cymbals, their flush'd faces hot,
> Smear'd from limbs torn in the glare
> Of blazing torches reeling through the smoke!
> Come, worshipt of our folk,
> Lord of the mellowing year! Come, for we come
> With ankles splash'd with vintage, honouring thee
> With must from foaming vats; bless now thy home,
> Dear as gray Thebes, or Nysa of sweet air,
> Thy own laughing Sicily!

They are a gentle people, living far from clamor and contest, and as we watch them moving to and fro, and dancing their shepherd dances, something of their own innocence seems to sink into the heart. It is this influence, this mood, that lifts the play out of the dust of common life and makes it poetry. It was this that made the audience feel that they had seen something new and memorable, and made the play successful. When the curtain fell, one heard on all sides, "How pretty!" "How beautiful!" "I would not have missed it for the world." It was not merely the play itself that gave one this feeling, for acting, scenery and verse were all a perfect unity. It was like a dream. There were details here and there that I would have wished different, though nothing important enough to take from the charm of the final impression. My literary personality is not the same as Dr. Todhunter's – no two men's are – and I could find fault, here and there, according to my different lights; but where I see so much to admire and be grateful for, I do not care to do otherwise than praise, and will not trouble *The Pilot* with the few small and mainly verbal changes I should like to see.

The acting deserves a paragraph to itself. Mrs. Edward Emery, who took the part of Amaryllis, won universal praise with her striking beauty and subtle gesture and fine delivery of the verse. Indeed her acting was the feature of the whole performance that struck one most, after the verse itself. I do not know that I have any word too strong to express my admiration for its grace and power. Miss Lily Linfield acted the part of Thestylis† with great verve and go, though her ear for verse was not by any means perfect. Her dance with cymbals before the statue of Bacchus was very fine, and well deserved its enthusiastic encore. The male parts were taken by amateurs. Mr. Paget, the artist, looked the athletic Alcander perfectly, and acted well, though not quite so well as the versatile and well known gentleman, journalist, solicitor, lecturer, novelist, authority on violins, writer on chiromancy and, I believe, war correspondent who prefers to remain hidden under the name of Mr. Smith. Mr. Paget's part was, however, much the more difficult. The music for the chorus was composed by Mr. Luard-Selby, the author of an admired church service and of a number of songs. The scenery was painted by Mr. Baldry and Mr. Arthur Lemon.[8]

W. B. Yeats

9   Rose Kavanagh:
Death of a Promising Young Irish Poet*

London, March 17

Miss Rose Kavanagh was, when she died, still a possibility, still – the future.[1] She has left but a very little bundle of songs and stories, the mere May blossoming of a young inspiration whose great promise was robbed of fulfillment, first by ill health and then by an early death. Readers of future anthologies of Irish verse will know the name of Kavanagh from "Lough Bray" and "St. Michan's Churchyard," but they will not know the noble, merry and gentle personality that produced them.[2] Death has robbed it of its clear expression. Is there anything sadder than unfulfilled promise? Is it not the very essence of all sadness? It makes one dream that maybe in the world we go to we shall carry to conclusion the tasks left uncompleted in the world we hasten from, that Christian will again take to his scrip and staff in that distant land, but gaily and with perhaps no little exultation.[3]

Miss Rose Kavanagh was born in Tyrone, at Killadroy, in the year 1860.[4] Presently the family moved to Mullaghmore, and the Avonban, the White River, gave place to the many fabled Blackwater, whose wandering course she has celebrated in lines that are tolerably well known through being included in Mr. Sparling's *Irish Minstrelsy*.[5] How prettily the poem tells of its rise,

> Fed with a thousand invisible rills,
> Girdled around with the awe of the hills.

The next verse is worth quoting, for in it Miss Kavanagh seems to me to have reached a delicacy of expression and thought that reminds one of Kickham at his best.[6] The lines, too, are full of

---

* This letter appeared in *BP* for 11 Apr 1891. HR title: "Rose Kavanagh."

that impassioned love for her country which was so deeply rooted
in her heart:

> Many a ruin, both abbey and cot,
> Sees in your mirror a desolate lot.
> Many an ear lying shut far away
> Hearkened the tune that your dark ripples play.
> One – I remember her better than all –
> She knew every legend of cabin and hall;
> Wept when the Law and the Famine-time met,
> Sang how the Red Hand was radiantly set
> Over the victors who fought at the Ford,
> Over the sweep of O'Neill's Spanish sword –
> O our own river! Where is she to-night?
> Where are the exiles whose homes are in sight?[7]

The last verse begins finely with

> Once in the Maytime your carol so sweet
> Found out my heart in the midst of the street;

and ends with a note of that tender sadness so very near to all
she has written. Was it a shadow of the tomb?

A little westward of her home was Knockmany, celebrated by
a wild, humorous tale of Carleton's, and not far off was the
homestead where he himself was born and bred.[8]

Miss Kavanagh came presently to Dublin, and studied art for
a time at the Royal Dublin Society, but before long began to
contribute articles and stories to the Dublin papers.[9] When the
Ladies' Land League had to find lady substitutes for imprisoned
journalists, she took a prominent part.[10] The Government even
did her the honor to appoint a special detective to watch her.
Strange Government to whom a bevy of young ladies was so
awe inspiring! It must have been at this time, or just before it,
that Miss Kavanagh inspired Kickham with his pleasant mock-
serious little song, "The Rose of Knockmany."[11] When the
Ladies' Land League had gone by, she contributed many short
stories to Irish magazines, notably to the now extinct *Irish
Fireside*, and for the last two or three years of her life managed
the Uncle Remus Club for children, started by Mrs. Dwyer Gray

in connection with *The Irish Fireside*, and continued in *The Weekly Freeman*.[12]

In 1888 a number of her poems were included in *Poems and Ballads of Young Ireland*, a little volume which has had a sale sufficient at any rate to warrant its present new and cheaper form.[13] It was planned out by a number of us, including Miss Rose Kavanagh, Miss Katharine Tynan, Miss Ellen O'Leary, Dr. Todhunter and Dr. Douglas Hyde, the Gaelic scholar, with the aim, I hope not altogether unfulfilled, of adding another link, however small, to the long chain of Irish song that unites decade to decade.[14] Every movement of Irish nationality has had its singers, and it seemed to us that our own times should not be dumb, even though the listeners were but few, and the singers' voices drowned in the roar of the market place. Miss Kavanagh's contributions were full of most delicate expression and tender music. At the time I often found myself repeating these lines from her "Lough Bray":

> The amber ripples sang all day,
> And singing spilled their crowns of white
> Upon the beach, in thin pale spray
> That streaked the sober sand with light.[15]

Perhaps, however, her most finished contribution was "St. Michan's Churchyard." It is hardly needful to tell Irish readers that Emmet is supposed to be buried in St. Michan's Churchyard.[16] The following are, I think, the best verses:

> Inside the city's throbbing heart
> One spot I know set well apart
> From life's hard highway, life's loud mart.
>
> A little, lonely, green graveyard,
> The old church tower its solemn guard,
> The gate with naught but sunbeams barred;
>
> While other sunbeams went and came,
> Above the stone which waits the name,
> His land must write with Freedom's flame.

The slender elm above that stone,
Its summer wreath of leaves had thrown
Around the heart so quiet grown.

A robin, the bare boughs among,
Let loose his little soul in song –
Quick liquid gushes, fresh and strong!

And quiet heart, and bird, and tree,
Seemed linked in some strange sympathy
Too fine for mortal eye to see –

But full of balm and soothing sweet,
For those who sought that calm retreat;
For aching breast and weary feet.[17]

The manner of such poetry much more closely resembles Kickham and Casey than Davis and Mangan.[18] Like most of the best Irish verse of recent years it is meditative and sympathetic, rather than stirring and energetic: the trumpet has given way to the viol and the flute. It is easy to be unjust to such poetry, but very hard to write it. It springs straight out of the nature from some well-spring of refinement and gentleness. It makes half the pathos of literary history. When one reads some old poem of the sort one says: "What a charming mind had this writer! How gladly I should have met and talked with such a one!" and then one gathers about one, like a garment, the mist of regret.

For the last year or so Miss Kavanagh was able to do but little writing. Consumption was gradually doing its work. The winter of 1889 she spent in the south of France in a vain search for health.[19] On her return to Ireland she went to live at her native village, where she died a few days ago.[20] Her last poem was a memorial lyric prefixed to the poems of her friend, Miss Ellen O'Leary, who had herself addressed to Miss Kavanagh a little poem beginning:

Brave eyes! brave eyes, how beautiful you are;
Not dark as night, or gleaming like a star,
But all alight with earnestness and truth,
And the fond, foolish dreams of fervid youth.

Brave eyes! brave eyes, and trustful too, as brave,
In which thought follows thought, as wave on wave;
True mirrors clear, reflecting every feeling,
Now bright, now blank, now full of soft appealing.[21]

W. B. Yeats

10   Some Recent Books by Irish Writers*

Your Celt in London has been so busy about certain affairs of his own that he has let months go by without sending you any of his random notes, and let quite a pile of Irish books collect and lie unreviewed upon his table. Among those on which the dust lies least thickly – for it is among the last arrivals – is *Lays of Country, Home and Friends* (Sealy, Bryers and Walker: Dublin),† a little green book of poems by Miss Ellen O'Leary.[1] She was able to partly correct the proofs, but did not live to look on the completed book; our Irish printers – or whoever was responsible – have been laggards indeed. If I remember rightly, Mr. Rolleston's introduction was written and in proof almost, if not quite, two years ago.[2] However, it is a book worth waiting for. I am distinctly of opinion† that Miss O'Leary was a better writer than either "Mary" or "Eva" of *The Nation*.[3] She had not the good fortune to live in a period when all Ireland was supremely interested in songs and ballads, when *The Nation* newspaper was filling the four corners of the land with lay and lyric. Had she done so, her name would long ago have been as well known as theirs. As it is, no maker of Irish anthologies will neglect this little green book. The following is a song in the old sense of the word, that is to say, a singable poem worthy of good music. The compilers of our songbooks, ballad sheets and the like, should garner it:

> I sit beside my darling's grave,
>   Who in the prison died,
> And tho' my tears fall thick and fast,
>   I think of him with pride:
> Ay, softly fall my tears like dew,
> For one to God and Ireland true.

---

* This letter appeared in *BP* for 18 Apr 1891 under the column heading "The Celt in London." HR title: "The Poems of Ellen O'Leary."

"I love my God o'er all," he said,
    "And then I love my land,
And next I love my Lily sweet,
    Who pledged me her white hand:
To each – to all – I'm ever true,
To God – to Ireland – and to you."

No tender nurse his hard bed smoothed
    Or softly raised his head;
He fell asleep and woke in heaven
    Ere I knew he was dead;
Yet why should I my darling rue?
He was to God and Ireland true.

Oh! 'tis a glorious memory,
    I'm prouder than a queen
To sit beside my hero's grave
    And think on what has been:
And, oh, my darling, I am true
To God – to Ireland – and to you.[4]

"The Emigrant's Return," "A Voice," "Home to Carriglea," "A Legend of Tyrone," "Ireland's Dead," and "My Own Galtees" are favorites of mine and will, I believe, drift into our song and ballad books. They are all written according to the Davis tradition, rather than the more elaborate one of Moore and his imitators.[5] Nothing could be more simple, nothing more sincere. The book has for frontispiece a good photograph of the author, and is introduced by Mr. T. W. Rolleston, who describes Miss O'Leary's connection with the Fenian movement, and by Sir Charles Gavan Duffy, who writes six pages of criticisms of the poems.[6]

Two books that have been lying on my table several weeks are *Poems* (Ward and Downey: London),† by John Francis O'Donnell, and *Whisper!* (Kegan Paul: London) by† Miss Wynne.[7] They differ in every way from the simple ballads I have just been noticing. They are elaborate, ornate and literary, and show a strong influence from English writers. The Southwark Irish Literary Club, who at great labor have gathered together O'Donnell's poems from old magazines and newspapers, must forgive my bracketing their bulky volume with Miss Wynne's little venture.[8] I know quite well that O'Donnell has stood the test of time to some extent, for he died as long ago as 1874, and that Miss Wynne is but a writer of pretty, skilful and rather trivial little verses. They both, however, belong to the same school of Irish writers. Both have read much English literature, and have taken from it, rather than from their own minds and the traditions of their own country, the manner and matter of their poetry. They have left behind them the simple national ballad manner, without proving strong enough to reach that more ample and subtle style the greatest writers learn, in part, from knowing and modelling themselves upon the best masters of verse and prose in every country of the world. To criticise Miss Wynne in this fashion is certainly rather like breaking a butterfly on a wheel; but O'Donnell had so much gift for expression that he might have reached it in some measure† in happier circumstances. A notion of what he might have done may be gathered from the following opening to an ode on "The Four Masters":

Where sleep the Four? What blessed earth –
What aisles, with burning windows, hold
In porphyry, or red rough gold,
The sages of the South and North?
Where rest the men who, whilst this Isle
Was barred with black oppression's cloud,
Faced death and dungeons with a smile,
Nor held their heads less straight and proud?
They crept to peace in far Louvain,
Shrouded in the Franciscan grain:
Caring no more to greet the sun,
The hand's work and the heart's work done.

Beside the sea of Donegal –
The coasts beloved of Gaul and Spain –
From sunrise to the sunset's wane,
Their shadows dropped from wall to wall
Through years of change. Few watched their toil,
And fewer still the glory prized
Of saving from a trampled spoil
The truths a warring world despised:
There in that narrow little room,

Our martyrs' palms took fresher bloom,
And o'er those rudely sanded floors
Moved poets, kings and warriors.[9]

Here is fulness of music and richness of phrase – despite a
commonplace metaphor here and there like that about "oppression's cloud"; but as the ode goes on, it becomes monotonous
and shows, like most of his work, frequent Tennysonian manner-
isms that spoil its originality.[10] With more leisure or more culture,
O'Donnell might have discovered a style quite his own. As it
was, he was stifled by journalism. "Talking of work," he wrote
in 1872, "since Sunday, two columns of notes, two columns of
London gossip, and a leader, one column, and two columns of
verse for *The Nation*. For *Catholic Opinion*, two pages of notes and
a leader. For *Illustrated Magazine*, three poems and five columns
of story."[11] A style is not picked up in this fashion. A career of
this kind for a man of imagination, if voluntary, is a crime; if
involuntary, the greatest of misfortunes; and yet O'Donnell
seems to have been rather proud of it. "I write verse faster than
prose," he said.[12] Oh thou great abyss of inane facility, how
many fine natures hast thou swallowed – above all, how many
Celtic ones? An unkind Providence has granted to us Irish folk
a terrible love of immediate results, wholly fatal to great work.
It will leave us with the approach of more orderly and successful
times. We shall learn then to trust the future sufficiently to work
for it. At present three sentences of mingled admiration and
blame, which I heard the wittiest Irishman of our day apply to
his countrymen, are in some manner true. "We are," he said,
"too poetical to be poets [great ones, he meant]. We are the
greatest talkers since the Greeks. We are a nation of brilliant
failures."[13] A love for immediate results makes us pour out our
faculties on the mere arts of life. Hence, perhaps, our humor and
that charm our bitterest enemies – Mr. Froude,[14] for instance –
are so ready to find in Irish character; but hence, too, the absence
of any very great epic and ample modern Irish book or poem.
We will change all that when prosperity has taught us to trust
in the morrow, and live for it. The Celt has done great works in
the past – witness *The Táin Bó*† and all that hoard of epic tales –
and will, beyond question, do great works in the future.[15]
Meanwhile he has created a modern ballad literature, no common
feat in these sophisticated times.

I find some token of a new state of things, such as I have foretold, in the fourth book that awaits mention. It is the last arrival, has only lain for about a month atop of O'Donnell's poems, waiting the writing of this letter. It is a collection of folk tales under the name of *Beside the Fire* (Nutt: London),† partly new and partly long expected translations of a portion of the *Leabhar Sgéulaigheachta*†, as Dr. Hyde has named his book of Gaelic stories.[16] If Dr. Hyde carries out his intentions, and continues to gather and write out, in that perfect style of his, traditions, legends and old rhymes, he will give the world one of those monumental works whose absence from modern Irish literature I have been lamenting. We have had Gaelic scholars of great learning, but none who have had the literary culture of Mr. Hyde. He has both knowledge and imagination, a somewhat rare combination, and I think he may be set down as the coming man in Gaelic scholarship. His name is gradually spreading beyond the four Sees† of Ireland. An English authority of note said to me a while since, when speaking of Dr. Hyde's telling of a particular legend, "There never was such a folk-lorist."[17] Certainly, at any rate, we have never had such a one, and if he makes his work as exhaustive as it is fine, no country of the world will have seen his master.

I may mention among forthcoming books an Irish historical romance by the younger Standish O'Grady. It deals with the Tyrone rebellion and the battle of Kinsale.[18] Your Celt in London vows some day to give it a whole column, if he can run so large a cargo across the harbor bar of editorial watchfulness.

W. B. Yeats

11 Dr. Todhunter's New Play*

London, June 27

Dr. Todhunter is known, or should be, to Irish people for his volume of Irish poems with its charming versions of "The Children of Lir" and "The Sons of Turann," but to the London public he is best known for his plays.[1] *Helena in Troas*, when acted four or five years ago, was an immense success. It not merely drew the cultivated public who care for poetry or for Greek drama, but filled the theatre with the ordinary run of theatre-goers. It was such a success, indeed, that several hundreds of pounds were taken at the first performance alone.

Much of this was doubtless due to the wonderful stage – the only exact reproduction of the stage of ancient Athens seen in the modern world – and to the no less wonderful stage management of E. W. Godwin.[2] Modern playgoers do not greatly care for poetry when it comes with no recommendation besides itself, but are ready enough to tolerate and, perhaps, even enjoy it, when they are lifted out of what Shelley called "the trance of real life" by beautiful and strange surroundings.[3] Hence they admired *Helena*, as before that they had admired the performance of Fletcher's *Faithful Shepherdess*, when acted in the open air at Combe by Lady Archibald Campbell's pastoral players.[4] There is a small, perhaps growing, public that does indeed care for poetry for its own sake, but it in no way resembles the great public of the theatres. Dr. Todhunter's *Sicilian Idyll*, when acted at Bedford Park last year, won the applause of this small body. For six or seven nights it filled the little theatre – a pleasant sight for all who hope to see true literary drama once more.

Now, however, Dr. Todhunter has tried to reach the common run of playgoers once more. Last week he revived the *Idyll* at the Vaudeville, and preluded it with a new play founded on

---

* This letter appeared in *BP* for 1 Aug 1891. HR title: "The Poison Flower."

Hawthorne's "Rappaccini's Daughter," and called *The Poison Flower*.[5] The small public who love poetry was there, and enthusiastic, and the larger public came also, but not in great numbers, and showed by the comments I could overhear how strange a thing poetry and romance have come to be in its ears, when not sanctioned by long usage, as is the case with Shakespeare, or made seem† possible by surroundings strange enough to break "the trance of real life."

Both the *Idyll* and *The Poison Flower* are much more dramatic than *Helena in Troas*, and lacked only its solemn staging, its rhythmic chorus and its ascending incense to move the audience much more powerfully. As it was, they needed†, coming in fresh from the trivialities of the world of shops and tea tables, the "once upon a time" that begins the make believe of fairy tales. Many people have said to me that the surroundings of *Helena* made them feel religious. Once get your audience in that mood, and you can do anything with them†.

I described *A Sicilian Idyll* to you at the time of its first performance, and so need only speak now of *The Poison Flower*. Dr. Todhunter has taken the story of the young girl who grew up among the poisoned flowers of the magician's garden until she, too, was poisonous as the flowers themselves, and added to it some hint of mystical significance, no less than much secondary incident. The story, as it is told in *Mosses from an Old Manse*, beautiful as it is, has always seemed to me a little fanciful and arbitrary. I never quite could get it out of my head that Hawthorne wanted to make one's flesh creep like the little boy in *The†* *Winter's Tale*, and did not much care how he managed it.[6] In the play it becomes a much more solid thing. One finds it quite easy to believe that this worn-looking Kabalist, who crosses the stage with cat-like tread, has in his mind some wild dream for the regeneration of men, and that he is bringing up in the garden, whose strange and exotic flowers rise before one, a new Eve to be mother of a new race to whom the poisons of the world – its diseases and crimes – shall do no hurt, for they will carry within themselves "the poison that drives out poison."[7] The copy of the Kabala that lies upon my own desk pleads for him, and tells us that such men lived, and may well have dreamed just such a dream, in the mystic Middle Ages. In becoming a thinker of a particular school, he has obtained the historical reality lacked by the Rappaccini of Hawthorne; and by the occult intention of his experiment being explained to us he has been united to many men in many ages. Even in our own day men dream of "the poison that drives out poison." Witness the recent rumor that some modern but still Italian Rappaccini had discovered the bacillus of old age.[8]

I hear some talk of the play being put on in America. It might prosper with you. Browning – I do not think any of his recent biographers have mentioned it – got three hundred and fifty dollars from the American revival of *A Blot in the 'Scutcheon*; not a large sum, but certainly more than it ever fetched in England.[9] You seem, indeed, to have much more liking for the verse drama than people have this side of the water. Dr. Todhunter's play does not pretend to be great poetry, but it is charming, romantic and interesting, and may please some portion of the many with you as ardently as it has pleased the few with us. You, however, will not have the chance of seeing the charming actress Dr. Todhunter has discovered and written the part of heroine for. Her performance of Beatrice, the girl who lived among the poisoned flowers, was as intense and passionate as her rendering of the rôle of Amaryllis, in the *Idyll*, was graceful and self-contained. She made her first appearance in any important part on the Bedford Park stage, but has since then become well known to theatre-goers through her acting in Ibsen's *Rosmersholm*†.[10] She will always, however, be best, I believe, in poetic drama, her exquisite recitation being no small part of her charm.

W. B. Yeats

12   The Celt in Ireland*

I do not head this letter "The Celt in London" as my wont is, for I am back in Ireland for the time being, and writing out on the lawn of an old Irish thatched farmhouse.[1] An apple tree covered with red apples shakes softly before me in the sunlight, and the paper on which I write rests on the stone top of a sundial. Behind me in the hedge a grasshopper has just lifted his shrill song. To talk of books at all on this green clover spotted grass seems sadly out of keeping, unless, indeed, it be some dreamy romance like *Marius the Epicurean*, whose golden sentences, laden as with sleepy sunlight, I have been reading slowly and fitfully since morning, taking the book up for a moment and then laying it down again, and letting my mind stray off to the red apples and the shadowing leaves before me.

But then *Marius the Epicurean* is not writ in my bond. With Irish literature and Irish thought alone have I to do. And yet the doctrines I have just been studying in Pater's jewelled paragraphs – the Platonic theory of spiritual beings having their abode in all things without and within us, and thus uniting all things, as by a living ladder of souls, with God Himself – have some relation to those very matters of Irish thought that bring me to Ireland just now.[2]

I am here looking for stories of the fairies and the phantoms, and are not these spiritual beings of Plato but the phantoms and fairies of philosophy? I have been away in County Down, looking almost in vain among its half-Scotch people for the legends I find so plentiful in the West. I heard, indeed, of two people who are said to have been killed by the fairies for taking up fairy thorn trees, in the last eight months, and of certain phantoms living among the marshes, but got no legends of any interest; and now I am faring somewhat better here in County Dublin.[3] A few minutes ago, an old woman came out of the kitchen and went into the yard, which I can see from my seat by the sundial,

* This letter appeared in *BP* for 12 Sep 1891. HR title: "A Ballad Singer."

and fed some chickens. In her childhood she was fairy-struck (she insists) on a fairy rath, and made ill for months. Yet people tell me that the belief in fairies is gone. Ah, no! There are still stories told with most entire faith in every quiet county barony. In the towns the fairy tradition is gone indeed, but even there the supernatural survives in visions and ghost-hauntings.

I was the other day sitting reading on the steps of the country house in Down where I was staying, when a ballad singer came up the avenue with his little fluttering strips of paper flying in the wind, and asked me would I like to hear an old Waterloo man sing a song. The man was clearly a liar, as he could not be more than forty or forty-five years old at most; but none the less I listened to him, and bought some of his ballad sheets.[4] The verses proved to be mainly rubbish of the usual kind, but there was among them one poem of great beauty. I at first thought it must be a reprint from some of our Irish poets; but then I do not remember having read it, and I know our Irish poets pretty thoroughly. It must, after all, be, I think, a genuine street ballad. Here are three of the verses:

> I'll sing to-night of that fairy land
>   In the lap of the ocean set,
> And of all the lands I have travelled o'er
>   It's the loveliest I have met;
> Where the willows weep and the roses sleep,
>   And the balmy breezes blow,
> For that dear old land, that sweet old land,
>   Where the ancient shamrocks grow.
>
> I'll sing of that lovely old churchyard,
>   Where my father's bones are laid,
> In clusters stand those ruins grand
>   Which tyrant foes have made;
> And I'll strike the harp with a mournful touch,
>   While the glistening tears will flow,
> For that dear old land, that sweet old land,
>   Where the ancient shamrocks grow.
>
> I'll sing of Ireland's ancient days,
>   When our sires were kingly men,
> Who led the chase and manly race

Through forest, field and glen;
Whose only word was the shining sword,
    And their pen – the patriot's blow!
For that dear old land, that sweet old land,
    Where the ancient shamrocks grow.

What infinite sadness there is in these verses! What wild beauty!
The man when he sold them to me did so timidly, mistaking
me, most evidently, for one of the loyal minority.[5] "There is a
deal of liberality in them," he said, in quaint apology.

The song about "The Ancient Shamrocks" is the best piece
of Irish literature I have met since I came to Ireland; much
better in every way, it certainly is, than this new Irish magazine –
The Irish Monthly Illustrated Journal – lying in its yellow cover
across the blue shadow of the dial before me. The thing is well
written enough, but what in the name of goodness has an Irish
magazine to do with Mr. Stead and the German Emperor?[6] If
people want to know about either, they will go to the English
periodicals. An Irish magazine should give us Irish subjects.
Have we no Irish sins to denounce, no Irish virtues to encourage,
no Irish legends to record, no Irish stories to tell, that we must
sing the praises of the Emperor of Germany and Mr. Stead, both
of them gentlemen who have no need of a trumpeter? Why
should we feebly imitate the methods and matter of English
magazines? At the same time I am very glad to see this new
monthly, especially as it is not all given up to foreign subject
matter, but does make some slight reference to Dublin men and
Dublin things. It has a very clever editor in Mr. Eyre, and it
may not be his fault that it is not more Irish. I do not know
what difficulties in the way of want of pence he, like most Irish
editors, has to contend against.

When I say that "The Ancient Shamrocks" is the best thing
I have seen this side of the water, I do not mean to belittle Miss
Katharine Tynan's *A Nun, Her Friends and Her Order* (Kegan
Paul).† I saw it before I left the other side. It is very picturesque
and charming, and brings the nunnery life most vividly before
the eyes of the reader. Well written as it is, however, it cannot
compete with Miss Tynan's verse. Her new book of poems, the
contents of which I have seen, will, I feel certain, give her a
higher position than anything she has yet done.[7] It will quite
overshadow this *Nun, Her Friends and Her Order*; and yet the *Nun*

is a good book, and I would say much more about it were I not
somewhat astray among those saints and holy people. Besides,
the grasshoppers have begun to chant in the hedge once more.
I listen to them and let all books and bookish things die away
out of my mind. What do they sing of so gaily? They were
singing before Troy was built, or seven-gated Thebes repelled
the encompassing armies; Socrates heard them on the banks of
the Ilissus; and still they sing on as of old.[8] What do they sing
of? Of the loves and wars of grasshoppers, and of the joy of men
living in the sunlight. I will put aside my pen and paper and let
my mind, listening to their song, go away and dream among the
green shadows and the red† apples.

W. B. Yeats

13   The Rhymers' Club*

In France literature divides itself into schools, movements and circles. At one moment the Decadents, at another the Symbolists, to-day the Parnassians, tomorrow the Naturalists, hold the public ear and win acceptance for their theory and practice of literature.[1] In England the writers do not form groups, but each man works by himself and for himself, for England is the land of literary Ishmaels.[2] It is only among the sociable Celtic nations that men draw nearer to each other when they want to think and dream and work. All this makes the existence of the Rhymers' Club the more remarkable a thing.[3] Into this little body, as about a round table of rhyme, have gathered well nigh all the poets of the new generation who have public enough to get their works printed at the cost of the publisher, and some not less excellent, who cannot yet mount that first step of the ladder famewards. Not that the Rhymers' Club is a school of poets in the French sense, for the writers who belong to it resemble each other in but one thing: they all believe that the deluge of triolets and rondeaus has passed away, and that we must look once more upon the world with serious eyes and set to music – each according to his lights – the deep soul of humanity. "What is the good of writing poetry at all now?" said the other day a noted verse writer whose fame was at its height ten years ago. "Sonnets are played out and ballades and rondeaus are no longer novel, and nobody has invented a new form."[4] All, despairing, cry of the departing age, but the world still goes on, and the soul of man is ever young, and its song shall never come to an end. The names of some few of the Rhymers may have already been blown across the Atlantic, though more probably they have not, for all but one are of the very newest literary generation. There is Arthur Symons, who has made the music halls of London and Paris his peculiar study, and set forth their gaieties and tragedies in even, deftest verse,

* This letter appeared in *BP* for 23 Apr 1892 under the column heading "The Celt in London." HR title: "The Rhymers' Club."

and John Davidson, who has just published a series of poems on a Scotch music hall.[5] In both writers one finds that search for new subject matter, new emotions, which so clearly marks the reaction from that search for new forms merely, which distinguished the generation now going out. "He is no poet who would not go to Japan for a new form," wrote a distinguished member of the Gosse, Lang and Dobson school.[6]

Arthur Symons is a scholar in music halls as another man might be a Greek scholar or an authority on the age of Chaucer.[7] He has studied them for purposes of literature and remained himself, if I understand him rightly, quite apart from their glitter and din. He has gone to travel among them as another man might go to travel in Persia, and has done it thoroughly, being familiar with those of many cities. John Davidson, upon the other hand, claims to have lived his verses. In the Prologue to his just published *In a Music Hall* (Ward and Downey),† one reads:

> I did as my desk-fellows did;
> With a pipe and a tankard of beer,
> In a music-hall, rancid and hot,
> I lost my soul night after night.
> It is better to lose one's soul,
> Than never to stake it at all.[8]

No two attitudes towards the world and literature could be more different, and despite the community of subject no two styles could be more dissimilar than those of John Davidson and Arthur Symons. One has more fire and enthusiasm, and the other more art and subtlety. Fine as much (notably the haunting and wonderful "Selene Eden") certainly is, I find my enjoyment checked continually by some crudity of phrase.[9] The din and glitter one feels were far too near the writer. He has not been able to cast them back in imaginative dimness and distance. Of Mr. Symons' method I will speak at length when his book comes to me. I have but seen stray poems and judge from them that, despite most manifest triumphs from time to time, he will sometimes fail through gaining too easily that very dimness and distance I have spoken of. He will, perhaps, prove to be too far from, as Mr. Davidson is too near to, his subject. I must say that the author of *In a Music Hall* is entirely successful in some

of the romantic poems that follow the "Music Hall" verses.
Notable is that radiant poem in which the gleeman tells how

> Starry truth
> Still maintains a changing strife
> With the purple dreams of youth;

and notable also are "For Lovers," and parts of "Anselm and
Bianca."[10]

Both writers are, whether they succeed or fail, interesting signs
of the times. Not merely are they examples of that desire for new
subject matter of which I have spoken, but of the reaction
from the super-refinement of much recent life and poetry. The
cultivated man has begun a somewhat hectic search for the
common pleasures of common men and for the rough accidents
of life. The typical young poet of our day is an aesthete with a
surfeit, searching sadly for his lost Philistinism,[11] his heart full
of an unsatisfied hunger for the commonplace. He is an Alastor
tired of his woods and longing for beer and skittles.[12]

The most like Alastor in appearance among the Rhymers is
certainly Richard Le Gallienne.[13] *The Review of Reviews* has made
many familiar with his refined Shelley-like face, and his own
Book-Bills† *of Narcissus* – a half romance, half autobiography –
with his moods and his history.[14] The longing for Philistine beer
and skittles has perhaps beset him less ardently than the bulk
of his fellows, and he still prides himself on wearing the ambrosial
locks of the poet. The longing for a new subject has filled him
as full as his neighbors, however, and has led him to publish a
book of poems, *Volumes in Folio*, which has dealt with nothing in
the world but the buying and treasuring of rare books.[15] A very
pleasant glamour of Keats-like romance did he weave about
them, too.[16] But *Volumes in Folio* is ancient history, and I have to
do but with the present and the future. Lionel Johnson, who has
somewhere about him a long poem called "Gloria Mundi," full
of Catholic theology, and George Greene, who is writing a whole
book of verse on the *Inferno* of Dante, are other typical members.[17]
Ernest Rhys, of Camelot fame, and T. W. Rolleston are constant
frequenters.[18] I need not multiply names. They will all be on the
title page of the forthcoming *Book of the Rhymers' Club* (Elkin
Mathews, Bodley Head, Vigo St.),† the manifesto of the circle.[19]

I said that all, with one exception, belong to the newest literary generation. That exception is important, for it is Dr. Todhunter, who has just published a shilling edition of his book of Irish poems,[20] and so concerns us more than all the others. If we do not take care of our own singers, who will? The book is called *The Banshee* and is sold by Sealy, Bryers and Walker, Middle Abbey Street, Dublin. I need not say much now about it, for it was reviewed enthusiastically and fully by all the Irish–American papers on its first appearance a couple of years ago. In it Dr. Todhunter follows in the footsteps of Sir Samuel Ferguson and gives us simple and stately versions of "The Children of Lir" and "Sons of Turann."[21] There is no better way of getting a knowledge of two of the most lovely of all the old Irish stories than from this book. May many follow in the road Dr. Todhunter has chosen. It leads where there is no lack of subjects, for the literature of Ireland is still young, and on all sides of this road is Celtic tradition and Celtic passion crying for singers to give them voice. England is old and her poets must scrape up the crumbs of an almost finished banquet, but Ireland has still full tables.

W. B. Yeats

14   The New "Speranza"*

London, July 9

England has indeed, as Mitchel phrased it, gained the ear of the world, and knows right well how to tell foreign nations what tale of Ireland pleases her best. By the mouths of her magnificent *Times*, and her countless tourists and sight-seers even from the wealthier and more conservative classes, she repeats to the admiring nations a ceaseless tale of English patience and Irish insubordination.[1] More than one Irishman has sought in vain to get a hearing for some Irish thoughts on the matter. The late Mr. Leonard tried all his life to make the people of Paris listen to the true story of England and Ireland, and with no very noticeable success.[2] But now Miss Maud Gonne, as eloquent with her tongue as was "Speranza" with her pen, has made her voice heard where so many have failed.[3] Every speech has been a triumph, and every triumph greater than the one that went before it. Thousands who come to see this new wonder – a beautiful woman who makes speeches – remain to listen with delight to her sincere and simple eloquence. Last week at Bordeaux, an audience of twelve hundred persons rose to its feet, when she had finished, to applaud her with wild enthusiasm. The papers of Russia, France, Germany and even Egypt quote her speeches, and the tale of Irish wrongs has found its way hither and thither to lie stored up, perhaps, in many a memory against the day of need. She is going through France addressing town after town, and beside spreading a better knowledge of Ireland and awakening a wider sympathy with our wrongs, has already, though this is not her main object, gained, I believe, a considerable sum for the evicted tenants.[4]

It is not, however, to describe her success that I write, but to review a supplement to *La Revue Catholique* which has just reached me. It is a verbatim report of her long speech at the Catholic

* This letter appeared in *BP* for 30 July 1892. HR title: "Maude Gonne."

University of the Luxembourg, and enables one to judge once for all whether she rule her audiences by the power of beauty alone, or whether she have indeed the genius of the orator.[5] I do not think that any one who reads through these twelve columns of clear and vigorous French will doubt the answer. I have heard many lady speakers, some of them being the most celebrated of their class, but do not remember finding in any of their words the same kind of faculty I find in these columns of *La Revue Catholique*. Miss Gonne is the first who has spoken on the platform wholly and undisguisedly out of a woman's heart. The speeches of the others might have been made by men, but this speech, while never weak, never sentimental in the bad sense of the word, is the kind of speech, both in its limitations and in its triumphs, which could only be made by a woman. From first to last it is emotional and even poignant, and has that curious power of unconsciously seizing salient incidents which is so distinguishing a mark of the novel writing of women. Its logic is none the less irresistible because it is the logic of the heart. Listen to her description of the famine of '48:[6]

The Middle Ages in the most sombre period of their history never beheld such misery. Men and women ate the dogs, the rats, and the grass of the field, and some even, when all food was gone, ate the dead bodies. Those who died were cast into great ditches so hurriedly opened and badly closed again that the pestilential odors helped to make death travel more rapidly. They were called the pits of the famine, for into them the famine cast all its harvest. Ireland was heroic in her suffering. Whole families, when they had eaten their last crust, and understood that they had to die, looked once upon the sun and then closed up the doors of their cabins with stones, that no one might look on their last agony. Weeks afterwards men would find their skeletons gathered round the extinguished hearth. I do not exaggerate, gentlemen. I have added nothing to the mournful reality. If you come to my country, every stone will repeat to you this tragic history. It was only fifty years ago. It still lives in thousands of memories. I have been told it by women who have heard the last sigh of their children without being able to lessen their agony with one drop of milk. It has seemed to me at evening on those mountains of Ireland, so full of savage majesty when the wind sighed over the pits of the famine where the thousands of dead enrich the harvests of the future, it has seemed to me that I heard an avenging voice calling down on our oppressors the execration of men and the justice of God.

The bulk of the spoken oratory of our time has, like the whole of our spoken drama, divorced itself from literature, but this passage has much of the serene beauty of good writing. Nor has it lost in gaining this any of its effectiveness as an oratorical appeal, for with rare mastery over the picturesque it unrolls incidents that compel attention and burn themselves into the memory. A man or woman trained on the political platforms of the day would have given figures and arguments and have been forgotten ten minutes after. But many who heard this passage will never forget as long as they live the skeletons huddled by the extinguished hearths and the great pits where lie thousands who make fertile the harvests of the future. Perhaps, too, some will remember the voice calling upon the mountain at evening, and if the need come, be ready in our service.

The whole speech shows this power of seizing upon the distinguishing incidents of an epoch and describing them in vivid and living sentences. It was no easy thing to give a clear picture of the history of Ireland in a speech of three-quarters of an hour, or an hour at most, without needless digression on the one hand or dry catalogues of events upon the other; yet this is what Miss Gonne has done with such perfect success. She takes her audience from incident to incident, from the bloodless conversion of pagan Ireland through the very bloody battle when hoariest Brian died in the moment of victory to the English invasion and down to our own day and the death of Parnell, and every event is described as vividly and simply as if it were all in some famous ballad of "old, unhappy, far-off things, and battles long ago."[7]

W. B. Yeats

15   The New National Library –
The National Literary Society – Mr. O'Grady's
Stories – Dr. Hyde's Forthcoming Book –
Themes for Irish Litterateurs*

Dublin, Nov. 6

Your Celt has written the greater bulk of his letters from the
capital† of the enemy, but he is now among his own people
again, and no longer "The Celt in London," but "The Celt in
Ireland." At this moment he is sitting writing, or trying to write,
in the big, florid new National Library with its stone balcony,
where nobody is allowed to walk, and its numberless stone
niches, in which there will never be any statues.[1] He is sitting
dreaming much, and writing a little from time to time, watching
the people come and go, and wondering what shall be born of
the new generation that is now so very busy reading endless
scholasticisms along the five rows of oak tables. An old fairy tale
which exists in many forms in many countries tells of a giant
whose life was hidden away in an egg, which was in its turn hid
in the mouth of a fish, or some such unlikely place.[2] The library
is just such an egg, for it hides under its white curved ceiling a
good portion of the scholastic life of student Dublin. Here they
come to read for examinations, and to work up their various
subjects. At my left hand is a man reading some registers of civil
service or other examinations; opposite me an ungainly young
man with a puzzled face is turning over the pages of a trigon-
ometry work; and a little beyond him a medical student is deep
in anatomical diagrams. On all sides men are studying the things
that are to get them bodily food, but no man among them is
searching for the imaginative and spiritual food to be got out of
great literature. Nobody, with the exception of a few ladies,

* This letter appeared in *BP* for 19 Nov 1892 under the column heading
"The Celt in Ireland." HR title: "The Irish National Literary Society."

perhaps, ever seems to do any disinterested reading in this library, or indeed anywhere else in Ireland. Every man here is grinding at the mill wherein he grinds all things into pounds and shillings, and but few of them will he get when all is done. Ireland, half through her own fault and half through circumstances over which she has no control, is not a reading nation, nor has she been so for many a long day. A single town in Scotland is said to buy more books than all Ireland put together, and surely nowhere out of Ireland will you find a great library like this given over completely to the student cramming for examinations.

Can we find a remedy? Can we not unite literature to the great passion of patriotism and ennoble both thereby? This question has occupied a good many of us this spring. We think that a national literary society and a series of national books like Duffy's Library of Ireland may do something, and have accordingly founded such a society and planned out, with the help of a number of well known men of letters, such a national series.[3] Our task should not, after all, be so difficult. These very students will do for the love of Ireland what they would not do for the love of literature. When literature comes to them, telling of their own country and of its history and of its legends, they will listen gladly enough. The people of Ireland have ever honored intellect, although they have no intellectual life themselves. I have heard a drunken fisherman tell a man that he was no gentleman "because nobody is a gentleman who has not been educated at Trinity College, Dublin." The people of Ireland have created perhaps the most beautiful folk-lore in the world, and have made a wild music that is the wonder of all men, and yet to-day they have turned aside from imaginative arts. Can we bring them to care once more for the things of the mind? Well, we are going to do our best to bring books to their doors and music, too, perhaps. Thomas of Erceldoune foretold the day when the gray goose quill would rule the world; and may not we men of the pen hope to move some Irish hearts and make them beat true to manhood and to Ireland?[4] Will not the day come when we shall have again in Ireland men who will not lie for any party advantage, or traffic away eternal principles for any expediency however urgent – men like the men of '48, who lived by the light of noble books and the great traditions of the past? Amidst the clash of party against party we have tried to put forward a nationality that is above party, and amid the oncoming roar of a general election we have tried to assert those everlasting principles of love of truth and love of country that speak to men in solitude and in the silence of the night.[5] So far all has gone well with us, for men who are saddened and disgusted with the turn public affairs have taken have sought in our society occasion to do work for Ireland that will bring about assured good, whether that good be great or small. We have met more support than we ventured to hope for, and there is no sign of its falling off.

The committee represents all parties and opinions which have any claim to be considered national. The Reverend T. A. Finlay of the Catholic University, Mr. John O'Leary, Sir Charles Gavan Duffy, Dr. Douglas Hyde, Dr. Sigerson, Count Plunkett, Miss Katharine Tynan, Miss Maud Gonne, so well known for her oratory and her beauty, and Mr. Richard Ashe King, the novelist, are among the best known. Books have been offered upon all manner of national epochs and events from the Ossianic days to our own time.[6]

Apart from the literary society altogether, things are not looking so badly for the future of our literature. Mr. Standish O'Grady, for instance, is doing better and better work. He has on hand an historical romance dealing with the invasions of Strongbow, and is contributing also from time to time singularly moving and picturesque little stories on events in Irish history to the Dublin papers. He will doubtless collect them into a volume before long. He has also written for Fisher Unwin's Children's Library a book called *Finn and His Companions*, which gives the most vivid pictures of the Ossianic age I ever hope to see. Caoilte, having survived to the time of St. Patrick by enchantment, describes to the saint the life of the Fenians, and tells numbers of the old tales out of the bardic poems in English both powerful and beautiful.[7]

Dr. Douglas Hyde has also a book on the legendary age in progress. It will give translations of bardic stories, and will be, I believe, but the first of a series if Dr. Hyde meets with proper support.[8] It is impossible to overrate the importance of such books, for in them the Irish poets of the future will in all likelihood find a good portion of their subject matter. From that great candle of the past we must all light our little tapers.

In England I sometimes hear men complain that the old

themes of verse and prose are used up. Here in Ireland the marble block is waiting for us almost untouched, and the statues will come as soon as we have learned to use the chisel. Our history is full of incidents well worthy of drama, story and song. And they are incidents involving types of character of which this world has not yet heard. If we can but put those tumultuous centuries into tale or drama, the whole world will listen to us and sit at our feet like children who hear a new story. Nor is this new thing we have to say in our past alone. The very people who come and go in this library where I write are themes full of new wisdom and new mystery, for in them is that yet uncultured thing – Irish character. And if history and the living present fail us, do there not lie hid among those spear heads and golden collars over the way in the New Museum, suggestions of that age before history when the art legends and wild mythology of earliest Ireland rose out of the void? There alone is enough of the stuff that dreams are made on to keep us busy a thousand years.[9]

W. B. Yeats

FROM THE *PROVIDENCE SUNDAY JOURNAL*

16   The Poet of Ballyshannon*

In this age of ambitious thoughts, this cosmopolitan age, when poets have ransacked the world for their themes, the author of this little volume has sung for the most part his own countryside and his seaboard towns:[1]

> A wild west Coast, a little Town,
> Where little Folk go up and down,
> Tides flow and winds blow:
> Night and Tempest and the Sea,
> Human Will and Human Fate:
> What is little, what is great?
> Howsoe'er the answer be,
> Let me sing of what I know.[2]

In many more verses, beautiful as these, he has sung it. To be read in this age you must have ambitious thoughts, offer some solution of the old riddle. You must draw heaven and earth into your net. That is as it should be, perhaps. It is certainly as it must be. It is possible we shall some day discover that these nineteenth century thoughts of ours are only bubble thoughts. But meanwhile we have so many things on our hands, so much to break and make, we can hardly listen at all to one who turning aside sings the folk-lore and memories of a little seaboard town. We – we are of the age. The spirit of the age has never been heard of down there. In their old crannie they still believe in spirits and fairies and ghosts. Hence has it come about, this poet of Ballyshannon has found few readers.[3] Children have loved him. They are always of the past ages – they and the very old. If they are wise children, to them it is of more importance to

---

* This letter appeared in *PSJ* for 2 Sep 1888 under the column heading "The Literary World. Book Reviews and News" and with the footnote "*Irish Songs and Other Poems*. By William Allingham. With Music. Reeves and Turner." HR title: "The Poet of Ballyshannon."

know that ghosts and fairies are not on speaking terms than to
have at your finger ends all notions that ever were cradled in
lecture rooms:

> The Moon was bright, the Sea was still,
> The Fairies danced on Fairy Hill;
> The Town lay sleeping far below;
> Ghosts went round it, sad and slow,
> Loth to leave their earthly place
> For the Wilderness of Space.
> The watch-dogs saw the Ghosts and howl'd,
> The Fairies saw the Ghosts, and cowl'd
> Their little heads and whirl'd away;
> No friendship between Ghost and Fay.
> Fairies lightly love Mankind,
> To mischief or to mirth inclined,
> They fear the Dead, by night or day.[4]

Perhaps, also, to fully understand these poems one needs to
have been born and bred in one of those western Irish towns; to
remember how it was the centre of your world, how the mountains
and the river and the roads became a portion of your life forever;
to have loved with a sense of possession even the roadside bushes
where the roadside cottagers hung their clothes to dry. That
sense of possession was the very centre of the matter. Elsewhere
you are only a passer-by, for everything is owned by so many
that it is owned by no one. Down there as you hummed over
Allingham's "Fairies" and looked up at the mountain where
they lived, it seemed to you that a portion of your life was the
subject. How much, too, did it not add to remember that old
Biddy So-and-So, at the river's side, laid milk and bread outside
her door every evening to wheedle into prosperity-giving humor
those same fairies of the song:

> Up the airy mountain,
>   Down the rushy glen,
> We daren't go a-hunting
>   For fear of little men;
> Wee folk, good folk,
>   Trooping all together;
> Green jacket, red cap,

And white owl's feather!

Down along the rocky shore
  Some make their home,
They live on crispy pancakes
  Of yellow tide-foam;
Some in the reeds
  Of the black mountain lake,
With frogs for their watch-dogs,
  All night awake.

High on the hill-top
  The old King sits;
He is now so old and gray
  He's nigh lost his wits.
With a bridge of white mist
  Columbkill he crosses,
On his stately journeys
  From Slieveleague to Rosses.[5]

And so on – such songs, the heart covers them with its ivy.

Many more such local themes are there in this last book of the poet of Ballyshannon: the pilot's daughter in her Sunday frock – the wake with the candles round the corpse and a cloth under the chin – the ruined Abbey of Asaroe, an old man who was of the blood of those who founded it, watching sadly the crumbled walls – girls sewing and singing under a thorn tree – the hauling in of the salmon nets – the sound of clarionet through the open and ruddy shutter of a forge – the piano† from some larger house, a jumble of old memories![6] Memories, be it noticed, of things and moments, more than of passions and persons. Everywhere the little hooks on which the heart catches.

This distance of the theme gives to the style its consciousness – more of Heine than of Burns there. His world was no longer one with the things of which he wrote. He consciously chose them. Hence he is an artist. Davis and Ferguson could not have written differently than they did. Their theme was appointed by those old spinners, the Fates.[7] This choosing and gathering of artistic moments, when he has a subject like "The Lady of the Sea," is not enough. We are not satisfied. The mermaid bride of Dalachmar has too little of sea wonder and mystery. She is too modern and pathetic, too cheap. One does not meet a mermaid every day, and one does not like to be disappointed.

The other long poem, "The Music Master," has the same fault, but we hardly notice it, the artistic moments are so beautiful. Witness these opening lines:[8]

> Music and Love! – If lovers hear me sing,
>   I will for them essay the simple tale,
> To hold some fair young listeners in a ring
>   With echoes gathered from an Irish vale,
> Where still, methinks, abide my golden years,
> Though I not with them, – far discern'd through tears.
>
> When evening fell upon the village-street
>   And brother fields, reposing hand in hand,
> Unlike where flaring cities scorn to meet
>   The kiss of dusk that quiets all the land,
> 'Twas pleasant laziness to loiter by
> Houses and cottages, a friendly spy,
>
> And hear the frequent fiddle that would glide
>   Through jovial mazes of a jig or reel,
> Or sink from sob to sob with plaintive slide,
>   Or mount the steps of swift exulting zeal;
> For our old village was with music fill'd
> Like any grove where thrushes wont to build.

Wistfulness and regret ever dominant in this poem throughout! The personal nature of this sadness again divides him from Davis and Ferguson. They were essentially national writers. Davis, looking into the future, saw Ireland free and prospering. Ferguson saw her in the past before the curse had yet fallen. For her were their hopes and memories and regrets. They ever celebrated the national life. No matter what they described you were made to feel its relation to that life. Allingham, though always Irish, is no way national. This widely affects† his work. Like Lever and Lover he does not take the people quite seriously.[9] Not so many miles from Ballyshannon – visible therefrom on clear days, I imagine – is the Mountain Nephin, where the blind Lynott warmed his vengeance for years. Ferguson chose that Lynott out, and wrote his "Vengeance of the Welshmen of Tirawley."[10]

Allingham noted down for us the sound of a clarionet through
the ruddy shutter of a forge, the fishers drawing in their net with
a silver wave of salmon, a bugle in a solitary valley, a peasant
in her Sunday dress – isolated† artistic moments.[11]

Besides this need of central seriousness, the narrative poems
are hardly one in matter and form. They are more versified
stories than poems. You feel the matter might have been told
differently, that matter and form have not grown up together.
They have been chosen, you imagine, each for itself. Indeed it
seems to me there is only one narrative poem in this book that
has, as wholly as the lyrics have, this unity of matter and form,
namely, the "Abbot of Inisfalen." Here everything, metre and
words alike, carries the same meaning, alike breathes of the days
when to every eye the blue of heaven seemed the floor whereon
the angel walked, and spirits seemed to come and go in shapes
of bird and beast. There is no more beautiful legend anywhere
than the monkish, many-countried tale, whereof Mr. Allingham
gives the Irish version, the Killarney version, for Mr. Allingham
has strayed far from his Ballyshannon this time.[12] Far south even
of bluest Nephin – blue as a wave of the sea sucked up by some
air-wandering Jotun – away into Kerry.[13]

The Abbot† of Inisfalen prayed at early dawn under the leaves.
All around, the island was still. He prayed for his sins forgiveness.
He prayed for his convent brothers. He prayed for Ireland. He
prayed for all mankind:

The Abbot of Inisfalen arose upon his feet;
He heard a small bird singing, and O but it sung sweet!
It sung upon a holly-bush, this little snow-white bird;
A song so full of gladness he never before had heard.
It sung upon a hazel, it sung upon a thorn;
He had never heard such music since the hour that he was
    born.†
It sung upon a sycamore, it sung upon a briar;
To follow the song and hearken this Abbot could never
    tire.
Till at last he well bethought him; he might no longer stay,
So he bless'd the little white singing-bird, and gladly went
    his way.

But when the Abbot came again to his Abbey everything was changed. On every side strange faces and the strange tongue of the Sassenach:

> Then the oldest monk came forward, in Irish tongue spake
>   he:
> 'Thou wearest the holy Augustine's dress, and who hath
>   given it to thee?'
> 'I wear the holy Augustine's dress, and Cormac is my
>   name,
> The Abbot of this good Abbey by grace of God I am.
> I went forth to pray, at the dawn of day; and when my
>   prayers were said,
> I hearken'd awhile to a little bird, that sung above my
>   head.'
> The monks to him made answer, 'Two hundred years have
>   gone o'er,
> Since our Abbot Cormac went through the gate, and never
>   was heard of more.
> Matthias now is our Abbot, and twenty have pass'd away.
> The stranger is lord of Ireland; we live in an evil day.'
> 'Days will come and go,' he said, 'and the world will pass
>   away,
> In Heaven a day is a thousand years, a thousand years are
>   a day.'
>
> 'Now give me absolution; for my time is come,' said he.
> And they gave him absolution, as speedily as might be.
> Then, close outside the window, the sweetest song they
>   heard
> That ever yet since the world began was utter'd by any
>   bird.
> The monks look'd out and saw the bird, its feathers all
>   white and clean;
> And there in a moment, beside it, another white bird was
>   seen.
> Those two they sang together, waved their white wings,
>   and fled.

Then they buried his body at the edge of the island at the

meeting of the grass and the water, "a carven cross at his head and a holly bush at his feet."[14]

Wonderful legend, breathing a piety as of old missals. Sometimes in those wooded lake islets one comes on ancient ivy-covered monastery walls – I have one such ruin in my mind where the ivy stems are many inches thick – green shadows surround them and cover them. Long grass blades† fondle their old stones. Century after century they are beaten down and washed away into universal nature, the symbols of man's age in the presence of the immortal youth of God. This old legend seems laden with the spirit of such a place – a legend of one standing before eternity without glory; a place where nature and God are persuasive.

There are many poems in this book beautiful as those I have quoted. "Lovely Mary Donnelly" (why has the astonishing change of "'tis you I love the best" into "my joy, my only best" in the first line been made?), and many another good story besides and some odd pages of old Irish mixed therewith.[15] They are so beautiful, these poems, I have hardly the heart to go back again to their nationalism or non-nationalism; and yet I must, for it is the most central notion I have about them. Yes, they are not national. The people of Ireland seem to Mr. Allingham graceful, witty, picturesque, benevolent, everything but a people to be taken seriously. This want of sympathy with the national life and history has limited his vision, has driven away from his poetry much beauty and power – has thinned his blood. In Mr. Allingham's two-volume poem, *Laurence Bloomfield*, announced for republishing, these things are very plain. Each figure as long as he is a background, a something to make artistic moments out of, is painted with most accurate and imaginative touch, but let him come into the foreground and all the magic is gone. Unless he is merely an ideal like the hero – a thing, not a nature – he is a child to be patronized with praise and blame. He may be playful, generous, pathetic, everything but a serious being, one fulfilling his own purpose with himself, choosing for himself between God and the devil. The landlord now, too! We do not believe in him much, this ideal hero. He is moderate not because of the clearness of his sight but rather from the nature of his sympathies. He, too, does not take seriously the people over whom he rules – they are all children, the misguided, the Celts.

Yet the poem is a good poem in its way, full likewise of much sound knowledge of the land question. Long ago it won the praise of Mr. Gladstone, it is said.[16]

What a sad business this non-nationalism has been! It gave to Lever and Lover their shallowness, and still gives to a section of Dublin society its cynicism. Lever and Lover and Allingham alike, it has deprived of their true audience. Many much less endowed writers than they have more influence in Ireland. Political doctrine was not demanded of them, merely nationalism. They would not take the people seriously – these writers of the Ascendancy – and had to go to England for their audience.[17] To Lever and Lover Ireland became merely a property shop, and to Allingham a half serious memory.

To the greater poets everything they see has its relation to the national life, and through that to the universal and divine life: nothing is an isolated artistic moment; there is a unity everywhere; everything fulfills a purpose that is not its own; the hailstone is a journeyman of God; the grass blade carries the universe upon its point. But to this universalism, this seeing of unity everywhere, you can only attain through what is near you, your nation, or, if you be no traveller, your village and the cobwebs on your walls. You can no more have the greater poetry without a nation than religion without symbols. One can only reach out to the universe with a gloved hand – that glove is one's nation, the only thing one knows even a little of.

W. B. Yeats

17   Dr. Todhunter's Latest Volume of Poems*

Dr. Todhunter in his last book has made a new departure indeed.[1] From the folk tale of Helen of Troy, transmitted to us through generations of poets, he has turned to "The Children of Lir" and "The Sons of Turann," folk tales entirely unknown to the readers of poetry. He claims a new kind of recognition. *Helena in Troas* was essentially an art product, the appeal of a scholar to the scholarly. It was acted on a stage fitted up to reproduce exactly the stage of Greece – everything done to rouse the historic imagination. What was new and creative was the attempt to apply the old conditions to the modern stage, to redeem the drama by mingling music and poetry, to add a new convention to the stage. But the poem itself dealt always with the oldest material, with personages who have figured in a hundred poems. The mind of the theatre-goer has grown numb on the side turned to poetry, and you can only rouse it possibly by striking where many painters and poets have struck before. Certainly Helen of Troy was still a name to conjure with, and Dr. Todhunter conjured successfully. Among the many hopeful signs of a revival of higher drama his *Helena* holds an important place.[2] We believe he intends to renew the attempt. If higher drama comes once more into existence, it will be in some such way, appealing first to the refined and cultivated and well-read, elaborating piece by piece its convention, then widening its range and gathering converts slowly among the many like a new book, not going to the public, but drawing them to itself. The modern author, if he be a man of genius, is a solitary; he does not know the everchanging public well enough to be their servant. He cannot learn their convention; they must learn his. All that is greatest in modern literature is soliloquy, or, at most, words addressed

---

* This letter appeared in *PSJ* for 10 Feb 1889 under the column heading "The Literary World. Book Reviews and News" and with the footnote "*The Banshee and Other Poems*. London: Kegan† Paul, Trench and Co., 1888." HR title: "The Children of Lir."

to a few friends. We must go to the stage all eagerness like a mob of eavesdroppers and to be inspired, not amused, if modern drama is to be anything else than a muddy torrent of shallow realism.

In some such mood did Goethe draw people to his Weimar stage, forbidding even applause, and great dramas were enacted there – his own, Schiller's and others' – till they were superseded one day by a performing poodle. On some such terms did Wagner find audience. The other day Renan described his ideal theatre: it should be subsidized by the State, in all matters be under the control of the greatest artists and poets and critics of the time, enact at stated intervals the greatest works of the greatest poets of all times, and announce each performance to the universe years beforehand.[3]

I have strayed far from "The Children of Lir" and "The Sons of Turann."[4] Nothing could be less like *Helena* than these "Children," *Helena* essentially belonging to what is called poetical poetry, everything seen through the spectacles of books, "The Children of Lir" almost too simple, almost too unelaborate. One is cosmopolitan, the other ethnic, falling on the cosmopolitan ear with an outlandish ring. One is written throughout in blank verse – most artificial if most monumental of forms – the other in strangely unstudied, fluid and barbaric measures.

Dr. Todhunter no longer comes to us as an art poet: he claims recognition as one of the national writers of the Irish race; as such we will consider him. In simplicity he resembles Ferguson. By right of fire and fortitude Ferguson stands alone, a singer of heroic things unrivalled in our days, the ballad Homer.[5] Fire and fortitude he needed, for he chose out the most epic incidents of Ireland's heroic age. Dr. Todhunter has chosen so far a different sphere. His legends belong to those mythic and haunted ages of the Tuatha De Danaan that preceded the heroic cycle, ages full of mystery, where demons and gods battle in the twilight. Between us and them Cuchulain, Conall Carnach, Conary, Ferdiad and the heroes move as before gloomy arras.[6]

In those mysterious pre-human ages when life lasted for hundreds of years; when the monstrous race of the Fomorians, with one foot, and one arm in the middle of their chests, rushed in their pirate galleys century after century like clouds upon the coast; when a race of beautiful beings, whose living hair moved with their changing thoughts, paced about the land; when the huge bulk of Balor had to be raised in his chariot, and his eyelid, weighted by the lassitude of age, uplifted with hooks that he might strike dead his foe with a glance – to these ages belongs the main portion of one legend supreme in innocence and beauty and tenderness, the tale of "The Children of Lir."[7]

Only one other modern poet has told the story – Miss Tynan's beautiful poem being a lyric treatment of a single episode; that other is the Catholic poet, Aubrey de Vere. His version is very readable, but over-embroidered, and lacking entirely the flavor of the original.[8] Dr. Todhunter has kept perfectly, on the other hand, all the old naïveté and unexpectedness.

He begins by telling how the Tuatha De Danaan had been defeated by the Milesian invaders:

> Sad were the men of De-Danaan,
> Sad from the sword of the Sons of Milith,
> In the fight of Tailtin,
> In the fight for lordship of the streams of Erin.
>
> To the hosting of the chiefs
> They drew together their war-sick banners,
> And said: "Let one be Lord,
> To the healing of us all."

Bov Derg, a southern chief, is chosen king; his rival, Lir of the White Field, retreats in wrath brooding upon his wrong.

> But those about Bov Derg were wroth at Lir, and
>   said:
> "Give us the word, Bov Derg, and Lir shall be an
>   heap
> Of bleaching bones, cast out and suddenly forgot."

"Not so," answered Bov Derg, "leave Lir the lordship of himself, to daunt Fomorian ships."[9] At last word came that the whole South was full of wailing. A cry had gone forth, "The wife of Lir is dead, and Lir like winter's frost that melts away in tears!" Bov Derg, that there might be peace between him and Lir, sent messengers offering one of his three daughters, Oova, Oifa, or Eva, as wife to Lir. Lir came and chose the eldest, for he would not wrong the first-born. Of this marriage were four

children: at the first birth Fianoula, a daughter, Oodh, a son; at
the second Fiachra and Conn, twin sons. But at the last birth
Oova died. Again the wail went forth, and Bov Derg, hearing
it, sent Oifa as wife to mother the babes of Oova. Lir cared only
for his children.

> By night he kept them near him, and oft ere dawn was
>   grey
> Hungry with love he rose, to lie down among his
>   children.

For a year Oifa nursed bitter jealousy. At last she mounted
into her chariot and came to a place of Druids, and said, "Come,
kill me now this plague," but the Druids drove her away. Then
she carried the children into a deep grove and drew her knife to
kill them. Conn looked up wondering and said, "Mother, what
means that knife?" "Wolves, wolves," she answered. The child
whirled his sling and said, "Lo, we are here; no wolf shall do
thee harm," and fearing to see their blood she threw the knife
away. They rode on and came to Derryvarragh Lough. The
afternoon was very hot, and she bid them bathe. While they
were plunging about in the water she paced, muttering a Druid's
mage† upon the shore,[10] and raising her witch wand, smote the
children, "and they were seen no more, but on the lake four
swans beheld their plumes, amazed." Over them she sang this
doom:

> The doom of the Children of Lir,
> Thus Oifa dooms them,
> Go pine in the feathers of swans
> Till the North shall wed the South.
>
> Three hundred years shall ye float
> On the stillness of Derryvarragh:
> On the tossing of Sruth-na-Moyle,
> Unsheltered, three hundred years.
>
> Three hundred years shall ye keene
> With the curlews of Erris Domnann;
> Till the bell rings in Inis Glory
> I curse you: nine hundred years!

They weep and pray her for some lightening of their doom, and she, being filled with terror of her own deed, grants, not from pity but from fear, that they shall have wonderful power of song:

> Sweet, sweet be your voices,
> Ye sorrowful Swans of Lir!
> Your song from the seas of Erin
> Shall comfort the sorrows of men.

Then Oifa drove on to the house of her father, Bov Derg. Lir passed by the lake and the swans saw him and came and told him of their doom, and, having stayed to weep with them that night, he also came to the house of Bov Derg. There he told his tale, and Bov Derg laid a spell on the tongue of Oifa that she might confess what shape she most abhorred.

> She writhed, compelled with pain,
> Crying with a ghastly shriek: "Demon of the air!"

Then he smote her with his wand, and "her blue eyes grew white as dazzling leprosy" and her form hideous and dragon-winged, and he sang over her a doom of ceaseless wandering, "an outlaw of the air."[11]

This brings us near the end of the second canto, or, as Dr. Todhunter calls it, "second duan." The remaining duans describe the troubles of the swans. The poem to the end of the fourth tells how they live three hundred years on Derryvarragh Lough, comforting their kin with sweet song, Bov Derg and Lir living near them all the while, for those divine races lived for hundreds of years; how they left Derryvarragh when their time came, and flew to Sruth-na-Moyle; how they dwelt on a rock among the seals:

> There dwelt they, with the seals, the human-hearted
>   seals,
> That loved the Swans, and far followed with sad soft
>   eyes,
> Doglike, in sleek brown troops, their singing, o'er the
>   sea;
> So for their music yearned the nations of the seals;

how they visited Manannan, the magician, on his island:

> Wizard to wizard, oft, Time in his cloudy cave
> He met; and he could spell some rune of things to
>   come.
> And in Fianoula's ear his mild prophetic word
> Breathed shell-like thunders dim from coming tides of
>   death.

The fifth duan describes how, another three hundred years having passed, the swans flew to Erris Domnann (an old name for a portion of the Connaught coast); how Ævric, a bard who had sought them all his life for love of their song, built a hut by the sea's edge where he lived listening to them; how at last feeling death draw nigh he went away to sing their songs "and keep the heart of Erin green"; how one winter night the sea was frozen round them, and in the midst of that frozen sea they sang a new song – a hymn to God – and while they sang the North "budded with phantom fire." Christianity was drawing westward; the old gods were flying before it. This duan brings to an end their wanderings. They fly home to the house of Lir only to find it desolate and weed-grown. They sing over it a song of lamentation and fly to Inis Glory of Brendan to await the coming of the faith.

> And all the tribes of birds were gathered to them there,
> And with sweet fairy singing there in the Lake of Birds
> They taught the airy tribes, and comforted their woes;
> Till, as the seals, they loved the singing of the Swans.
> Far was their flight by day; along the wild west coast
> They roamed to feed, as far as Achill, and at night
> Flew back to Inis Glory; and wheresoe'er they moved
> Thick waved the following wings of loving flocks of
>   birds.

The two final duans describe how they dwelt there in peace until the coming of St. Patrick, when a priest sent of God came to the island of Inis Glory; how for six days worked the priest, Mochaom Og by name, building a church with no man to help, and very sad, for he knew not why he was sent of God:

Marvellous was his work; for great strength in his
    hands
God put; and there by night, no shelter for his head,
But sheltering as he might the Church's holy things,
He laid him down to sleep, wet with the rain and the
    dew.

And like the birds he lived, no better than the birds.
Toiling, yet keeping still, matins, and nones, and
    primes.
Then by God's finished house he built himself a hut,
Where like the birds he lived, no better than the
    birds.

On the seventh day he consecrated the bread and wine and
rang his bell. The swans heard the sound, and at first Oodh,
Fiachra and Conn were filled with fear, but Fianoula comforted
them. It was God's bell, she said, the bell that brought them
peace. They dwelt thereafter for a time with Mochaom Og,
hearing mass and keeping the canonical hours. At last the
prophecy of the North wedding the South was fulfilled, for
Lairgnen, King of Connaught, took to wife Deoch, daughter of
the King of Munster. The new Queen of Connaught pined for
the singing of the swans and sent Lairgnen to carry them off.
Lairgnen came to Inis Glory and seized them in spite of Mochaom
Og.

But lo! a wondrous thing: suddenly from the Swans
Slack fell their feathery coats, and there once more they
    stood,
Children; yet weird with age, weird with nine hundred
    years
Of woe: four wistful ghosts from childhood's daisied
    field!
Four children there they stood, naked as when in
    glee
They plunged into the lough. And Mochaom Og in
    haste
Clad them in spotless fair white robes of choristers.
But Lairgnen curst he loud, with Deoch, for their
    sin.

The four children were baptized, and, having taken the sacrament, they sang away their souls that night.

> And in one grave he laid, keeping Fianoula's word,
> The four Children of Lir; and masses for their souls
> He said, and wrote their names in Ogham on their
>   stone;
> And in the church he hung the four white shapes of
>   swans.

In Gaelic-speaking days this poem was a national epopee known from Fair Head to Cape Clear, told in the poor man's hut and the rich man's castle.[12] So famous it was that down to this day an old-fashioned peasant would think it most unlucky to injure a swan. In Dr. Todhunter's version it may again grow into a national epopee. There is not a more beautiful story anywhere extant; it is like a breath of morning air.

It is strange how an inspiration seizes many people at the same time. In the present century many Irish tales have received metrical clothing, but this children† of Lir remained neglected until a few years ago, when came de Vere's embroidered song, and then in a single year Miss Tynan began a lyrical poem thereon, an Irish lady artist covered the walls of a Dublin hospital with frescos of the swan children, Dr. Todhunter wrote his epopee, and, rumor has it, the Gaelic *skolawr*, Mr. Douglas Hyde, commenced a long version.[13]

We do not believe any version will supersede in simplicity and tenderness this present epopee. It may grow in time to be something of a household word in Ireland, to stand beside the poems of Ferguson and Davis and Mangan. Not quickly, however, will it come to its own, being too simple, too breezy and ancient, too free aired, too altogether different from the close back parlor atmosphere of nineteenth century life. Its very virtues will be in the scale opposite to its popularity. Its faults will not injure its success much with most readers. People at first will read it for the story probably, not noticing how Dr. Todhunter in his longing for simplicity in all things has sometimes lost the fullness of perfectly developed metre – the sound as of smitten bronze. His lines are a little tentative and timid like the drawing in old pictures. Ferguson in his best poems, even in his masterpiece, "Conary," fell into a kindred fault.[14] In his dislike for the self-conscious variations and over-elaboration of modern meter, he made his lines often a little monotonous.

The other long poem in the book, "The Lamentation for the Three Sons of Turann," is divided like an old Irish keen into "The Little Lamentations," "The First Sorrow," "The Second Sorrow," "The Great Lamentation." It is as completely pagan as the other is Christian, being the history of an implacable vengeance. The three sons of Turann are sent by the hero, Cian, to do for him various mighty tasks about the world in penalty for having slain his father. A sort of court of the chiefs had given them into his power. In the doing of the last of these tasks they are slain as he had intended. This poem is the lamentation their father, Turann, makes for them.

The following description of the eldest carrying away the enchanted spit from the sea spirits is fine and musical. He has laid on himself a spell that he may walk through the sea:

> Days twice-seven was he treading
> The silent gloom of the deep,
> His lanterns the silver salmon
> To the sea-sunk Isle of Finchory.
>
> Soft shone the moony splendour
> Of the magic lamps of Finchory.
> There sat in their hall of crystal
> The red-haired ocean-wraiths.
>
> Twice-fifty they sat and broidered
> With pearls their sea-green mantles;
> But Brian strode to their kitchen
> And seized a spit from the rack.

Dr. Todhunter has also, he says in the preface, written a Deirdre, but did not print it with these poems as it is of more epic nature.[15] It was a pity to keep it back. It would have been pleasant to have in one book what were called in ancient Ireland "The Three Sorrows of Story-Telling."

There are some fine short poems. The best without any doubt is "Aghadoe." Had it appeared in *The Nation* in Young Ireland times it would now be in every collection of Irish ballads:[16]

There's a glade in Aghadoe, Aghadoe, Aghadoe,
There's a green and silent glade in Aghadoe,
Where we met, my love and I, love's fair planet in the
    sky,
O'er that sweet and silent glade in Aghadoe.

There's a glen in Aghadoe, Aghadoe, Aghadoe,
There's a deep and secret glen in Aghadoe,
Where I hid him from the eyes of the red-coats and their
    spies,
That year the trouble came to Aghadoe.

Oh! my curse on one black heart in Aghadoe, Aghadoe,
On Shaun Dhuv, my mother's son, in Aghadoe!
When your throat fries in hell's drouth, salt the flame
    be in your mouth,
For the treachery you did in Aghadoe!

For they tracked me to that glen in Aghadoe, Aghadoe,
When the price was on his head in Aghadoe,
O'er the mountain, by the wood, as I stole to him with
    food,
Where in hiding lone he lay in Aghadoe.

But they never took him living in Aghadoe, Aghadoe;
With the bullets in his heart in Aghadoe,
There he lay – the head my breast feels the warmth
    of, where 'twould rest.
Gone, to win the traitor's gold, from Aghadoe!

I walked to Mallow town from Aghadoe, Aghadoe,
Brought his head from the gaol's gate to Aghadoe,
Then I covered him with fern, and I piled on him the
    cairn,
Like an Irish king he sleeps in Aghadoe.

Oh! to creep into that cairn in Aghadoe, Aghadoe!
There to rest upon his breast in Aghadoe,
Sure your dog for you could die with no truer heart
    than I,
Your own love, cold on your cairn, in Aghadoe.

The name poem, too, is fine, the Banshee being taken as a type of Ireland and her sorrows, and there is a fine description of a stormy night in "The Coffin Ship." On the whole, however, these shorter poems are not so good as the longer ones: they are not so rich in association and allusion.

But in all, whether epopee or ballad, is the same charm of sincerity, of Celtic sympathy. There is no trying for effect, no rhetoric, no personal ambition, no posing. Their writer never tries to compel but always to win attention. All this simplicity and directness comes from great sympathy with his own creations. They fill him with so much pity and interest – these mournful adventurers† – that he has not time to hang purple draperies or embroideries, or consider his own attitude to the world. In this we believe he is a Celt, or at any rate of a type more commonly found in Ireland than in England. The Saxon is not sympathetic or self-abnegating; he has conquered the world by quite different powers. He is full of self-brooding. Like his own Wordsworth, most English of poets, he finds his image in every lake and puddle. He has to burthen the skylark with his cares before he can celebrate it.[17] He is always a lens† colored by self. But these poems are altogether different with their simplicity and tenderness. They rise from the same source with† the courtesy of the Irish peasant; and because there is no egotism in them there is no gloom. Their sadness is nature's, not man's – a limpid melancholy. It is the sentiment that fills morning twilight. They are Greek-like and young – as young as nature. *Helena* was as old as mankind.

Old with words and thoughts and reveries handed down for ages; complex with that ever-increasing subdivision of thought and complexity of phrase that marks an old literature. It was as old as the old man in the Irish folk-tale, who, having wandered for centuries in the form of a beautiful stag, when once the spell was broken crumbled into dust and was blown away in pieces by the wind.[18] It belonged to old England and old age; these poems belong to Ireland and youth. As a literature ages it divides nature from man and sings each for itself. Then each passion is taken from its fellows and sung alone, and cosmopolitanism begins, for a passion has no nation. But in these poems man and nature are one, and everywhere is a wild and pungent Celtic flavor. When a literature is old it grows so indirect and complex that it is only a possession for the few: to read it well is a difficult pursuit, like playing on the fiddle; one† needs especial training. But these poems should rouse each one so far as he is human and imaginative.

W. B. Yeats

18 Irish Wonders*

Mr. McAnally does not treat his material with sufficient respect; he is too eager to embroider everything with humor, to steep everything in a kind of stage Irish he has invented.[1] All this is very disappointing. When will Irishmen record their legends as faithfully and seriously as Campbell did those of the Western Highlands?[2] Mr. McAnally with his material might have made a book that students would turn to for years to come, but he has been content to blow a bubble for the circulating libraries. It is a good bubble, as bubbles go. There is not a dull chapter in the book. But no Irish peasant ever pronounced English as Mr. McAnally makes him. The very same dialect is put into the mouths of peasants from most different counties. Why, the children of one county laugh at the pronunciation of another! It is a foreigner's idea of Ireland. Neither does folk-lore like the following seem to ring true:

> Near Colooney, in Sligo [says Mr. McAnally], there is a "knowlageable woman," whose grandmother's aunt once witnessed a fairy ball, the music for which was furnished by an orchestra which the management had no doubt been at great pains and expense to secure and instruct.
>
> It was the cutest sight alive. There was a place for thim to shtand on, an' a wondherful big fiddle av the size ye cud slape in it, that was played be a monsthrous frog, an' two little fiddles, that two kittens fiddled on, an' two big drums, baten be cats, an' two trumpets, played be fat pigs. All round the fairies were dancin' like angels, the fireflies givin' thim light to see by, an' the moonbames shinin' on the lake, for it was be the shore it was, an' if ye don't belave it, the glen's still there, that they call the fairy glen to this blessed day.[3]

* This letter appeared in *PSJ* for 7 July 1889 under the column heading "The Literary World. Book Reviews and News" and with the footnote "*Irish Wonders*. By D. R.† McAnally. Houghton, Mifflin and Co. Boston and New York, 1889." HR title: "Irish Wonders."

When were fireflies imported into Ireland, where even
glowworms are scarce? When a writer is certainly inaccurate in
his dialect, and makes old women see fireflies in Ireland, one is
inclined to doubt everything, and certainly to doubt this piece
of folk-lore. It is far too ingenious, and sounds like a modern
nursery tale from German sources. Fairies are described by the
peasantry as much like mortals: sometimes a man will meet
them and dance with them before he knows who they are. They
are only occasionally small, and even then are much like small
mortals. But this cat and fiddle business seems to belong to a
quite different person – the fairy of literature. I have collected
fairy tales, if not at Colooney itself, within a mile of it, and have
lately given some months to reading all written Irish folk-lore,
so far as I could find it, whether in books or old newspapers and
magazines, but have never found anything like these fiddle-
playing animals.[4] Even so I would not doubt but for that firefly.
Mr. McAnally has not the convincing art.

However, some of the chapters are of much interest, sometimes
throwing quite a new light on some old belief. It is very pleasant
to hear that the Donegal fairies conduct the souls of the dead as
far as the gates of heaven and then return disconsolate like the
poor earth-bound creatures they are.[5] In some other counties,
they have rather a different belief about fairies and the newly
dead. One old man in County Sligo told me a story of a man
who saw all who had died out of his village for years, sitting in
a fairy rath one night. The gentry, as he called the fairies, had
enticed them away into the dim fairy world. There are probably
many races of supernatural beings, some kindly, some unkindly,
according to present belief. It must be some quite different
race than those pleasant Donegal *sheeoges*, for whom the Sligo
peasantry, at the death of a child, sprinkle the threshold with
the blood of a young chicken that they may be drawn away from
the weak soul of the child. Perhaps they are evil spirits, these
soul-thieves, and not fairies at all.[6]

Mr. McAnally has really added much to our knowledge of the
leprechaun, that shoemaking fairy who has so many treasures
under the ground. The chapter on the leprechaun contains
indeed the most minute descriptions of that creature extant.[7] He
is the child, it appears, of a debased fairy and an evil spirit. In
northern counties he wears the uniform of some British infantry
regiment, a red coat and white breeches, and a broad-brimmed,

high pointed hat. Sometimes, when he has played off some more than usually successful piece of mischief, he mounts onto a house or wall and spins round on the point of his hat with his heels in the air. In Kerry he is very fat, and wears a red cutaway jacket with seven rows of buttons, seven buttons in each row, and when in full dress wears a helmet much too large for him. In Monaghan he is called the cluricaune, if indeed the cluricaune is not, as Croker believed, a quite different kind of fairy, and wears a cone-shaped hat, the point of which he sometimes drives into the eye of one who offends him, though generally he but abuses him in a loud voice, the abused one seeing nothing, but hearing the voice. In Clare and Galway his favorite amusement is riding sheep and goats and dogs.[8] If a sheep or dog looks tired in the morning, the shepherd knows that the leprechaun has been riding on some distant errand. He is always old and withered and dapper like an old beau. In one of Mr. McAnally's stories he appears as a lady-killer.

The fairies of Lough Erne once stole away a baby called Eva. She grew up amongst them and was very well treated, and was given a dance every night. At last she fell in love with an old leprechaun. The fairy queen, wishing to find her a better husband, let her walk on the shores of the lake. There she met the mortal, Darby O'Hoolighan, and loved him and married him with the queen's consent. The queen gave them riches in plenty, pigs and sheep and cattle, and told her to tell him that if ever he struck her three blows without reason she would return to the fairies. After they had lived happily together for seventeen years, one day when she and Darby were going to a wedding she was slow and he struck her a slap on the shoulder. She began to cry. He asked her what ailed her; she said he had struck her the first of the three blows. One day when he was teaching one of his boys to use a stick she stood behind him and got hit with the shillalagh.

That was the second blow, an' made her lose her timper, an' they had a rale quarl. So he got mad, sayin' that nayther o' thim blows ought to be counted, bein' they both come be accident. So he flung the shtick agin the wall, "Divil take the shtick," says he, an' went out quick, an' the shtick fell back from the wall an' hit her an the head. "That's the third," says she, an' she kissed her sons an' walked out. Thin she called the cows in the field an' they left grazin' an' folly'd her; she called the oxen in the shtalls an' they quit atin' an' come out; an' she shpoke to the calf that was hangin' in the yard, that they'd killed that mornin' an' it got down an' come along. The lamb that was killed the day afore, it come; an' the pigs that were salted an' thim hangin' up to dhry, they come, all afther her in a shtring. Thin she called to her things in the house, an' the chairs walked out, an' the tables, an' the chist av drawers, an' the boxes, all o' thim put out legs like bastes an' come along, wid the pots an' pans, an' gridiron, an' buckets, an' noggins, an' kish, lavin' the house as bare as a 'victed tinant's, an' all afther her to the lake, where they wint undher an' disappared, and haven't been seen be man or mortial to this blessed day.

Wanst in a while she'd come to the aidge av the lake whin they were clost be the bank an' spake wid thim, fur aven, if she was half a fairy, she'd the mother's heart that the good God put in her bosom; an' wan time they seen her wid a little attomy av a man alang wid her, that was a Leprechawn, as they knewn be the look av him, an' that makes me belave that the rale rayzon av her lavin' her husband was to get back to the owld Leprechawn she was in love wid afore she was marr'd to Darby O'Hoolighan.[9]

In the chapter on the Banshee the word "fearshee" is translated "man of peace." This is entirely wrong. Feeling puzzled by this translation (Campbell makes the same blunder with a kindred word in Scotch Gaelic), I wrote to an accomplished Irish scholar, who is also perhaps the best Irish folk-lorist living, and asked him about it. He answered: "There is no such person as the 'man of peace' in Irish mythology; it is only a mistranslation of 'fairy man.' 'Shee' means 'peace' as well as 'fairy,' but this is accidental, and the words have no connection, I am certain. 'Sidh' (shee), 'a fairy,' is, I believe, nearly the same word as the Sanskrit."[10]

Mr. McAnally gives a notation of the Banshee's cry somewhat different from that given by Mr. and Mrs. S. C. Hall in their *Ireland*.[11] He is wrong in saying that the Banshee never follows Irish families abroad. There are several recorded stories of its doing so, one, for instance, I forget where, of an Irish family settled in Canada who are still followed by their Banshee.[12] And one of the most distinguished of British anthropologists told me that he has not only heard but seen it in a Central American forest. It came to announce the death of his father, who had just died in England. It was dressed in pale yellow and had grey hair and seemed very old. It vanished as he rode towards it. He had since then twice seen and heard it in London.[13]

Mr. McAnally is wrong in saying that the Banshee is invariably a ghost. Cleena of Ton Cleena, queen of the monster fairies, is the Banshee of the O'Donovan family. The great antiquarian, father of O'Donovan of Merv, claimed her for his family in a since-published letter.[14] But Mr. McAnally's mistake is fortunate, as it led to the following most interesting passage:

> The spirits of the good wander with the living as guardian angels, but the spirits of the bad are restrained in their action, and compelled to do penance at or near the places where their crimes were committed. Some are chained at the bottoms of the lakes, others buried under ground, others confined in mountain gorges; some hang on the sides of precipices, others are transfixed on the tree-tops, while others haunt the homes of their ancestors, all waiting till the penance has been endured and the hour of release arrives.

I wish the name of the part of Ireland, of the very village, where Mr. McAnally was told that the spirits of the lost were hung on the sides of precipices and transfixed on the points of trees had been given. For it is a new and very strange piece of folk-lore. It should have been recorded with a reverent exactness as to place and time. It is strange enough for the *Mahabharata* or the *Inferno* of Dante.[15]

The belief that the less holy dead are compelled to haunt the scenes of their transgressions is universal. The good also, Mr. McAnally might have added, may be earth-bound by some care or untold secret. In all parts of Ireland one hears stories of mothers who have "appeared" because of their orphan children being neglected by the husbands. One such case occurred lately in Tyrone. The children told the priest of their mother's coming to them continually. He asked were they sure it was their mother. They answered, "Would we not know our own mammy?"[16] At Howth a little while ago a woman was said to have appeared to a neighbor because her children had been sent to the workhouse.

She also asked that three masses be said for the repose of her soul. "If my husband does not believe you, show him that," she said, touching the neighbor's arm with three fingers; the places where they touched swelled up and blackened.[17] This seems to be a favorite way the dead have of impressing the living with their reality. In the Beresford ghost story the phantom of her lover caught the wrist of Lady Beresford and it withered. In parts of Ireland these earth-bound souls are compelled to obey the living. A man at Ballysodare, a Sligo village not far from Coloony, said once to me: "The stable boy up at Mrs. G——'s there met the master going round the yards after he had been two days dead, and told him to be away with him to the lighthouse, and haunt that; and there he is far out to sea still, sir. Mrs. G—— was that mad about it she dismissed the boy."[18]

The lighthouse is a very desolate one. The ghost must have a bad time of it on windy nights. Those who die suddenly very often are said to become haunting ghosts, or *thivishes*, as they call them in Gaelic. Mr. McAnally tells a pathetic tale about such a one. There was a pretty girl who was drowned tragically at Cashel. She was trying to escape from her father, who was bringing her away to make her marry a rich farmer whom she did not love. When she was struggling to escape from her father's grasp, the bank of a stream gave way and they were both drowned. There was a great wake and funeral, but her own true lover, the one her father did not wish her to marry, did not go to either: he sat as in a dream. At last he went to his mother, and told her that Nora, the dead girl, had come to him and laid her hand on his brow and said, "Come to Cashel, Paddy dear, and be wid me." He went thither. On the rocks of Cashel he tended Nora's grave, and then because they were buried near her, all the graves. In the day time he used to hide and sleep, at night to walk up and down in the chapel with her spirit. He had no friends, but the people used to leave potatoes and bread where he would find them. On these he lived. He was sixty years on the rock. When there was a burying he would sometimes show himself in the daytime and say, "You have brought me another friend."

When he got owld, an' where he cud look into the other worruld, Nora came ivery night an' brought more wid her, sper'ts av kings an' bishops that rest on Cashel, an' ther's thim that's seen the owld man walkin' in Cormac's Chapel, Nora holdin' him up an' him discoorsin' wid the mighty dead. They found him wan day, cowld an' still, on Nora's grave, an' laid him be her side, God rest his sowl, an' there he slapes to-day, God be good to him.

They said he was only a poor owld innocent, but all is aqualized, an' thim that's despised sometimes have betther comp'ny among the angels than that of mortials.[19]

Mr. McAnally tells this story very well. His phrasing is usually genuinely Irish, though the pronunciations be too often, as we have said, stage Irish. "Mighty dead" is, however, surely not good Irish at all but modern poetic. It is notable that the girl was drowned. There is something mysterious about the ghosts of the drowned that I do not well know. They seem to have a more intense life in them than other ghosts, or to be under the power of the fairies, or in some other way distinguished among the commonality of ghosts. It is said to be unlucky to have much to do with the drowned. Drowned cattle are sometimes supposed to be carried away by the fairies.

In one way Mr. McAnally does take his legends more seriously than Croker and his school did: he never rationalizes; he has no theories, and why should he?[20] The Irish peasant believes the whole world to be full of spirits, but then the most distinguished men have thought not otherwise. Newspapers have lately assured us that Lord Tennyson believes the soul may leave the body, for a time, and communicate with the spirits of the dead.[21] The Irish peasant and most serene of Englishmen are at one. Tradition is always the same. The earliest poet of India and the Irish peasant in his hovel nod to each other across the ages, and are in perfect agreement. There are two boats going to sea. In which shall we sail? There is the little boat of science. Every century a new little boat of science starts and is shipwrecked; and yet again another puts forth, gaily laughing at its predecessors. Then there is the great galleon of tradition, and on board it travel the great poets and dreamers of the past. It was built long ago, nobody remembers when. From its masthead flies the motto, *semper eadem*.[22]

W. B. Yeats

19   *A Sicilian Idyll* – Dr. Todhunter's New Play – A New Departure in Dramatic Representation*

London, May 5

A few years ago Dr. Todhunter's *Helena in Troas*† was the talk of a London season. Its solemn processions, smoking incense and stately verse combined to produce a semi-religious impression new to the London stage. On Monday last Dr. Todhunter again came before that circle of listeners who still remain faithful to the rightful muses of the stage and have not wholly bowed the knee to those two slatterns farce and melodrama. His little play, *A Sicilian Idyll*, is drawing artistic and literary people from all parts of London. There have been three performances this week, on Monday, Wednesday and Friday, respectively, and every time the little club theatre of Bedford Park has been crowded from end to end by a decidedly distinguished audience; and it is no easy thing to draw social and dramatic notables so far from town as this little red brick, Queen Anne suburb, on Friday.[1] I noticed the creator of the part of Beatrice in the "Shelley Society's" performance of the *Cenci*, Miss Alma Murray, and a little further off Miss Winifred† Emery, now performing in Buchanan's *Tomboy*† and Mr. Cyril Maude and Mr. Terriss,† just returned to the Lyceum fold for a time, and Lady Archibald Campbell of pastoral drama celebrity.[2] Among social and literary notables Mrs. Jopling† Rowe, Miss Mathilde† Blind, whose translation of Marie Bashkirtseff's diary is making such a stir, Mrs. Charles 'Hancock of "the Woman's Liberal Association," Mr. Theodore Watts, the critic, and Miss May† Morris, the daughter of the poet.[3] One saw faces here and there who are seldom to be met with at ordinary play houses – people for whom poetry and subtle dialogues have charms impossible to mere prose. The long room with its black panels covered with

---

* This letter appeared in *PSJ* for 8 June 1890.

gilt cupids has suddenly become a sacred place where the muses still walk.

When the curtain lifted there was a murmur of admiration at the beautiful scene, the work of Mr. Baldry and Mr. Arthur Lemon. The distant glimpse of the blue Mediterranean†, the statue of Bacchus against the pillars of the arbor, the overhanging festoons of grapes and vine leaves, and the white marble seat to the right, made it like a picture of Alma-Tadema's†. It was a veritable dream of peace and loveliness. The story was taken from Theocritus, and was very, very simple.[4] A shepherd dressed in leopard skins and a white-robed shepherdess come on the stage. Daphnis, the shepherd, is in love with a shepherdess, Amaryllis, who does not care in the least for him. He bewails his sorrow with the pretty extravagance of the old pastoral drama. The white-robed shepherdess, Thestylis, offers to comfort him, and he gives ready consent. He will woo her, in sport, and see if that will bring him forgetfulness. Then follows a scene in which a number of shepherds and shepherdesses sing to Bacchus in thankfulness for the vintage, and Thestylis dances with cymbals before the statue of the god. An wonderful dance, enthusiastically encored. Thestylis and the heroine, Amaryllis, are then brought together – the shepherds and shepherdesses with their crooks and their wands topped with pine cones having trooped away. The two girls talk together of marriage. Thestylis tries to soften the heart of Amaryllis toward Daphnis, and only succeeds in revealing to her that she loves him herself. Amaryllis rails against all men, and accuses her friend of being faithless to their friendship. Had they not sworn never to marry? She talks eloquently of "the tragedies of woman's lives," and of the soon decay of married love. Thestylis leaves her to go and comfort the sighing Daphnis, and so closes a very fine piece of dialogue. Amaryllis remains alone. Alcander,† a shepherd from a distant country, rough and burly, having on his head the "Phrygian bonnet," comes on. Whence has he come? Amaryllis questions. "Out of the fires of Troy, whose siege blind Homer sung," he answers. "O wonderful! so many centuries old, and not yet gray," she makes reply. "My stock, I mean. Alcander is my name."[5] He proves to be the shepherd who carried off the prizes at the last shepherds' game. He has heard of the fame of Amaryllis and has come to be cured of the love it has filled him with. He has loved the beauty of many women before he saw them, but always the first sight made him cease to care for them, they were so much less beautiful than rumor made them. He finds out who she is, and being from a far country different from gentle Sicily, kisses her against her will. This kiss is the theme of the play. When he sees how angry she is he goes away full of penitence and she remains alone with her anger.

Then follows a five-minute interval, when we talk to our neighbors and praise the acting of the heroine and the cymbal dance of Thestylis and the writing of the dialogue between the girls. When the curtain next rises it is no longer the bright daylight of the previous scene. The stage is flooded with moonlight, broken and dwindled by overhanging leaves. Thestylis and Alcander come on together. She is telling how, in spite of her anger, Amaryllis loves him, when she catches sight of Daphnis in the background and bids Alcander woo her, and so win Daphnis by jealousy from his mock love for Amaryllis and make him discover instead a real love for her. Alcander makes love very charmingly, promising true "Arcadian" gifts – lambs and goats.[6]

At this moment the figure of Amaryllis in her deep crimson dress appears in the distance. She is filled with anger. It was then only in mockery that he kissed her, she thinks, and the blood-red figure glides away again with a vow of vengeance. This entrance is a particularly fine piece of acting. Meanwhile Thestylis, who has seen nothing, has carried her point. Daphnis is furiously jealous, and has quite forgotten his love for Amaryllis. He rails at her in the most violent way. He goes away threatening to live "away from the savage men," far from pastoral Sicily, and she follows him.[7] The next few passages are the finest in the play. The wronged Amaryllis comes on to the dim stage, now once more empty. An old woman in perfect silence places a flaming tripod in the centre and goes out. Amaryllis calls on the gods to avenge her, and, pacing round and round, weaves an incantation to draw Alcander dying to her feet. He is carried in by two shepherds and laid before her. They are then left alone. A fine situation well worked up to. She is filled with remorse, and tries to break her spells. She extinguishes the flame in the tripod and he finds partial relief. There is only one thing, he tells her, that can cure him – her love. But did he not woo Thestylis, she asks. He explains and they are reconciled. She leans upon his breast and cries that she has "come into a new

country" and love has made her "a woman."[8] Daphnis and
Thestylis come on together. They, too, have been reconciled,
and the play closes with the singing of the chorus of shepherds
and shepherdesses, who crown the lovers with amaranth and
myrtle, and the curtain falls, amid loud applause and calls for
actors and author. On all sides one hears nothing but "how
pretty," "how beautiful," "I would not have missed it for the
world."

The whole play was indescribably lovely – a veritable vision
of the golden age.[9] From first to last one's interest never strayed.
Every dialogue was full of nature and drama; yet what slight
materials – a kiss taken unwillingly, an incantation that comes
to nothing, and a reconciliation. Prose would have made nothing
of such slight materials. Verse has made of them a charming
poem, an absorbing drama; none the less absorbing because a
glamour of other-world beauty was over it all. Dr. Todhunter
has had several requests – in the case of one of which he
consented – for leave to revive† *Helena*, and will, I believe, have
a still larger number in the case of the present work. He has, I
believe, already had one, on the first performance.

It only remains to speak of the acting. Mrs. Edward Emery,
who took the part of heroine, was above all praise. Her subtle
and delicate acting and striking beauty were upon all lips. Miss
Lily Linfield's† rendering of the role of Thestylis was vivacious
and full of "go." Her ear for verse is not, however, as good as
Mrs. Emery's, or that of the versatile Mr. Heron-Allen† – solicitor,
well-known writer on palmistry, lecturer, war correspondent,
novelist and a recognized authority on old violins – who went
through his new role of actor with all the success that seems to
follow him everywhere. Mr. Paget,† the artist, gave his lines well
and looked the athletic Alcander to perfection. The music was
much praised. The author is Mr. Luard-Selby†, well known for
his songs and the admired church service used in Salisbury
Cathedral.[10] On the whole, it will be long before I forget this
pastoral play or any of its accessories, scenery, dances, songs
and leopard-skin robes. It reminds one of the great days of the
stage, when poetry was thought to be not undramatic, and
literature not wholly out of place in the glare of the footlights.

W. B. Yeats

20   A Scholar Poet*

In Victor Hugo's *Shakespeare* occur these sentences:[1] "'He is sober, discreet, temperate. He can be trusted.' Is this the description of a domestic? No; of a poet."[2] In these words the greatest modern representative of that school of poets that looks upon poetry as a direct message from the Most High, and amenable to no law but its own, poured out his scorn on those critics who consider it a purely human art, a criticism of life by subtle and refined thinkers. When Ezekiel lay upon his side and ate dung in order, as Blake says, to make men believe that there is an infinite in all things, he belonged to the first school.[3] When Matthew Arnold defined God as "a something not ourselves that makes for righteousness," he exemplified, as always in his writings, the opposite habit of mind.[4] It is not necessary to debate the point at issue. It would take many pages. Perhaps one would not be far from some truth bearing on the matter in saying that as nature has night and day, action and repose, light and shadow, so the mind of man has two kinds of shepherds: the poets who rouse and trouble, the poets who hush and console. It is often pleasant to turn to the latter; to turn, when bewildered by the gigantic, to men who have nothing extravagant, exuberant, mystical; to turn from the inspired to the accomplished. For most men the divine fire glows in regions of unstable equilibrium. They cannot rest there.

Among the younger men who follow the Matthew Arnold tradition, there is not one who has produced more scholar-like and accomplished poetry than an almost unknown writer, William Watson. In technique it is perfect. No ill-chosen word ever jangles its serene and solemn meditation. No diffuseness

* This letter appeared in *PSJ* for 15 June 1890 under the column heading "The Literary World. Book Reviews and News" and with the footnote "*Wordsworth's Grave and Other Poems*. By William Watson. Cameo Series. T. Fisher Unwin, Paternoster Square." HR title: "A Scholar Poet."

dims its slow, burning fire – a fire that will not warm our hearths, but gives a thin flame, good to read by for a little, when wearied by some more potent influence.

I first heard of William Watson about five years ago. A friend, Professor Dowden, I think, lent me a little book of quatrains, *Epigrams* it was somewhat misnamed, there being nothing epigrammatic in the ordinary sense of the word about them – no vivacity, no sharpness in their deliberate art.[5] The book, I was told, had made illustrious friends. Dante Gabriel Rossetti had praised it, and a certain famous hedonist had written a letter on scented note paper to say it was "the most perfect book that had come from any press for twenty years," or some such words.[6] The book seemed all the more attractive, perhaps, because, praised by the many among the few, it had not made even a few friends among the many. It was a scholar's book, and would perforce remain so. To know it at all implied almost a knowledge of signs and passwords – membership of some mysterious scholars' Brotherhood of the Rose.[7] Before long I knew its hundred quatrains by heart, and do not find they have lost anything in five years. It still seems to me more beautiful than any other work of its author's.

At odd times these last five years William Watson's name has reached the more alert among us. At the time of General Gordon's death he contributed to *The National Review* a series of sonnets, written from the Conservative point of view, that were hailed by an evening Tory paper as the greatest political poetry since Milton.[8] In slow moving, stately rhetoric they lamented the fate of Gordon and his men, telling how their dust was

> Grown
> A portion of the fiery sands abhorred;

cast elaborate invective against all whom their author believed to be the enemies of England – Russia and the like; grew wroth with cosmopolitans, proclaiming their author's pride in "Insularity," his loving care for men of whom he can say:

> Born of my mother England's mighty womb,
> Nursed on my mother England's mighty knees,

And lull'd as I was lull'd in glory and gloom
With cradle song of her protecting seas.[9]

It was clearly scholars' politics. He would have written quite otherwise if Wordsworth and Milton had not written political sonnets before him. The thought and feeling were in no way new or personal, nor are they at any time throughout his poems.

A little later, one heard he had finished for the same review a poem on Wordsworth's grave, but kept it back for polish. Two years passed, and he was still polishing it. Last year it appeared, and has now been followed by a thin octavo, Number Three of Unwin's Cameo Series, containing a general selection of his poems, with the "Wordsworth's Grave" as title poem.[10] I do not think it has been much reviewed as yet, but it is certainly finding a welcome among that small circle of people – may their shadows never grow less – who still find time to read poetry by new writers.

As one turns over the pages, and catches sight of page after page devoted to metrical criticism of Shelley and Wordsworth, and Landor and Keats, or lights on an epigram comparing Marlowe and Shakespeare, or weaving metaphors for the play of *King Lear*, one sees at once that the book has sprung from the critical rather than the creative imagination.[11] For this writer a scholar and his scholarly feelings are the microcosm, and the books he reads make up the whole of it; and the books he reads include by no means even the entire world of letters. He is insular, as his sonnet puts it. For him Goethe's "proud, elaborate calm," as he calls it, means less than "Byron's fire," and France has little to please him with her "Hugo-flare against the night."[12] Among modern English writers, Wordsworth is the one he loves. In his own work he is no less deliberate than the sage of Rydal: no emotion is ever extreme; no belief is held immoderately, unless it be Tory patriotism; no violent emotion ever tips the beam of his balance. I turn to the section containing twenty "epigrams," selected from his first book, and find his evident ideal in the very first:

'Tis human fortune's happiest height to be
  A Spirit melodious, lucid, poised, and whole;
Second in order of felicity
  I hold it, to have walk'd with such a soul.[13]

And these epigrams still remain, I believe, the most perfect and spontaneous expressions he has yet found, having less rhetoric than the sonnets, less elaboration than the title poem, less artifice than the lyrics. They certainly contain lines that should live. They are all full of style, and some of solemnity. Witness the following:

> In mid whirl of the dance of Time ye start,
>   Start at the cold touch of Eternity,
> And cast your cloaks about you, and depart;
>   The minstrels pause not in their minstrelsy.

Or this on Byron:

> Too avid of earth's bliss, he was of those
>   Whom Delight flies because they gave her chase.
> Only the odour of her wild hair blows
>   Back in their faces hungering for her face.

Or this on Antony at Actium:

> He holds a dubious balance: – yet *that* scale,
>   Whose freight the world is, surely shall prevail?
> No; Cleopatra droppeth into *this*
>   One counterpoising orient, sultry kiss.

Or, perhaps, finest of all, the following on the play of *King Lear*:

> Here Love the slain with Love the slayer lies;
>   Deep drown'd are both in the same sunless pool.
> Up from its depths that mirror thundering skies
>   Bubbles the wan mirth of the mirthless Fool.[14]

There are two poems in the section of lyrics that perhaps go nearer than he has gone elsewhere to seeing life and nature direct, and without the spectacles of books. The first, on "Life without Health," is weighty and impressive:

> Behold life builded as a goodly house
>   And grown a mansion ruinous,
> With winter blowing through its crumbling walls!

The master paceth up and down his halls,
And in the empty hours
Can hear the tottering of his towers
And tremor of their bases under ground.
And off he starts and looks around
At creaking of a distant door
Or echo of his footfall on the floor,
Thinking it may be one whom he awaits
And hath for many days awaited,
Coming to lead him through the mouldering gates
Out somewhere, from his home dilapidated.

In the second, "World Strangeness," one finds an exquisite expression of a sensitive nature and of its trouble over the riddle of things, a nature that is refined, inquiring, subtle – everything but believing. It is a nature admirable for most things that man has to do – except found religions or write the greatest kind of poetry. I quote the poem entire:

Strange the world about me lies,
    Never yet familiar grown –
Still disturbs me with surprise,
    Haunts me like a face half known.

In this house with starry dome,
    Floored with gemlike plains and seas,
Shall I never feel at home,
    Never wholly be at ease?

On from room to room I stray,
    Yet my host can ne'er espy,
And I know not to this day
    Whether guest or captive I.

So between the starry dome
    And the floor of plains and seas,
I have never felt at home,
    Never wholly been at ease.[15]

I believe that this little book – it is not more than seventy-five thinly printed pages – is a distinct addition to contemporary literature, and that it will for years to come continue to charm and irritate alternately, but at all times interest, the few whom it was intended for. It is not promise, but complete accomplishment. There is not one ragged or slovenly line. All is perfectly scholarly, perfectly cultivated. It will interest some people because it expresses their thoughts, and some because it does not, but gives them instead a glimpse into a quiet scholar's room, where everything is well arranged, where no fierce emotion has ever come. One thinks, when reading it, of a small house full of books somewhere in a pastoral country, with ivy falling over the windows and an owl somewhere in the deep shadow under the eaves. Taking it all in all, it is, perhaps, the most polished achievement of any among the youngest generation of poets. It is all the more to be treasured, too, because there will hardly be another book of the same type written in the coming generation. The struggle of labor and capital, of mysticism and science, and many another contest now but dimly foreshadowed, will more and more absorb or deafen into silence all such cloistered lives – the products of periods of rest between two worlds, "one dead, one powerless to be born."[16]

W. B. Yeats

21   The Arts and Crafts:
An Exhibition at William Morris's*

The movement most characteristic of the literature and art and to some small extent of the thoughts, too, of our century has been romanticism.[1] We all know the old formal classicism† gave battle to it and was defeated when Hernani's horn rang out on the French stage.[2] That horn has been ringing through the world ever since. There is hardly a movement in which we do not hear its echo. It marked the regained freedom of the spirit and imagination of man in literature. Since then painting in its turn has flung aside the old conventions. The arts of decoration are now making the same struggle. They have been making it for some years under the leadership of William Morris, poet, Socialist, romance writer, artist and upholsterer, and in all ways the most many-sided man of our times.[3] But for these "arts and crafts" exhibitions, of which this is the third year, the outer public would hardly be able to judge of the immense change that is going on in all kinds of decorative art and how completely it is dominated by one man of genius. Last Saturday was the private view. The handsome rooms† of the new art gallery with their white pillars and leaping fountain were crowded by much that is best and most thoughtful of London society – above all with whatever is "advanced" in any direction – literature, politics, art. It was this future paying homage to one man who had turned aside for a little from his dreams of a Eutopia of Socialism for the poor, to create a reality of art scarcely less beautiful for any rich man who cares for these heavy tapestries and deep-tiled fireplaces, for these hanging draperies and stained-glass windows that all seem to murmur of the middle ages, and the "olden times long ago." Only a small part of the exhibits are from Morris and Co., and yet all the numberless people who send work from the well-known firm that made the huge fireplace in

* This letter appeared in *PSJ* for 26 Oct 1890.

the north gallery to the lady who illuminated the copy of Coventry Patmore's poems in the balcony are under the same spell.[4] The melancholy beauty of *The Earthly Paradise* is everywhere. "The Idle Singer of an Empty Day" has neither sung nor wrought idly.[5]

The south gallery is chiefly notable for the cartoons for stained glass and for Cobden Sanderson's book binding.[6] Along the south wall goes a huge design by Burne-Jones for a window at Jesus College, Cambridge. The window itself is to be executed by Morris and Co. The subject is the ninefold "Hierarchy" of angels, archangels, cherubim, seraphim, thrones, dominions, principalities, powers and vertues. It is full of medieval symbolism difficult for modern ignorance to remember and understand. The figures are of course full of that peculiar kind of subtle expression and pensive grace runs through all Burne-Jones's work, but it is hard to judge of the final effect with its blazing and jewel-like color from these uncolored drawings. One can but remember the windows from the same hand at Oxford and fill in the reds, and gold, and blues out of one's head; but then the Oxford windows I have in mind were done when Burne-Jones was young, and his manner almost indistinguishable from that of Rossetti, whereas these angels and archangels are in his most recent and decorative style.[7] They have not the intensity of feeling of the early work, but are, on the other hand, much less crabbed in drawing and crowded in composition. In the same room are other window designs from the same hand – would that they were colored – of subjects like "The Annunciation of the Shepherds," "Lazarus and Mary," "Rachel and Jacob."[8] The windows themselves in each instance being the work of Morris and Co. The case of artistic book covers is charming. In few handicrafts has there been greater need of reforms, the book covers of this century have been for the most part pretentious and foolish, with their gilding smeared hither and thither in purposeless and conventional forms. These Cobden Sanderson books are, however, simple and artistic, but also not cheap. One expects illuminated pages like G. E. Renter's† six specimen sheets of Morris's romance, *The Roots† of the Mountains* to be as dear as you please, but there seems to be no reason why the covers of books should not be designed by good artists and yet remain not altogether beyond the purse of the poor student for whom, after all, books chiefly exist.[9] In comparison to the immense bills for paper, and printing, publishing, illustrating, and writing, the expense of the cover designer should count for little.

The feature of the west gallery is distinctly a huge green marble mantel piece, with a sculptured figure of Fouque's "Undine" in the centre. In some ways, perhaps, the most interesting exhibit of all. It is the work of Messrs. Farmer and Brindley†.[10] In the same room is Mr. Parnell's contribution, the Irish national banner, designed by Walter Crane. The subject is the "Sunburst," breaking into a Celtic cross, enclosed by an Irish harp, surrounded with the motto "Children of the Gael shoulder to shoulder," the four-quarters of the banner contain the shields of the four provinces.[11] In the right hand is Mr. Parnell's now familiar autograph. The banner may look fine enough when blown out in the wind but it certainly looks over-glaring in color and formal in design among the soft greens and rich golds of estheticisms.

In the north gallery is the furniture, oaken and cushioned alcoves, deep fireplaces pannelled with every kind of form and colors, heavy curtains, carved writing tables and desks and all stamped with the same signet of romanticism and medievalism. There is nothing to remind one that the formal classicism of the eighteenth century, with its legacy to the nineteenth, of dismal mahogany and pallid coloring ever existed anywhere.

Upstairs in the balcony are more book-bindings and book illumination, too, to make us remember that the art of the old world has been revived in our day. There is also an etching from Madox Brown's *Dream of Sardanapalus*, a picture seldom seen, though among the finest he has painted, and to my mind much more interesting than his big cartoons in the south gallery.[12] *The Baptism of Eadwine†*, a picture that I cannot persuade myself to like chiefly, I think, because I have a violent hatred for "Eadwine†" himself, with his clerical beard, and because I do not know what he has done with his feet in that very small fount they have immersed him in. Not that the cartoon is not full of that curious realism of pose and fullness of light that marks the Father of Prae-Raphaelites.[13]

On the whole, then, we have in this exhibition the last echo of Hernani's horn – the long-waited-for deliverance of the decorative arts.

W. B. Yeats

22 The Poetic Drama – Some Interesting Attempts to Revive It in London – Dr. Todhunter's Important Work in *The Poison Flower**

London, July 13

It is one of the queer things about our age that with all our education and respect for literature we have no modern poetic drama. We still go to see Shakespeare, but then we have made him one of our superstitions. When any adventurous person puts verse upon the stage, the theatre-goer – if the verse be worth anything and not mere prose cut into lengths – begins to yawn and say it is all very pretty, but it is not dramatic. It is the poet's fault, he insists, that he does not like the play. He then goes on, if he be a bookish man, to explain that the Elizabethan poets were quite different and understood the stage and people like him, and that until poets of their sort take to play making once more he prefers *The Lights of London*, or *Judah*, or *The Silver King*, or *Jane*, or whatever the popular play of the time may be.[1] Sometimes he happens to be critic for one of the morning papers, in which case he says all this at great length and with an evident sense of superiority. But after all is it mainly the fault of the poet? Did the Elizabethan poet write for the sort of stage this man admires, or understand people like him, or even use the word *dramatic* in the same sense? Read Chapman's dramas if you would know the answer.[2] They were popular in their day, and yet there are pages on pages in them of sheer poetry, long speeches that have no dramatic justification of any kind except their beauty. The fact is the age of Elizabeth was one of the great poetic ages. Every one, from the pot boys to the noblemen, thought imagination a high and worthy thing. Thomas Dekker

---

* This letter appeared in *PSJ* for 26 July 1891. HR title: "A Poetic Drama."

in one of his prose tracts describes the honor and glory it brought a man in one of the eating houses of the day to be thought a poet by his fellow diners, and gives amusing directions for getting up such a reputation with the least possible amount of talent.[3] The knowledge and love of poetry were then a necessary part of good breeding, for commercialism and puritanism had not yet set their brand on England.

Dr. Todhunter has heroically attempted to bring back our listless and conventional public to something of the high thinking and high feeling of the playgoers of the time of Elizabeth. It is somewhat uphill work, naturally, and must for some time tend to resemble, for both author and audience, the famous adventures of Jack and Jill.[4] He has, however, had more than one unexpected success. Some few people are growing tired of perpetual *Lights of London*. I chronicled for you some time ago the triumphant production of *A Sicilian Idyll* at Bedford Park.[5] For a small number of performances – twice as many as were originally arranged for – he filled from end to end the little club theatre. Nor did they come with "paper," these just people who had not bowed the knee to farce or melodrama, but paid well for their seats and went home rejoicing, and bade their friends go and pay likewise. Now Dr. Todhunter has had the *Idyll* acted at the Vaudeville, one of the big Strand theatres, and preluded it for this occasion with a play of still more romantic and passionate nature.[6] It was a great change from the men and women of culture who thronged the club theatre to the Philistines – oh, that some philanthropist would invent a new name for "our friends the enemy" – who dropped in out of curiosity at the Vaudeville and were good enough to sit there in the body while their hearts were with *Jane* afar.[7] Instead of appealing to them with a play as closely resembling what they were used to as would be compatible with its being poetry, he decided to give them something which would challenge their hostility with every line. The motive of *The Poison Flower*, as he calls the new piece, must seem to them wild, exotic and obscure. An Elizabethan would have found it all obvious enough, for his age knew all the gamut of unhappy love from the deep bass notes of realism to the highest and most intense cry of lyric passion. It knew that romantic art alone when in its wildest and most fantastic mood can give us these lyric intonations. The Londoner, on the other hand, can only open his eyes and murmur, "The man must have been mad when he wrote that." The audiences that loved Ben Jonson's Masks, Chapman's *Bussy D'Ambois* or the love scenes of *Old Fortunatus* would have wished for more numerous set passages of poetic oratory, and more audacious metaphors; the Victorian public, on the other hand, by the mouth of a morning paper accustomed to pronounce its mandates, asks for more "matter of fact" conversations.[8] Yet Dr. Todhunter may, on the whole, congratulate himself upon having gone as near success as could be expected. In spite of the burning July heat, a certain portion of the regular public did go to see it; a still smaller portion did forget *Jane* and find the shadow of old romance a fine thing; and some papers of good standing have worked themselves up into very fair enthusiasm. In his *Helena in Troas*, some few years ago, Dr. Todhunter drew the multitude in great numbers – there being three hundred pounds in the house the first day – but then he had to help him the most wonderful stage manager of our time, E. W. Godwin, and the curiosity that was roused by his exact model of a Greek theatre, and the patronage of the Prince of Wales, to bring in the crowd.[9] This time he has had nothing to rely upon but dramatic poetry soundly acted; and he has gone near enough to success to make it seem probable that we shall yet have a genuine public, however small, for poetic drama, and that we may see once more the work of poets put upon the stage as matter of regular business, and have plays of heroic passion and lofty diction, instead of commonplace sentiments uttered in words which have at the very best no merit but successful mimicry of the trivial and unbeautiful phraseology of the streets and the tea table. We may again – for genius can never be exhausted – experience dramatic movements mighty as the last agony of Faustus when burned was "Apollo's laurel bough," and cut "the branch that might have grown full straight," where now real fire engines driven by real firemen find worthy setting in absurd plays.[10] When things are at their worst, philosophy, popular and otherwise, assures us they begin to mend, and realism has had rope enough to hang itself these latter years, and we have still some coils left if it wants to do it decoratively.

The Poison Flower was suggested by Hawthorne's "Rappaccini's Daughter." There is the garden of flowers whose breath is poison, and the young girl who dwells among them until she, too, is poisonous as the flowers, and the old magician who has planned out the garden; but the story is worked out with much greater detail, and a number of secondary incidents are added. In the midst of the garden, for instance, is a mysterious tree, "this new Eden's tree of life," in† which dwells the soul of a dead mistress of the magician's, his familiar, with whom he talks and learns the wisdom of the dead people. The magician himself is more completely realized than was possible in Hawthorne's dreamy little story, and the garden is made significant with hints of allegory.[11]

Rappaccini, we are told, has brought his daughter up in this garden of poisons that she may grow impervious to all the poisons – the sins and diseases – of the world and drive them out as "poison drives out poison." Giovanni Guasconti, allured by the beauty of the magician's daughter, makes his way by a secret stair into the garden. He is at first almost slain by the poisonous flowers, but Beatrice, the magician's daughter, gives him an amulet that preserves him until he, too, has absorbed the nature of the flowers and grown deadly as they are. He then discovers that he has been lured into the garden to be the husband of Beatrice, and father of the new race that is to redeem the world. He is horror-stricken to find himself shut off from his fellows. A friend follows him to rescue him if possible, and gives him in the short while he dares to stay an antidote strong enough to drive out the magician's poison. He persuades Beatrice to drink it, and she dies; for her nature had become so intermixed with the poisonous life of the flowers that the antidote drove away life also. Giovanni Guasconti then drinks the poison of her breath and dies with the words,

> See, I plunge after, and will follow thee,
> Æons on Æons, till my flaming feet
> Bear me to thy pure presence.

I wonder when anything so startling as this play must seem to the Philistines was seen before on the London stage. Certainly it has given the few who care for poetry and romance more pleasure than anything for a long time. A friend who happened to come in since I began this article tells me he has seen it three times. Much of this charm is in the play itself, but some comes, undoubtedly, from the form – from the greater compression and suggestiveness that give verse its advantage over prose as a dramatic vehicle. If we had a poetic drama I should probably be more critical. I do not think, for instance, that Dr. Todhunter has a quite firm enough grasp of the significance of his allegory. He has not made me quite certain of its meaning, at any rate. He need not have suggested an allegoric significance at all; but having done so, it should have been more completely worked out. Then again, I find the conversation between the lovers in Scene Two rather circular in its motion: it does not press on to an event as dramatic dialogue should do. It is a little desultory. It contains many things that are wanted, but somehow they are not brought in with perfect success. These are, however, slight matters when weighed against the great charm of the total effect.

The acting was worthy of the play. Miss Florence Farr, who made her first appearance in any important part in the Amaryllis of *A Sicilian Idyll* last year, and won more general recognition by her versions of *Rosmersholm*† at the Vaudeville this spring, acted with subdued passion in the character of Beatrice. She is an almost perfect poetic actress. All her gestures are rhythmic and charming, and she gives to every line its full volume of sound. Her one fault is a slight tendency to underact. She has shown by one magnificent rendering of the incantation scene in the *Idyll* that she has power enough for anything, but does not seem as yet quite sure of herself. On Friday, the last performance of the two plays, she gave the incantation with a force that added vehemence and beauty, whereas on Tuesday she underacted it sadly. Bernard Gould†, who took the part of Giovanni, had all his usual power of utterance and all the statuesque grace of his not unpleasantly conventionalized gesture.[12]

There is a chance of the play being put on the stage in America. Dr. Todhunter holds, I believe, that the American public cares more for poetry than the English – an opinion borne out by the success of *A Blot in the 'Scutcheon* in America after its utter failure in England. Browning received (I do not know that this has been pointed out by his recent biographers) seventy pounds from the American performances – not a large sum, but certainly more than it brought him in this country.[13]

W. B. Yeats

NOTES

These notes provide information about names, places, historical events, titles, quotations, and allusions that are not identifiable from their immediate contexts in *Letters to the New Island*. Because of the wide variation in knowledge among the prospective international readers of the volume, even names and titles relatively familiar to many, such as Shakespeare and *King Lear*, are identified. Although such annotation can never be purely objective and factual, we have kept overt interpretation to a minimum.

Because Yeats often wrote about the same subjects for both *BP* and *PSJ*, a number of the notes contain cross-references to other notes. We regret any inconvenience to readers caused by this format, but the only alternative would entail excessive repetition. Occasional repetition will be found in notes where the information itself occupies little more space than a cross-reference would require. The notes also include a number of references to other works by Yeats in which topics mentioned in *Letters to the New Island* reappear. These notes are intended to assist readers who wish to trace a given subject elsewhere in Yeats's *oeuvre*.

The abbreviations used in the notes are identified in the List of Abbreviations at the beginning of the book. The notes themselves are numbered in a separate sequence for each of Yeats's letters, are cued in the text by superscript numerals, and appear below under the item number and title assigned to each letter in this edition. Cross-references to notes in the same sequence give the note number only; cross-references to other notes give the item number followed by a point and the number of the pertinent note (e.g. note 22 to item 2 is cross-referenced as note 2.22).

Epigraph: the German epigraph may be translated as, "What one wishes in youth, one has the fullness of in old age."

1 PREFACE

1. The writer and teacher Horace Reynolds (1896–1965) edited the first and only previous edition of *Letters to the New Island* (Cambridge, Mass.: Harvard University Press, 1934; repr. 1970). Yeats had sailed from Southampton on 21 Oct 1932 for his last lecture tour of the United States. Reynolds attended Yeats's lecture at Wellesley College on 8 Dec 1932 and interviewed him at his hotel in Boston the next day. The American newspapers were the Boston *Pilot* and *Providence Sunday Journal*.

2. Passage of the Chace Act by the United States in 1891 enabled foreign authors for the first time to enjoy American copyright protection.

3. Bedford Park, where Yeats lived 1879–81 and again 1888–95, was a garden suburb of London reflecting some of the principles of the aesthetic movement, particularly in interior design. Its Clubhouse, built in 1879, saw the first production of John Todhunter's *A Sicilian Idyll* in May 1890. Todhunter (1839–1916) entered Trinity College, Dublin, in 1861; there he befriended John Butler Yeats (see note 5) and won the Vice-Chancellor's prize for verse three times. He served 1870–4 as Professor of English at Alexandra College, Dublin, and settled in 1879 in Bedford Park. Of Todhunter's literary works – which included poems, plays, translations, and studies of Shelley and Heine – *A Sicilian Idyll* most impressed Yeats.

4. The actress Florence Farr (1860–1917) played the part of Amaryllis in *A Sicilian Idyll*. She later acted in several of Yeats's plays and shared his occult interests as well. Books by the amateur actor and palm-reader Edward Heron-Allen (1861–1943) include *Violin-Making* (1882) and *A Study Manual of Cheirosophy* (1885); he was co-author of *Chiromancy* (1883). "Some woman engaged from some London theatre" was Lily Linfield, dancer and actress.

5. William Morris (1834–96), the prominent writer and designer, influenced Yeats more by his taste for medievalism and romance than by his socialism. John Butler Yeats (1839–1922), the poet's father, was a well-known portrait painter of the Irish revival. Dante Gabriel Rossetti (1828–82) was a leading Pre-Raphaelite poet and painter.

6. Percy Bysshe Shelley (1792–1822) was the Romantic poet who Yeats said "shaped my life" (*E&I* 424). His play *The Cenci* (1819, but first produced by the Shelley Society in 1886; see note 8.4) featured the tormented Beatrice Cenci persecuted by her father; his *Epipsychidion* (1821) presented a Dantesque treatment of idealized Romantic love. Alfred Tennyson (1809–92), first Baron Tennyson, served as Poet Laureate. His tragedy *Becket* (1884) treated the quarrel between Henry II and Archbishop of Canterbury Thomas Becket; his lyric poem "The Lotos-Eaters" (1832) elaborated a passage from the *Odyssey*, book IX, into a portrait of languorous longing for escape from life's rigors.

7. Yeats's play was first published in 1892 as *The Countess Kathleen* and later

much revised. In it the Countess sells her soul to the demons to feed her starving people but is redeemed at the end.

8. The writer and preacher George MacDonald (1824–1905) and his family gave frequent performances from 1877 onwards of his wife Louisa's dramatic adaptation of John Bunyan's allegory *The Pilgrim's Progress* (1684).

9. The Royal Academy of Arts, founded under the patronage of George III in 1768, was regarded by the painters surrounding the young Yeats as the center of official, sterile art.

10. William Holman Hunt (1827–1910) was one of the founding members of the Pre-Raphaelite Brotherhood. Many of his paintings are on religious or literary subjects.

11. With the help of T. W. Rolleston, Yeats founded the Irish Literary Society, London, in late 1891 as a renewal of the Southwark Irish Literary Club (see note 10.8); the inaugural General Meeting was held in May 1892. That spring and summer he campaigned for the founding of the National Literary Society in Dublin to promote Irish culture, particularly literature.

12. Founded in 1877, the National Library of Ireland officially opened its building in Kildare Street, Dublin, on 29 Aug 1890.

13. Yeats abridges and misquotes the title and credits of *The Works of William Blake: Poetic, Symbolic, and Critical*, edited with lithographs of the illustrated "Prophetic Books" and a memoir and interpretation by Edwin John Ellis and William Butler Yeats (London: Bernard Quaritch, 1893). Containing two volumes of commentary and one of text, this edition includes the long poem *Vala* and substantial extracts from *An Island in the Moon*, neither of which had been published before.

14. Michael Butler Yeats was born on 22 Aug 1921. He attended St. Columba's College, Rathfarnham, before entering Trinity College, Dublin.

15. William Blake (1757–1827) was one of the two great Romantic influences on Yeats (the other was Shelley). Emmanuel Swedenborg (1688–1772) was a Swedish mystical philosopher and scientist who influenced both Blake and Yeats; so, too, did the German mystic Jacob Boehme (1575–1624).

16. Yeats worked on *The Shadowy Waters*, eventually published in very different forms as both a poem and a play, for over a quarter of a century, from the early 1880s until 1907. Its plot concerns the search for a perfect and eternal union between the lovers Forgael and Dectora.

17. Yeats studied at the Metropolitan School of Art in Dublin from 1884 to 1886.

18. *CT* contains poems, essays, and stories on folk and fairy themes.

2 IRISH WRITERS WHO ARE WINNING FAME

1. William Congreve (1670–1729) and Richard Brinsley Sheridan (1751–1816) were among the leading dramatists of their day. Oliver Goldsmith (1728 or 1730–74) wrote with distinction in a number of genres, including comedy; William Wills adapted Goldsmith's novel *The Vicar of Wakefield* for his own drama *Olivia* (1878).

2. William Gorman Wills (1828–91) had successive careers as journalist, portrait painter, and dramatist, eventually being appointed "Dramatist to the Lyceum" (the theater where Henry Irving acted the principal male roles). The appropriately named Dion(ysius Lardner) Boucicault (1820–90) was a popular playwright best known for his favorable if sentimental revision of the stage-Irishman type.

3. First produced at the Princess's Theatre in December 1883, Wills's play *Claudian* is a melodramatic adaptation of the story of the Wandering Jew.

4. In 1881 and 1883 earthquakes struck the island of Ischia, 16 miles southwest of Naples. For an account of Wills's trip to Rome see the memoir by his brother Freeman Wills, *W. G. Wills: Dramatist and Painter* (London: Longmans, Green, 1898) ch. XVII.

5. Wills's collaborator on *Claudian* was the playwright and novelist Henry Herman (1832–94), who provided the plot; he was also Wilson Barrett's manager at the Princess's Theatre.

6. The "well known dramatist" has not yet been identified.

7. Ellen Alice Terry (1847–1928) was a famous actress who played the leading female roles at the Lyceum Theatre. Sir Henry Irving (1838–1905) paid Wills £800 for his play *King Arthur* but then chose not to produce it; Guinevere was King Arthur's wife. Shakespeare's tragedy *Macbeth* (first acted in 1606) presents Macbeth's usurpation of the crown and eventual downfall. The Irish hero Robert Emmet (1778–1803) was a United Irishman executed for his leadership of the abortive uprising of 1803; Wills does not seem to have written a play about him.

8. Sir Francis Cowley Burnand (1836–1917) served as editor of the weekly comic magazine *Punch* from 1880 until 1906. The poet and biographer Henry Austin Dobson (1840–1921) was a close friend of the critic Sir Edmund William Gosse (1849–1928), who is now best remembered for his autobiographical *Father and Son* (1907). Herbert Spencer (1820–1903) was the founder of evolutionary philosophy, a social application of Darwinism. Yeats disliked Gosse's embrace of Ibsenism and Spencer's scientism.

9. The dramatic critic Edward Dutton Cook (1829–83) worked on the *Pall Mall Gazette* from 1867 to 1875 and then on the *World* from 1875 to 1883. "Miss S——" has not yet been identified.

10. The "very distinguished poet" who remarked on book prices has not yet been identified, but may have been William Morris, A. C. Swinburne, or Coventry Patmore.

11. The many books of the poet Aubrey Thomas de Vere (1814–1902) include *Legends of St. Patrick*, which was published in London by Cassell in 1889 and Macmillan in 1892.

12. The long sequence of poems *The Angel in the House* (1854–63) by Coventry Kersey Dighton Patmore (1823–96) celebrates married love. The first two cantos of *My Beautiful Lady* (1863) by the sculptor and poet Thomas Woolner (1825–92) were originally published in the Pre-Raphaelite journal the *Germ*, to which Patmore also contributed. *Ça ira*: French, "It [the Revolution] shall go on," the burden of a French revolutionary song composed about 1789.

13. Joseph Skipsey (1832–1903), the self-taught English collier poet, worked as a boy in the Northumberland coalpits. Walter Scott's edition of Skipsey's

Carols from the Coal-Fields (London, 1886) was republished as *Carols, Songs and Ballads* in 1888.

14. For Rossetti see note 1.5. Rossetti, who knew Skipsey, repeatedly praised his poetry, as in a letter to the author calling it "poetry coming really from a poet of the people who describes what he knows and mixes in" – Robert Spence Watson, *Joseph Skipsey: His Life and Work* (London: T. Fisher Unwin, 1909) pp. 53–4.

15. James Clarence Mangan (1803–49) was one of the leading Irish poets of his age; his stirring lyric "Dark Rosaleen," based on an Old Irish original, is one of his best-known works. Yeats ranked him with Thomas Davis and Sir Samuel Ferguson in his own poem "To Ireland in the Coming Times."

16. A Special Commission of Parliament (Sep 1888–Nov 1889) investigated charges against the Irish leader Charles Stewart Parnell (1846–91) stemming principally from letters forged by the Dublin journalist Richard Pigott; in Feb 1890 the Commission's report found Parnell innocent of all charges. The Irish National League, inaugurated by Parnell in 1882, became the constituency organization of the Irish Parliamentary Party. Clondalkin is a village a few miles west of Dublin.

17. Appointed Archbishop of Dublin in 1885, the nationalist cleric William J. Walsh (1841–1921) gave important evidence to the Special Commission which helped expose Pigott's forgeries.

18. The "quiet shoemaker" was Pat Gogarty (*c.*1849–91), whom Katharine Tynan described in both *The Middle Years* (1916) and *A Cluster of Nuts* (1894). See *CL1* 54.

19. The influential Victorian sage Thomas Carlyle (1795–1881) published his six-volume biography of Frederick the Great of Prussia 1858–65; in his unflattering portrait of the barrister and orator John F. Taylor (*Au* 214) Yeats described Carlyle as "the chief inspirer of self-educated men in the 'eighties and early 'nineties." Ralph Waldo Emerson (1803–82), the American Transcendentalist, included his essay "The Over-Soul" in *Essays, First Series* (1841). Yeats included *Flitters, Tatters, and the Councillor* by May Laffan (later Hartley) under the "Novels and Romances" section of his 1895 "List of the Best Irish Books" (*UP1* 386). She was born in Dublin and later lived in London; during the eleven years from 1876 to 1887 she published anonymously five books of fiction about Ireland, the others being *Hogan, M. P.* (1876), *The Hon. Miss Ferrard* (1877), *Christy Carew* (1880), and *Ismay's Children* (1887).

20. Thomas William Rolleston (1857–1920), poet and translator, played important roles in both the Irish Literary Society and the Rhymers' Club. His *The Teachings of Epictetus* first appeared in 1886 and *A Life of Lessing* in 1889. Rolleston collaborated with the German-American scholar Karl Knortz on *Grashalme* (Zürich: Schabelitz, 1889), the first major translation of Whitman's poems into German. For Whitman see note 6.11.

21. Rolleston's "pretty Wicklow house" at the time was Fairview, in Delgany, County Wicklow. As a boy he had lived in Glasshouse, near Shinrone, 7 miles from Roscrea; after leaving the Department of Agriculture in 1905 he retired to Hollywood House in Glenealy, County Wicklow.

22. Ellen O'Leary (1831–89), sister of the Fenian John O'Leary, shared his

nationalism in politics and literature; her posthumous *Lays of Country, Home and Friends*, edited by Rolleston, appeared in 1891.

23. After his return to Ireland in 1885, the Fenian nationalist John O'Leary (1830–1907) exercised a major influence on Yeats's political and literary views; Yeats memorably commemorated him in the refrain to "September 1913": "Romantic Ireland's dead and gone, / It's with O'Leary in the grave" (*PNE* 108).

24. The Fenians were a republican organization founded in New York in 1858 at the same time as the Irish Republican Brotherhood in Dublin; the name in general usage included both organizations and became associated with the use of physical force to secure nationalist aims. Both O'Learys worked for the movement; John was arrested with other Irish leaders in 1865, imprisoned, and then exiled for his role. Sir Charles Gavan Duffy (1816–1903), a journalist who helped lead the Young Ireland movement of the 1840s, spent a quarter-century in a distinguished Australian political career before returning to Europe; he was Yeats's great antagonist in the New Irish Library scheme. Duffy's article "A Celtic Singer," reprinted from the *Dublin University Review* for Dec 1886, appeared not as appendix but immediately following Rolleston's Introduction to *Lays of Country, Home and Friends*.

25. William Wordsworth (1770–1850), the English Romantic poet, advocated a poetic language approaching common speech. The distinguished critic who compared Miss O'Leary to Wordsworth may have been Edward Dowden (1843–1913), who held the first Chair of English Literature at Trinity College, Dublin.

26. The novelist Charles Joseph Kickham (1828–82) first joined the Young Ireland movement and later the Fenians; like John O'Leary, he was arrested in 1865 and sentenced to penal servitude. His well-known ballad "The Irish Peasant Girl" (also known as "She lived beside the Anner," after its first line) first appeared in the periodical the *Celt* in Aug 1859.

27. The poet, patriot, and journalist Thomas Davis (1814–45) led the Young Ireland movement and wrote some of the most stirring Irish nationalist ballads and lyrics. Along with Charles Gavan Duffy and John Blake Dillon he founded the *Nation*, an important nationalist periodical.

3   SOME FORTHCOMING IRISH BOOKS

1. Brighton is a popular seaside resort about 50 miles south of London.
2. Lady Jane Francesca Wilde (1826–96) published articles and verse in the *Nation* under the pen-name "Speranza"; under her own name she published several works on folklore.
3. The surgeon and antiquary Sir William Robert Wills Wilde (1815–76) and his wife Lady Jane (see note 2) were the parents of the famous writer Oscar Fingal O'Flahertie Wills Wilde (1854–1900), an important early influence on Yeats.
4. The failure of the uprising of 1848 precipitated the collapse of Young Ireland. William Carleton (1794–1869), Samuel Lover (1797–1868), and

Charles James Lever (1806–72) all wrote novels on Irish subjects. Yeats particularly admired Carleton's *Fardorougha the Miser* (1839).

5. For Thomas Davis see note 2.27.

6. Grafton Street is a principal shopping street on the south bank of the river Liffey in Dublin.

7. The poet John Keegan (1809–49) wrote public poetry, often with the voice of a peasant speaker, published in periodicals such as the *Nation*. Edward Walsh (1805–50), one of the best early translators of Irish folk poetry, also published there.

8. David Fitzgerald (1843–1916) contributed two articles on "Popular Tales of Ireland" in 1879–80 and one on "Early Celtic History" in 1884 to the *Revue celtique*. His book was apparently never published. Founder of the Gaelic League and later first president of the Republic, the scholar–poet and translator Douglas Hyde (1860–1949) produced as his first book *Leabhar Sgéulaigheachta* (1889), a collection of Irish folk material. He had translated three stories from the Irish for Yeats's collection *FFT* the previous year.

9. Turlogh Carolan (1670–1738) is perhaps the best remembered of the Gaelic harpists and composers; he spent most of his time in Connacht and Ulster.

10. Hyde began to publish "Songs of Connacht" in the *Nation* in 1890 and continued them in the *Weekly Freeman* in 1892–3; *Love Songs of Connacht* (Dublin: Gill; London: Fisher Unwin) appeared in 1893. Connacht (or Connaught) is one of the four historic provinces of Ireland and lies to the north-west.

11. Hyde contributed six poems in English to the anthology *PBYI* (1888), an early gathering of the emerging literary revival. A. R. Stritch's *Lays and Lyrics of the Pan-Celtic Society* was published in 1889.

12. For Duffy see note 2.24. His biography *Thomas Davis* was published in London by Kegan Paul in 1890. Park Lane is a fashionable street near Hyde Park in London.

13. *Political Prisoners* by Dr. George Sigerson (1836–1925) was published by Kegan Paul in 1890. Yeats knew the Sigerson family; the poet, essayist, and historian Dr. Sigerson himself was Maud Gonne's doctor in the 1890s and later served with Yeats as a Free State senator. In his autobiography Yeats described him as "learned, artificial, unscholarly, a typical provincial celebrity, but a friendly man" (*Au* 202).

14. The Dublin newspaper the *Freeman's Journal*, which also appeared in a weekly edition, cautiously supported the Land League and Home Rule; after its plant was destroyed by the Irish Republican Army in 1922 it was incorporated into the *Irish Independent*.

15. Edmund Dwyer Gray (1845–88) was succeeded by his son Edmund Dwyer Gray, Jr., as editor and owner of the *Freeman's Journal*. *The Treatment of Political Prisoners in Ireland* appeared in 1889 with a preface dated 3 Aug of that year.

16. George John Shaw-Lefevre, Baron Eversley (1831–1928), held various Cabinet posts in Liberal governments; he had been Postmaster General before his defeat in the general election of 1885. Dr. Jonas Dryasdust, whose name suggests his character, is the fictitious antiquarian to whom

Sir Walter Scott addressed the prefaces of several novels, including *Ivanhoe*.
17. The Radicals made up the more extreme wing of the Liberal Party and drew particular strength from the Nonconformist middle classes and some trade unions.
18. The Pillars of Hercules are the two promontories guarding the eastern passage to the Strait of Gibraltar.

4   WHAT THE WRITERS AND THINKERS ARE DOING

1. For the O'Learys see notes 2.22 and 2.23. Ellen O'Leary's ballad "To God and Ireland True," which appeared in the posthumous 1891 collection, presents a young woman's lament for her beloved who died in prison and her pledge to continue faithful both to him and to the Irish cause. The poem is reprinted in the text of item 10 in the present volume.
2. Halloween or Hallow Eve falls on the evening of 31 Oct and precedes Allhallows or All Saints Day on 1 Nov.
3. The American Colonel Henry Steel Olcott (1832–1907) founded the Theosophical Society along with Madame Blavatsky (see note 4) and William Quan Judge in 1875. Olcott had lectured in Dublin first on "Theosophy" and then on "Irish Fairies"; Yeats describes here the second lecture, which was given at the Antient Concert Rooms in Dublin on 19 Oct 1889.
4. The founder of the Theosophic movement, Helena Petrovna Blavatsky (1831–91), had returned to London somewhat neglected in 1887, when Yeats met her. He joined the Esoteric Section of the Theosophical Society in Dec 1888 and was expelled in Oct 1890 for unapproved psychical experiments and for criticism of the Society.
5. The "London wit" has not yet been identified but may have been Oscar Wilde.
6. Jersey is one of the Channel Islands; Birmingham is a large industrial city in the English Midlands.
7. Donegal is the north-western county of Ireland, known for its rugged scenery. The town of Donegal lies at the head of Donegal Bay. The unnamed friend may be George Russell (AE); in a letter to Douglas Hyde (25 Oct 1889) Yeats describes his informant for the story of the O'Byrnes as "a young artist who has been staying in Donegal" (*CL1* 194).
8. One of the leading men of letters in London, the Scottish-born Andrew Lang (1844–1912) published extensively on folklore; today he is perhaps best remembered for his translations of Homer and for his fairy tales.
9. Slieve League (elevation 1972 feet) is a mountain overlooking the Donegal coast; in the letter to Hyde, Yeats identifies the rath as *Cahel enore*.
10. The Irish poet and prose writer Katharine Tynan (1859 or 1861–1931) first met Yeats in June 1885 and became an important early friend and collaborator; in 1893 she married his sometime schoolmate Henry Hinkson. Until her marriage she lived at Whitehall Farm at Clondalkin, just west of Dublin. Yeats's early letters to her contain important statements of his

literary aims. Trained as a teacher, Clara Commer (1856–1937) lived at the time with her brother Ernst, a professor in Breslau. Her many books include *Kleeblätter* (Breslau: Gorlich and Coch, 1890), a translation of Tynan's *Shamrocks*.

11. See note 3.12.
12. The Camelot Classics was a sixty-four volume series of classical and modern writings edited by Ernest Rhys (1859–1946) and published by Walter Scott from 1886 onwards; *Prose Writings of Thomas Davis*, ed. T. W. Rolleston, appeared in 1890. For Rolleston and Duffy see notes 2.20 and 2.24.
13. The English poet and novelist Amy Levy (1861–89) committed suicide in her parents' house on 10 Sep 1889. Best remembered for her novel of Jewish life *Reuben Sachs* (1888), she published several volumes of verse, including the posthumous *A London Plane-Tree and Other Verse* (London: T. Fisher Unwin, 1889).
14. In Greek mythology, Lethe is a river of the Underworld; drinking its waters causes forgetfulness of life on earth.
15. "A Cross-Road Epitaph" appeared in Amy Levy's *A Minor Poet and Other Verse* (London: T. Fisher Unwin, 1884) p. 94, with the following readings different from Yeats's: l. 1, no comma; l. 2, "he"; l. 3, "wax'd"; l. 4, full point instead of semi-colon.
16. Yeats quotes the last quatrain of "A Dirge" from Levy's *A Minor Poet* volume, p. 80, where the first line lacks the comma at the end.
17. Margaret Mary Ryan (1848–1932) dedicated *Songs of Remembrance* (Dublin: Gill, 1889) to the memory of her brother, the Very Revd. John Ryan DD, VG, who died in 1887; she often used the pseudonym "Alice Esmonde." Yeats knew the Dublin-born Elsa D'Esterre-Keeling (d. 1935), author of *In Thoughtland and in Dreamland* (London: T. Fisher Unwin, 1890); he describes a visit to her and her sister in a letter to Katharine Tynan, 6 Nov 1889 (*CL1* 196). When James Anthony Froude printed the lyric "To a Swallow Building under Our Eaves" for the first time in his *Thomas Carlyle: A History of the First Forty Years of His Life 1795–1835* (London: Longmans, Green, 1882, 2 vols), he attributed it to Jane Welsh Carlyle (II, 291–92); modern scholars assign it to Thomas Carlyle instead. Froude gives the fourth stanza as follows:

> What was it, then? some mystic turn of thought,
> Caught under German eaves, and hither brought,
> 		Marring thine eye
> For the world's loveliness, till thou art grown
> A sober thing that dost but mope and moan
> 		Not knowing why?

18. Yeats quotes the third stanza of "Reveries," from *Songs of Remembrance*, p. 96, where the third line reads "Sweet Virgin, crowned with gracious power,".
19. In 1873 Matthew Russell, SJ (1834–1912) founded the *Irish Monthly* to encourage an Irish national and Catholic literature, though he also

welcomed Protestant writers. For Katharine Tynan see note 10. The
prolific Rosa Mulholland, later Lady Gilbert (1841–1921), produced many
books of fiction and poetry, often dealing with the peasantry of the West.
In contrast, Frances Marcella O'Brien (1840–83), most of whose poems
and stories appeared under the name "Attie O'Brien," wrote primarily for
periodicals.
20. Yeats, who obviously had not seen Elsa D'Esterre-Keeling's novel, mistakes
its title, *Three Sisters; or, Sketches of a Highly Original Family* (Leipzig:
Tauchnitz, 1884, and New York: G. Munro, 1885).

5   CHEVALIER BURKE – "SHULE AROON" –
CARLETON AND THE BANIMS' NOVELS –
AN AUTOGRAPH SALE AT SOTHEBY'S –
WILLIAM ALLINGHAM – MISS ELLEN O'LEARY

1. The novel *The Master of Ballantrae: A Winter's Tale* by Robert Louis
Stevenson (1850–94) first appeared in 1889. One of Stevenson's popular
Scottish romances, it has a convoluted and picaresque plot concerning a
bitter feud between two brothers on opposite sides in the Stuart uprising
of 1745 and their subsequent animosity. Chapters 3 ("The Master's
Wanderings") and 7 ("Adventure of Chevalier Burke in India") purport
to be extracts "From the Memoirs of the Chevalier de Burke."
2. The term "English garrison" refers to Protestant settlers in Ireland and
their descendants, particularly those strongly committed to the British
connection and involved in the government of the country.
3. The Hell-Fire Clubs were rakish and often blasphemous associations
drawing heavily from the upper-class and military in the eighteenth
century, chiefly around London; the most famous was at Medmenham
Abbey. Ireland had one club in Limerick and another in Dublin, the latter
flourishing from about 1735 and founded by Richard Parsons (the first
Earl of Rosse) and Colonel Jack St. Leger. Yeats wrote about the Dublin
club, which had a lodge on Mount Pelier in the Dublin hills, in his 1891
essay "A Reckless Century. Irish Rakes and Duellists," repr. in *UP1* 198–
202. The English historian James Anthony Froude (1818–94), author of a
twelve-volume history of England, also wrote *The English in Ireland in the
Eighteenth Century* (1872–4, rev. 1881) in three volumes. For remarks similar
to those recalled by Yeats see II, 192–3, and III, 514–15, of the 1881 edition
(London: Longmans).
4. "Shule Aroon" is an anonymous eighteenth-century ballad in which a
young girl bemoans her beloved's absence in France.
5. The "common friend" of Yeats and Stevenson was almost certainly William
Ernest Henley (1849–1903), poet and editor of the *Scots Observer* (after 1890
the *National Observer*). The "well known authority on Irish songs" was
Patrick Weston Joyce (1827–1914), professor at a teachers' training college
in Dublin, who wrote extensively on Irish lore. For Charles Gavan Duffy

see note 2.24; his anthology *The Ballad Poetry of Ireland* (Dublin, 1845) contained the same text of "Shule Aroon" printed by H. H. Sparling in *Irish Minstrelsy* (London: Walter Scott, 1887) pp. 232–3, and by Yeats himself in *BIV* 231–2, with slight variations in the Gaelic refrain.

6. The first quotation is from *The Master of Ballantrae* (London: Cassell, 1889) p. 119. The second may most easily be found in the facsimile reproduction of the fortieth edition (1869) of *The Ballad Poetry of Ireland* (Delmar, New York: Scholars' Facsimiles and Reprints, 1973) p. 121. In HR Reynolds included a footnote translating the Gaelic line as "And mayest thou go, my little darling, safe!"

7. John (1798–1842) and Michael (1796–1874) Banim wrote twenty-four volumes of fiction depicting Irish cabin life in which they often sought to render Irish grievances for an English audience without falsifying Irish character. Their *Tales by the O'Hara Family* (1825, 1827) contained considerable Irish folklore, albeit colored by sentimentality and caricature. Yeats included John Banim's novels *The Nowlans* and *John Doe* in his letter to the *Daily Express* (Dublin) of 27 Feb 1895 recommending a list of thirty Irish books; he particularly commended *The Nowlans*, which he noted was out of print.

8. For Carleton see note 3.4; he came of a peasant background and was educated at a hedge school. Yeats included both *Fardorougha, the Miser* and *The Black Prophet* on the list for the *Daily Express* with the notation that they were out of print. Yeats's own edition of *Stories from Carleton* was published in Aug 1889; he wrote in John Quinn's copy, "I thought no end of Carleton in those days & would still I dare say if I had not forgotton him. W. B. Yeats, 1904."

9. The two novels appeared among the eight by Carleton included in a list of "Popular Works" advertised for sale at a 40 per cent discount at the *BP* office in an advertisement appearing in *BP* on 7 Sep 1889 (p. 8).

10. The auction house of Sotheby's is a center for the sale of rare books and art objects in London.

11. The letters were by the dramatist Richard Brinsley Sheridan (1751–1816), the statesman and orator Edmund Burke (1729–97), the writer Oliver Goldsmith (1728 or 1730–74), former Prime Minister Benjamin Disraeli, first Earl of Beaconsfield (1804–81), the poet Percy Bysshe Shelley (1792–1822), the essayist Charles Lamb (1775–1834), and the poet and engraver William Blake (1757–1827); Burke, Goldsmith, Shelley, and Blake were particularly important to Yeats.

12. The writer, politician, and dandy Edward George Earle Lytton Bulwer-Lytton (1803–73) was the first Baron Lytton. The source of the quotation "The secret worm ne'er ceases, / Nor the mouse behind the wall" has not yet been identified.

13. William Blake's *America* (1793) was the first of his poems to be designated "a prophecy" and is one of the most beautiful of his illuminated works.

14. All but the last paragraph of this famous letter of Blake to George Cumberland, 12 Apr 1827, was first published by Yeats and Edwin Ellis in *The Works of William Blake* (I, 162–3). In the present text, Yeats quotes excerpts from the first and last paragraphs of the letter, which in the standard modern edition read: "I have been very near the Gates of Death

& have returned very weak & an Old Man feeble & tottering, but not in Spirit & Life, not in The Real Man The Imagination which Liveth for Ever. In that I am stronger & stronger as this Foolish Body decays . . . . Flaxman is Gone & we must All soon follow, every one to his Own Eternal House." See *The Letters of William Blake with Related Documents*, ed. Geoffrey Keynes, 3rd edn (Oxford: Clarendon Press, 1980) pp. 168–9. The same letter includes *America* at £6 6s. in a price list of Blake's works. The sculptor and draftsman John Flaxman (1755–1826) was a friend of Blake's who was created Professor of Sculpture at the Royal Academy in 1810; Blake engraved Flaxman's illustrations to Hesiod in 1817.

15. Yeats read the verse of the novelist and poet George Meredith (1828–1909) extensively in the fall of 1888, praising Meredith's "suavity and serenity" and "curious intricate richness" but finding him "so suggestive ones mind wanders." Upon meeting Maud Gonne early in 1889, Yeats found her "very Irish, a kind of 'Diana of the Crossways' " (*CL1* 97, 108, 137).

16. Joseph Bonaparte (1768–1844), brother of Napoleon, was made King of Naples and King of Spain by his brother.

17. The poet William Allingham (1824–89), whose friends included Carlyle, D. G. Rossetti, Patmore, and Tennyson, is now best remembered for his short lyric "The Fairies" ("Up the airy mountain"). For an elaboration of Yeats's early views on Allingham, see his review of *Irish Songs and Poems* for *PSJ* (item 16 in the present volume). William Gladstone (1809–98) was leader of the Liberal Party and four times Prime Minister of Britain.

18. In 1887–90 Reeves and Turner published Allingham's work in four volumes: *Irish Songs and Poems* (1887), *Flower Pieces and Other Poems* (1888), *Life and Phantasy* (1889), and *Laurence Bloomfield* (1890). In 1890 the same firm published *Thought and Word and Ashby Manor* and the 1884 *Blackberries* collection, making a total of six volumes.

19. The English poet Robert Herrick (1591–1674) wrote highly crafted lyrics.

20. William Allingham, *Irish Songs and Poems* (London: Reeves and Turner, 1887) p. 136. Yeats reprinted "Let Me Sing of What I Know" (the opening section of "A Stormy Night. A Story of the Donegal Coast") as the first entry in his *Sixteen Poems by William Allingham* (Dundrum: Dun Emer Press, 1905). For Ballyshannon see note 6.21.

21. For Ellen and John O'Leary see notes 2.22 and 2.23. Drumcondra is a northern suburb of Dublin.

6   BROWNING – A NEW SCHOOL – EDWARD CARPENTER – MR. CURTIN'S *IRISH MYTHS AND FOLKLORE* – LADY WILDE'S *ANCIENT CURES* – ALLINGHAM

1. The great Victorian poet Robert Browning (1812–89) had died at Venice on 12 Dec and was buried in the Poets' Corner of Westminster Abbey on

the 31st. This is the longest of over fifty references to him in Yeats's published prose; he also cited Browning explicitly in the late poem "Are You Content."

2. The "great friend of Browning's" has not yet been identified; see note 5.

3. Yeats particularly admired "the great reverie of the Pope" which constitutes book x of Browning's long poem *The Ring and the Book* (1868–9) and which hints at a cyclical view of history.

4. In the Advertisement (later a note) to the original 1842 edition of *Dramatic Lyrics* Browning described his method as follows: "Such Poems as the majority in this volume might also come properly enough, I suppose, under the head of 'Dramatic Pieces'; being, though often Lyric in expression, always Dramatic in principle, and so many utterances of so many imaginary persons, not mine" – Robert Browning, *The Poems*, ed. John Pettigrew, supplemented and completed by Thomas J. Collins, 2 vols (New Haven, Conn.: Yale University Press, 1981) i, 347.

5. The acquaintance of Yeats who called Browning a mystic has not yet been identified; among Yeats's circle, Stopford Brooke, Edward Dowden, John Nettleship, William Sharp, and Arthur Symons all wrote books about Browning.

6. For Spencer see note 2.8. He tried to reconcile utilitarian with evolutionary ethics.

7. This scene takes place not in Goethe's *Wilhelm Meister's Apprenticeship* but in its sequel, *Wilhelm Meister's Travels*, ch. 14, which Yeats probably read in Carlyle's widely reprinted translation (1827).

8. The Fellowship of the New Life (or New Fellowship), out of which the Fabian Society partly sprang, made an effort to found a new school in Abbotsholme House, on the banks of the Dove near Rocester in Staffordshire. One of its prime movers was Edward Carpenter (see note 9). Abbotsholme House stood on the edge of the Peak District, which is formed by the termination of the Pennines in Derbyshire.

9. The social reformer Edward Carpenter (1844–1929) was a fellow of Trinity Hall, Cambridge (not Oxford), and curate to F. D. Maurice before resigning his fellowship in 1874 to become a University Extension lecturer and then to settle at Millthorpe, near Chesterfield, where he pursued his ideals of socialist and community fellowship.

10. Stepniak (or Stepnyak) was the pseudonym of Sergei Mikhailovich Kravchinski (1852–95), Russian writer and nihilist who stabbed General Mezentsev. After a stay in Switzerland and Italy, he settled in London in 1884.

11. *Leaves of Grass* by the American poet Walt Whitman (1819–92) had a profound impact on Carpenter, who first read him in an edition of 1868 edited by William Michael Rossetti; later, Carpenter met and corresponded with Whitman. Ruskin, Morris, and Thoreau were other important influences. The "little patch of land" was Millthorpe (see note 9) and totalled about 7 acres. Despite Yeats's assertion, Carpenter never married; he settled at Millthorpe with the scythe-maker Albert Fearnehough and his family.

12. The American naturalist and Transcendentalist Henry David Thoreau

(1817–62) is best known for his book *Walden* (1854), which Carpenter admired, as did Yeats.

13. The article appeared in the magazine *Pioneer* in Jan 1889 and was reprinted as the title essay in Carpenter's volume *Civilisation: Its Cause and Cure, and Other Essays* (London: Swan Sonnenschein) later that year. The book went through seven editions by 1902.

14. Born in Detroit of Irish parents, Jeremiah Curtin (1835–1906) published his *Myths and Folklore of Ireland* in 1890; *Hero Tales of Ireland* followed in 1894 and *Tales of the Fairies and of the Ghost World* in 1895. He was influenced by Douglas Hyde. Yeats cited *Myths and Folklore of Ireland* as source for his poem "Cuchulain's Fight with the Sea" (*VP* 799) and praised "Curtin's fine collections" in the *National Observer*, 28 Feb 1891 (*UP1* 188).

15. Educated at Eton and the University of Edinburgh, John Francis Campbell of Islay (1822–85) insisted that folk tales should be transcribed exactly as they were told, as in his four-volume *Popular Tales of the West Highlands* (Edinburgh: Edmonston and Douglas, 1860–2).

16. Yeats numbered both Sir John Rhys's *Lectures on the Origin and Growth of Religion as Illustrated by Celtic Heathendom* (1888) and Henri d'Arbois de Jubainville's *Le Cycle mythologique irlandais et la mythologie celtique* (1884) with Alfred Nutt and Kuno Meyer's *The Voyage of Bran* (1895) as "the three books without which there is no understanding of Celtic legends" (*UP2* 119). Beginning in 1877, Rhys (1840–1915) served as the first Jesus Professor of Celtic at Oxford. De Jubainville (1827–1910) was Professor of Celtic Language and Literature at the College de France and founder of the *Revue celtique*.

17. For Lady Wilde see note 3.2. *Ancient Cures, Charms, and Usages of Ireland* was published in 1890 (London: Ward and Downey).

18. Yeats quotes two proverbs from p. 250 of Lady Wilde's book; the first quotation should read: ". . . the swan . . . the bridle . . . the wool." Saadi or Sadi (d. 1291 or 1292) was a Persian poet about whom little is known biographically; his principal works are *Bustan* (*Tree Garden*), *Gulistan* (*Rose Garden*), and *Diwan* (a collection of lyrics).

19. For Fitzgerald see note 3.8, and for Hyde see notes 3.8 and 3.10–11. Hyde's *Beside the Fire* (London: David Nutt, 1890) included English translations of about half the stories in *Leabhar Sgéulaigheachta* together with half a dozen other Irish tales.

20. Yeats had included "Teig O'Kane and the Corpse" along with two other translations by Hyde in his own *FFT*, where in a headnote he called it a "magnificent story."

21. For Allingham see note 5.17. He was born in the west-coast town of Ballyshannon, where his family had lived for generations and where he served as customs inspector until 1870, when he moved to London. The unnamed brother of Allingham's was probably Hugh, one of two younger brothers by his father's second marriage. Hugh Allingham lived in Ballyshannon, took over his father's place as manager of the Provincial Bank of Ireland, and wrote *Ballyshannon: Its History and Antiquities* (Londonderry: J. Montgomery, 1879).

22. Edward Allingham, the poet's other younger brother by his father's second marriage, took his BA from Trinity College in 1862, his MB in 1874, and

practiced in Belfast. He published *New and Original Poems* (London: Reeves and Turner, 1890). Originally appearing in *Fraser's Magazine* in 1862–3, Allingham's poem on landlord–tenant relations, *Laurence Bloomfield*, went through several changes in subtitle before its final form as *Laurence Bloomfield; or, Rich and Poor in Ireland* (London: Reeves and Turner, 1890). In it, young Bloomfield inherits an estate in Lisnamoy and in a blend of *noblesse oblige* and benevolence tries with his wife to stimulate better relations between tenants and unresponsive landowners.

7   IRISH WRITERS OUGHT TO TAKE IRISH SUBJECTS – *A SICILIAN IDYLL*

1. For Todhunter see note 1.3. His *A Sicilian Idyll: A Pastoral Play in Two Scenes* (London: Elkin Mathews, 1890) was first produced in the Clubhouse on 5 May 1890. The play is based upon the Second Idyll of the Greek pastoral poet Theocritus (third century BC) and takes the names of some characters from the Third Idyll. See items 8 and 19 in this volume, "Plays by an Irish Poet" (*UP1* 190–4), and "Dr. Todhunter's New Play," *Nation* (Dublin), XLVIII, no. 20 (17 May 1890) 2, for other reviews by Yeats, and see *Au* 119–23 for a retrospective account.
2. For Bedford Park and the club theatre see note 1.3.
3. Florence Farr (see note 1.4) acted the part of Amaryllis.
4. The organist and composer Bertram Luard-Selby (1853–1918) was best known in his own day for his incidental music to Todhunter's *Helena in Troas* and for a musical duologue *Weather or No* performed at the Savoy in 1896; in 1900 he became organist of Rochester Cathedral.
5. The Bavarian-born Sir Hubert von Herkomer (1849–1914) came to England in 1857 and served as Professor of Fine Art at Oxford 1885–94. He had a house at Bushey in Hertfordshire. There he also started a school and built a private theater, at which his own operas or "musical plays" were performed in 1888–90 and works by others in 1890–3.
6. A mountainous region in the central Peloponnese, Arcadia is in Classical literature the idealized location of pastoral verse, as in Virgil's *Eclogues*. Yeats set his first major published work, *The Island of Statues* (1885), there.
7. In Classical mythology Bacchus, or Dionysus, was the son of Zeus and Semele; he was the god of wine, associated with a mythic cult.
8. Yeats probably did not see the performance of *Helena in Troas* (London: Kegan Paul, 1886), which opened in London 17 May 1886 at Hengler's Circus in Great Pulteney Street. For its "incomparable staging" see note 11.2.
9. Exeter, a cathedral city in Devon, was the site of many University Extension lecture courses sponsored by Cambridge University in the 1880s and 1890s, prior to the foundation of University College, Exeter, in 1901.
10. Politician and journalist as well as novelist and historian, Justin McCarthy (1830–1912) served in the Irish Party under Parnell; in the party split of 1890 following the O'Shea divorce case, he led the anti-Parnellite group.
11. In Irish legend, Cuchulain was the warrior hero of the Gaelic epic the

Táin Bó Cuailnge (Cattle Raid of Cooley) in the Red Branch or Ulster-cycle of tales. Yeats wrote poems and plays about him, including both his first death fighting the waves after unwittingly killing his son and – years after his rescue by his wife Emer from that drowning – his final demise after battle. The rebel leader Michael Dwyer (1771–1826) took part in Wolfe Tone's rising of 1798 and in Robert Emmet's abortive one in 1803; he surrendered and was transported to Australia. Yeats may be thinking of John T. Campion's melodramatic novel *Michael Dwyer; or, The Insurgent Captain of the Wicklow Mountains* (Glasgow and London: Cameron and Ferguson, 1869) or of Katharine Tynan's poem "The Grave of Michael Dwyer," *PBYI* 7–11.

12. Tempe is a valley in Greece used by Classical poets to represent an idealized pastoral dale.

13. The Norman invasion of Gaelic Ireland took place 1166–72.

14. A major early influence on Yeats, the historian and novelist Standish James O'Grady (1846–1928) wrote *History of Ireland: The Heroic Period* (London: Sampson Low, Searle, Marston, and Rivington; Dublin: E. Ponsonby, 1878) and many other works on Irish history and lore. In the late poem "Beautiful Lofty Things" Yeats remembered "Standish O'Grady supporting himself between the tables / Speaking to a drunken audience high nonsensical words" (*PNE* 303). The educator Sophie Bryant (1850–1922), the first woman to take a DSc. in Moral Science (1894), published *Celtic Ireland* (London: Kegan Paul) in 1889. Lady Mary Catherine Ferguson (1823–1905), wife of Sir Samuel Ferguson and author of a memoir of him, wrote *The Story of the Irish before the Conquest* (London: Bell and Daldy, 1868; 2nd, enlarged edn Dublin: Sealy, Bryers and Walker, 1890).

15. Richard de Clare (d. 1176), second earl of Pembroke, known as Strongbow, was asked for aid by Dermot Macmurrough, the Irish king of Leinster, and thus initiated the Norman conquest of Ireland.

16. Brehon law, the customary oral legal system of the Celtic peoples, functioned wherever native power prevailed up to the time of the Tudor conquest; St. Patrick (389?–461) began his mission to convert Ireland to Christianity in 432; the bards were the traditional singers of Gaelic culture.

17. The children of Lir were changed into swans by their stepmother for 900 years, until the establishment of Christianity in Ireland (for Yeats's retelling of the story in his review of Todhunter's poem see item 17 in the present volume). The tragic love between Deirdre and Naoise led to the death of Naoise and his brothers at the hands of King Conchubar; Yeats treated the subject in his play *Deirdre*.

18. For the *Tain Bo* see note 11. The Royal Irish Academy was founded in 1785 by the Earl of Charlemont to advance the studies of science, literature, and antiquities.

19. The poet Sir Samuel Ferguson (1810–86) ranked among the first to put Irish legends into verse; he became President of the Royal Irish Academy and had a successful career as a lawyer. Yeats wrote his first two pieces of published prose on Ferguson's poetry, which he also acknowledged in the refrain of "To Ireland in the Coming Times." Ferguson's most ambitious poem, *Congal: A Poem in Five Books* (1882), recounts the rebellion of young

King Congal against High King Domnal, to whose daughter he is betrothed; the shorter "Conary," included in *Poems* (1880), renders the bardic story "The Raid on Da Derga's Hostel" freely into blank verse. First published in four installments in *Transactions of the Royal Irish Academy* from 10 Nov 1884 to 9 Feb 1885, Ferguson's work on Patrician documents was republished as *The Remains of St. Patrick: The Confessio and Epistle to Coroticus Translated into English Blank Verse* (Dublin: Sealy, Bryers and Walker, 1888).

20. For Aubrey de Vere see note 2.11. In the essay on Ferguson for *Essays: Chiefly Literary and Ethical* (London: Macmillan, 1889) de Vere wrote, "It would be difficult to find, amid our recent literature, a poem which at once aims as high as 'Conary,' and as adequately fulfils its aim" (p. 106). Yeats repeated his own praise of Ferguson's "Conary" in *BIV*, where he called it "the best Irish poem of any kind" (p. xix).

21. An anonymous report entitled either "Dublin Letter" or "Notes from Ireland" was a weekly feature of the *Daily Graphic* from its inception in January 1890. Yeats here attributes the authorship of the report to Standish James O'Grady (see note 14). Yeats refers specifically to "Notes from Ireland. (By Our Dublin Correspondent)," *Daily Graphic*, 88 (16 Apr 1890) 13, which includes a review of the spring agricultural exhibition of the Royal Dublin Society (see note 9.9).

22. Descriptions of Finn's hound Bran are frequent in literature of the period; the exact source of O'Grady's quotation has not yet been identified.

23. The term "West British" refers to those in Ireland, usually Protestant, who identified with English rather than Irish culture and were strongly committed to the Imperial connection. Despite both the hopes of Yeats and his own growing disillusionment with the landlord class, O'Grady remained a Unionist, convinced that Ireland belonged in the Empire and hopeful that Ascendancy stock could regenerate itself.

24. For Carlyle see note 2.19. Works of his such as *On Heroes, Hero-Worship, and the Heroic in History* glorified the role of the great man; despite some affinities, Yeats often deprecated Carlyle.

25. In *Red Hugh's Captivity: A Picture of Ireland, Social and Political, in the Reign of Queen Elizabeth* (London: Ward and Downey, 1889) O'Grady told the story of Red Hugh O'Donnell (*c.*1571–1602). Taken hostage through the trickery of the Elizabethan viceroy Sir John Perrott in 1587, Red Hugh escaped, became chief of the O'Donnells in 1592, and with Hugh O'Neill led the fight for the Irish cause. After the battle of Kinsale he travelled to Spain for further Spanish help and was poisoned there in 1602. His antagonist Sir John Perrott or Perrot (*c.*1527–92) served as Lord Deputy of Ireland 1584–88; his fortunes later declined, and he returned in disgrace to London, where he died in the Tower.

26. For John Keegan see note 3.7. The son of a small farmer, Keegan was educated by hedge-schoolmasters; his difficult life included an unfortunate marriage, great suffering during the Famine, and an impoverished early death of cholera in 1849. His ballad "Caoch O'Leary," more usually known as "Caoch the Piper," was first printed in the *Irish National Magazine* in 1846; it recounts a small boy's love of the blind but merry piper and their melancholy reunion twenty years later. The letters had been provided

to Yeats by Sir Charles Gavan Duffy, for whom see note 2.24.

27. For Mangan see note 2.15. Mangan's life of urban poverty in Dublin matched Keegan's experience of rural penury and was exacerbated by alcoholism. Like Keegan, he died during the cholera epidemic of 1849, probably of malnutrition.

28. For the Fenians see note 2.24. James Stephens (1825–1901) was the chief founder of the Fenians; Thomas Clare Luby (1821–1901) and the novelist Charles Joseph Kickham (1828–82) were prominent Fenians, appointed by Stephens to the supreme executive of the movement together with John O'Leary.

29. For John O'Leary see note 2.23. His *Recollections of Fenians and Fenianism* (London: Downey) appeared in 1896.

30. For Sir Charles Gavan Duffy see note 2.24; Michael Davitt (1846–1906) founded the Irish National Land League; William O'Brien (1852–1928) edited the Land League journal *United Ireland* and was elected MP in 1883; Sir Charles Russell (1832–1900), later Baron Russell of Killowen and the first Catholic Lord Chief Justice of England since the Reformation, was the leading counsel for Parnell before the Parnell Commission (see note 2.16); Joseph Allen Galbraith (1817 or 1818–90), a Trinity academic of mildly nationalist leanings, was one of the founders of the Home Government Association with Isaac Butt in 1870; the poet George Francis Savage-Armstrong (1845–1906), Professor of English at Queen's College, Cork, wrote numerous books, including *Stories of Wicklow* (London: Longman, 1886); the Revd John Gwynn (1827–1917) served as Dean of Raphoe and Derry, and from 1888 to 1907 as Regius Professor of Divinity; for Parnell see note 2.16.

8 DR. TODHUNTER'S *SICILIAN IDYLL*

1. For Blake see note 1.15. Yeats refers to *Jerusalem* (1804–?20), the last and greatest of the mythological and symbolic poems which Blake called his Prophetic Books. Yeats quotes from book II, plate 41, ll. 29–30.

2. For Todhunter see note 1.3. For *Helena in Troas* see notes 7.8 and 11.2.

3. The Muses are nine Greek goddesses who preside over the arts and sciences. The "rightful Muses" of poetic drama are Thalia, muse of comedy and pastoral poetry, and Melpomene, muse of tragedy. For *A Sicilian Idyll* and Theocritus see note 7.1. After its Bedford Park performances the play was presented at Aubrey House, Kensington (24 June 1890), St. George's Hall (1 July 1890), and the Vaudeville Theatre (see note 11.5).

4. Shelley's *The Cenci: A Tragedy in Five Acts* (see note 1.6) received its first production on 7 May 1886 at the Grand Theatre, Islington. The Shelley Society of London sponsored not only the production but also a new edition of the play (London: Reeves and Turner, 1886), with an introduction by Alfred and H. Buxton Forman and a prologue by Todhunter. Alma Murray (1854–1945) played Beatrice Cenci; a few weeks later she also acted the title role in *Helena in Troas*.

5. Winifred Emery (1862–1924) played Fanny Hoyden in *Miss Tomboy* by

Robert Buchanan (1841–1901) when it opened at the Vaudeville Theatre on 20 Mar 1890. Her husband, Cyril Maude (1862–1951), was an actor and theater-manager. Actor and playwright William Terriss (1847–97) gave 260 performances in the role of Romeo at the Lyceum Theatre; he was later stabbed to death outside the stage door of the New Adelphi Theatre by a revengeful actor named Prince. For Lady Archibald Campbell see note 11.4.

6. Painter and poet Louise Jopling Rowe (1843–1933) helped design the set and costumes of *Helena in Troas* and performed (along with Mrs. Oscar Wilde) as a member of the chorus. Her memoir *Twenty Years of My Life: 1867 to 1887* (London: John Lane, 1925) recalls the production in some detail. Mathilde Blind (1841–96) translated *The Journal of Marie Bashkirtseff*, 2 vols (London: Cassell, 1890); she also wrote poetry, edited the works of Byron and Shelley, and published a book on George Eliot (1883). Marie Bashkirtseff (1859–84) was a Russian artist whose introspective diary was first published in French in 1887. On 28 Apr 1888 Yeats attended a large "Home Rule" party at the South Kensington home of Mr. and Mrs. Charles Hancock, where Mrs. William Gladstone and other Liberal Party dignitaries spoke on electoral prospects and Home Rule for Ireland (*CL1* 64). Theodore Watts-Dunton (1832–1914), literary critic, was the protector of A. C. Swinburne during the poet's later years. May Morris (1862–1938) instructed Yeats's sister Susan Mary (Lily) in the art of embroidery; for William Morris and *The Earthly Paradise*, see notes 1.5 and 21.5.

7. In the Golden Age of Greek legend, mankind was ideally happy and innocent. For Bacchus, see note 7.7. Yeats misquotes several of Todhunter's lines: "Before this insult grows a shepherd's tale!" (*A Sicilian Idyll*, p. 28); "I wooed her but in pretty sport" (p. 33); "And purple clusters nodding round thy brow, / Welcomed with every seasonable rite, / Dances, and pastoral mirth!" (p. 11).

8. For Mrs. Edward Emery, or Florence Farr, and for Lily Linfield see note 1.4. Henry Marriott Paget (1856–1936), painter, illustrator, and brother-in-law of Florence Farr, took the role of Alcander. In the preceding year, 1889, Paget painted the portrait of Yeats which is reproduced at the beginning of this book. The "well known gentleman" who played Daphnis was Edward Heron-Allen (see note 1.4). For Bertram Luard-Selby see note 7.4. Alfred Lys Baldry (1858–1939), painter, critic, and stage-manager, learned to represent Hellenic scenes in the studio of the Victorian Neoclassical painter Alfred Moore. Baldry was the husband of Lily Linfield. Landscape painter Arthur Lemon (1850–1912) specialized in Italian pastoral scenes.

9 ROSE KAVANAGH:
DEATH OF A PROMISING YOUNG IRISH POET

1. The young poet Rose Kavanagh (1859–91) died of consumption on 26 Feb 1891; Yeats's article is dated 17 Mar. She was a close friend of the O'Learys and of Katharine Tynan. For Yeats's personal reaction to her death and

plan for this article, see his letter to Katharine Tynan, 5 Mar 1891 (*CL1* 244–5).

2. Lower and Upper Lough Bray are small mountain lakes south of Dublin, between that city and Glendalough; St. Michan's Churchyard is the Dublin cemetery where Robert Emmet was supposed to be buried without epitaph, in accord with the closing words of his famous speech from the prisoner's dock: "When my country takes her place among the nations of the earth, then and not till then let my epitaph be written." Yeats discusses Rose Kavanagh's poems about both sites below (see notes 15 and 16).

3. Christian is the hero of John Bunyan's allegory *The Pilgrim's Progress* (1684), in which he flees the City of Destruction and after an eventful pilgrimage arrives at the Celestial City.

4. County Tyrone lies in Ulster, the northern province of Ireland; Killadroy is situated 3 miles south-east of the town of Omagh.

5. The Avonban (White River) is a noisy stream by Killadroy; Mullaghmore, near Augher in County Tyrone, lies on the banks of the Blackwater. The river Blackwater, which flows into Lough Neagh, witnessed many important battles, including the victory of Hugh O'Neill at the Yellow Ford in 1598 and of his great-nephew Owen Roe O'Neill at Benburb in 1646. Kavanagh's poem "The Northern Blackwater" was included in H. Halliday Sparling's anthology *Irish Minstrelsy* (London: Walter Scott, 1887) pp. 295–7. Yeats's three following quotations comprise the first couplet of the third stanza, the entire fourth stanza, and the first couplet of the fifth stanza, respectively.

6. For Kickham see note 2.26; to Yeats, "The Irish Peasant Girl" showed Kickham "at his best."

7. The text in *Irish Minstrelsy*, pp. 296–7, contains three variants from Yeats's quotation: "its" for "a" in l. 2; "ev'ry" for "every" in l. 6; and "where" for "Where" in l. 11.

8. Knockmany is a hilltop in County Tyrone. For Carleton, see notes 3.4 and 5.8. Carleton was born at Prillisk, near Clogher, County Tyrone. The "wild, humorous tale" was "A Legend of Knockmany," in which a bumptious Fin M'Coul outsmarts his rival Cucullin; Yeats included it in his anthology *FFT*.

9. The Royal Dublin Society was established in 1731 for "improving husbandry, manufactures and other useful arts and sciences"; it was incorporated by Royal Charter in 1750 and assumed the title "Royal" in 1820 under patronage of George IV. Responsible for such important institutions as the National Library, National Museum, National Gallery, and Botanic Gardens, it also established the first school of art in Ireland, now the National College of Art. Rose Kavanagh was most closely associated with the *Weekly Freeman*; she also wrote for many other periodicals, including *BP*.

10. The Ladies' Land League was founded in 1881 as the Central Land League of the Ladies of Ireland by Anna Parnell at the urging of Michael Davitt; its members included Yeats's friend Katharine Tynan. When Davitt, Charles Stewart Parnell, and other leaders of the land movement were imprisoned in 1881–2, the women temporarily ran the movement and its newspaper *United Ireland*, but they were disbanded in Aug 1882.

11. For Kickham see note 2.26. By 1879 Rose Kavanagh had moved to Dublin,

where she became friends with the aged and infirm Kickham. "The Rose of Knockmany" may be consulted in *The Valley Near Slievenamon: A Kickham Anthology*, ed. James Maher (Mullinahone, Co. Tipperary: James Maher, 1942) pp. 95–6.

12. Rose Kavanagh contributed the regular feature "Uncle Remus to His Nieces and Nephews" to the *Irish Fireside*, which she also edited; after the demise of that journal in 1889, the column was continued in the *Weekly Freeman*. Mrs. Dwyer Gray was the wife of the editor and owner of the *Freeman's Journal* (see note 3.15).

13. *PBYI* was originally published by M. H. Gill and Son (Dublin, 1888) and included three poems by Rose Kavanagh as well as work by such other members of the Yeats circle as Rolleston, Todhunter, Tynan, Hyde, and Yeats himself. In 1890 Gill brought out a "New Edition" consisting of the sheets of the first edition with a new title page.

14. For Tynan, Ellen O'Leary, Todhunter, and Hyde see notes 4.10, 2.22, 1.3, and 3.8, respectively.

15. Yeats quotes the third of the seven stanzas comprising the poem (*PBYI* 33–4).

16. Robert Emmet (1778–1803) was a leader of the United Irishmen; he was hanged in 1803 and buried in St. Michan's Churchyard (see note 2).

17. Yeats quotes all but the second and the last stanzas of the poem (*PBYI* 60–1).

18. The popular Fenian poet John Keegan Casey (1846–70) is perhaps best remembered for his nationalist ballad "The Rising of the Moon." For Kickham, Davis, and Mangan see notes 2.26, 2.27, and 2.15, respectively.

19. Rose Kavanagh spent the winter of 1889–90 at Arcachon, on the Bay of Biscay.

20. See notes 1 and 4.

21. For Ellen O'Leary see note 2.22 and the following essay by Yeats in the present volume. Kavanagh's memorial poem is the three-stanza "Ellen O'Leary," which faces the title page of O'Leary's *Lays of Country, Home and Friends* (Dublin: Sealy, Bryers and Walker, 1891). Yeats quotes the first two of the four stanzas comprising O'Leary's "Brave Eyes: Inscribed to Rose Kavanagh" (p. 93), where the text lacks the comma after "brave eyes" in the first line of both stanzas.

10   SOME RECENT BOOKS BY IRISH WRITERS

1. Published 1891. For Ellen O'Leary see note 2.22; she had died on 16 Oct 1889 at Cork.

2. For Rolleston see note 2.20. Yeats had referred to the book and its introduction in the last paragraph of his first *BP* article, dated 10 July 1889 and reprinted as item 2 in the present volume.

3. The famous periodical the *Nation* (1842–92) was founded by Sir Charles Gavan Duffy, Thomas Davis, and John Blake Dillon. Many of its women poets wrote under pseudonyms; "Mary" was Ellen Mary Patrick Downing (1828–69), and "Eva" was Mary Anne Kelly (*c.*1825–1910).

4. Yeats quotes "To God and Ireland True," p. 38 of O'Leary's book, where the last line of stanza two lacks a dash after "Ireland."

5. For Davis see note 2.27. Byron's friend Thomas Moore (1779–1852) was the most famous Irish poet of his day; his *Irish Melodies* appeared in ten volumes, 1808–34.

6. For Rolleston and Duffy see notes 2.20 and 2.24, respectively. Rolleston's Introduction gives a helpful biographical account, and Duffy's critical remarks include the following account of "To God and Ireland True": "Here is such a little song, which might move a peasant to tears, or a peer or philosopher whose heart had not grown hard. A few years ago there died suddenly in his sleep in Milbank gaol, a political prisoner, convicted of appearing in arms against the Crown, who is affectionately remembered as the 'Fenian Emmet,' for, like Emmet, he sacrificed a great passion to a greater one. This is the lament of the one loved and left behind" (pp. xxvii–xxix). The volume is dedicated to Duffy.

7. The poet and journalist John Francis O'Donnell (1837–74) published poems in the *Nation* at the age of seventeen. His books include *Emerald Wreath* (1865) and *Memories of the Irish Franciscans* (1871), in addition to the posthumous collection *Poems* (London: Ward and Downey, 1891). Katharine Tynan's friend Frances Alice Wynne (1863–93) published poems in various periodicals, including *PSJ*; *Whisper!* (London: Kegan Paul, 1890) was her only volume of verse.

8. The Southwark Irish Literary Club (see note 1.11) was founded in 1883; Charles Gavan Duffy, Douglas Hyde, John Todhunter, Katharine Tynan, Oscar Wilde, and Yeats all lectured there.

9. Yeats quotes the first two of the seven stanzas of "The Four Masters" (O'Donnell, *Poems*, pp. 101–2, where the first stanza has a comma at the end of l. 2, lacks the comma after "who" in l. 5, and capitalizes the "O" of "Oppression" in l. 6). The Four Masters consisted of Micheál Ó Cléirigh and three assistants who from 1632 to 1636 compiled the *Annalá Ríoghachta Éireann* (Annals of the Kingdom of Ireland) at a time when it was feared that ancient records might be lost.

10. For Tennyson see note 1.6; Yeats often viewed him as contaminated by discursiveness, moralism, and abstraction.

11. Yeats quotes from Richard Dowling's Introduction to O'Donnell's *Poems*, p. xix, where the passage, from a letter of 19 July 1872, reads: "Talking of work – since Sunday, 2 cols. notes, 2 cols. London gossip, and a leader 1 col., and a col. of verse for the *Nation*. For *Catholic Opinion*, two pages of notes and a leader. For *Illustrated Magazine*, 3 poems and a five col. story." In 1872, O'Donnell also became London correspondent of *BP*.

12. Yeats is probably paraphrasing from p. xiv of Dowling's Introduction to O'Donnell's *Poems*: " 'Why,' said I, 'you write verse as fast as prose!' 'Faster,' said he . . . . ' "

13. "The wittiest Irishman of our day" was Oscar Wilde (see note 3.3), who according to Yeats made the remark to him at Christmas dinner in 1888 (*Au* 135).

14. For Froude see note 5.3.

15. For the *Tain Bo* see note 7.11.

16. For Hyde see note 3.8; Yeats refers here to *Beside the Fire: A Collection of Irish Gaelic Folk Stories* (London: David Nutt, 1890).

17. The "English authority of note" was Frederick York Powell (1850–1904), a don at Christ Church and from 1894 Regius Professor of Modern History at Oxford; Powell lived in Bedford Park 1881–1902 and was a friend of John Butler Yeats. In a letter of 23 Aug 1889 Yeats wrote to Hyde, "York Powell said to me last week – 'there was never a Folk lorist like him'" (*CL1* 182). The "particular legend" was probably "Teig O'Kane and the Corpse."

18. On 24 Dec 1601 an English army under Mountjoy routed combined Spanish and Irish forces at the battle of Kinsale; the Irish were led by Hugh O'Neill and Red Hugh O'Donnell (see note 7.25). The forthcoming romance by O'Grady (see note 7.14) was probably *Ulrick the Ready*, which did not finally appear until 1896 (London: Downey).

11 DR. TODHUNTER'S NEW PLAY

1. For Todhunter see note 1.3. For "his volume of Irish poems" and its contents see item 17 in the present volume.

2. For Todhunter's *Helena in Troas* (see note 7.8) Edward William Godwin (1833–86), architect, theatrical designer, and passionate Hellenist, built a large replica of a classical Greek theater inside Hengler's Circus. The frieze on the stage pediment consisted of live figures miming the attitudes of the Parthenon sculptures. The production attempted to capture the religious spirit of the Greek theater by employing music, choral dancing and singing, incense, and authentic costumes (but no masks). Godwin also helped to plan Bedford Park, supervised Lady Archibald Campbell's private theatricals, and fathered director Gordon Craig by actress Ellen Terry.

3. For Shelley see note 1.6. We have not located the phrase "the trance of real life" in Shelley's writings. In l. 344 of *Adonais* he speaks of "the dream of life" and in l. 347 of "mad trance." Yeats may have conflated these two expressions.

4. Lady Archibald Campbell (d. 1923) was a painter and the author of *Rainbow Music; or, The Philosophy of Harmony in Colour-Grouping* (London: Bernard Quaritch, 1886). She sponsored private, open-air theatricals in wooded settings at Coombe in Surrey and on Wimbledon Common. Supervised by E. W. Godwin, these pastoral productions included Shakespeare's *As You Like It* in 1884, John Fletcher's *The Faithful Shepherdess* in 1885, and *Fair Rosamond* in 1886. The influence of these productions upon Todhunter's *Helena in Troas* and *A Sicilian Idyll* is described by John Stokes in *Resistible Theatres* (London: Paul Elek, 1972) pp. 51–6, 65–7. *The Faithful Shepherdess* by Fletcher (1579–1625) was first published in 1610.

5. *A Sicilian Idyll* (see note 7.1) and *The Poison Flower* were performed at the Vaudeville Theatre 15–19 June 1891. *The Poison Flower* is based upon "Rappaccini's Daughter," a short story by American novelist Nathaniel Hawthorne (1804–64) originally published in *Mosses from an Old Manse*

(1846). Hawthorne's son Julian (1846–1934), also a novelist, had lived in Bedford Park during the late 1870s. Todhunter's adaptation was published in *Isolt of Ireland: A Legend in a Prologue and Three Acts and The Poison Flower* (London and Toronto: J. M. Dent, 1927). For another review by Yeats of *The Poison Flower* see item 22 in the present volume.

6. In William Shakespeare's *The Winter's Tale* (1611) ii. i, Mamillius tells his mother: "A sad tale's best for winter. I have one / Of sprites and goblins." Hermione replies: "Come on, sit down; come on and do your best / To fright me with your sprites; you're powerful at it."

7. In the book of Genesis, Eve is the first woman created by God and thus the mother of the human race. Yeats misquotes Todhunter's line "So poison casts out poison" (*Isolt of Ireland and The Poison Flower*, p. 133). Yeats's friend Samuel Liddell MacGregor Mathers (1854–1918) translated Knorr von Rosenroth's *Kabbala Denudata* (1677) into English as *The Kabbalah Unveiled* (London: George Redway, 1887).

8. The rumor and the Italian scientist to which Yeats refers remain unidentified. Research on micro-organisms in milk began about 1890 and later led a number of scientists to conclude that a lactic acid bacillus is responsible for "a direct connection between the use of soured milk [or yoghurt] and longevity"; see Loudon M. Douglas, *The Bacillus of Long Life* (New York and London: G. P. Putnam's Sons, 1911) pp. 12–14. The bacillus was thought to counteract poisons generated within the intestinal tract.

9. *A Blot in the 'Scutcheon* (1843) by Robert Browning (see note 6.1) is a tragedy arising from mistaken notions of honor and purity in an aristocratic English family. It was revived in Boston, Massachusetts, on 16 Mar 1885.

10. In the double bill at the Vaudeville, Florence Farr (see note 1.4) played both Beatrice Rappaccini in *The Poison Flower* and Amaryllis in *A Sicilian Idyll*. She also played Amaryllis in the original Bedford Park production of *A Sicilian Idyll*. In the spring of 1891 she appeared at the Vaudeville in the first British production of *Rosmersholm* (1886) by Norwegian dramatist and poet Henrik Ibsen (1828–1906).

12   THE CELT IN IRELAND

1. From 10 to 16 Aug 1891 Yeats visited Whitehall, the family farm of Katharine Tynan near Clondalkin in County Dublin. Her description of the farm appears in *Twenty-five Years: Reminiscences* (London: Smith, Elder, 1913) p. 31.

2. Yeats was reading *Marius the Epicurean: His Sensations and Ideas*, 2 vols (London: Macmillan, 1885) by English essayist and novelist Walter Pater (1839–94). Yeats refers to passages in chs xix and xx which mention the Greek philosopher Plato (427–347 BC).

3. Many residents of County Down in Ulster descend from Scottish immigrants. Yeats repeats the story of the two people killed by the fairies in *IFT* 225.

4. The battle of Waterloo, in which allied armies commanded by the Duke of Wellington decisively defeated the army of Napoleon Bonaparte, took

place in 1815. We have not been able to trace the ballad quoted by Yeats.

5. By "minority" Yeats means those loyal to the union of Ireland with England.

6. *The Irish Monthly Illustrated Journal* remains unidentified. "Mr. Eyre," mentioned by Yeats as the magazine's editor, may be John Richard Eyre, Dublin journalist and author; see *CL1* 136n. William Thomas Stead (1849–1912), English journalist, author, and social reformer, edited the *Pall Mall Gazette* from 1883 to 1889 and founded the *Review of Reviews* in 1890. He met Madame Blavatsky in 1888 and shared Yeats's interests in spiritualism, theosophy, and automatic writing. The German emperor in 1891 was Wilhelm II.

7. Katharine Tynan (see note 4.10), *A Nun, Her Friends and Her Order: Being a Sketch of the Life of Mother Mary Xaveria Fallon* and *Ballads and Lyrics*, both published in London by Kegan Paul, 1891.

8. In Greek legend the ancient city of Troy in Asia Minor was besieged and eventually destroyed by a Greek army, whereas the city of Thebes in Greece survived a siege by seven allied armies, each of which attacked one of the city's main gates. In Plato's *Phaedrus* the Greek philosopher Socrates (d. 399 BC) hears cicadas as he walks along the Ilissus River near Athens.

13 THE RHYMERS' CLUB

1. All the groups Yeats mentions belong to the second half of the nineteenth century. The Decadents exhibited morbid or perverse tastes, unconventional social behavior, and hyperaesthetic temperaments in their personal lives while advancing an ideal of pure art; for Yeats the most influential French Decadent was Joris Karl Huysmans (1848–1907), author of the novel *À Rebours* (*Against the Grain*). Although the poets Stephane Mallarmé (1842–98), Paul Verlaine (1844–96), Arthur Rimbaud (1854–91), and the dramatist Phillipe-Auguste Villiers de l'Isle Adam (1838–89) are also associated with the term "Decadence," they more properly belong to the Symbolist movement, which took Charles Pierre Baudelaire (1821–67) as precursor. In stressing suggestion, evocation, symbolism, and musical wordplay the Symbolists reacted against the restraint, precision, and objectivity sought by Parnassians such as Charles-Marie-René Leconte de Lisle (1818–94). Primarily interested in prose fiction, Naturalists such as Émile Zola (1840–1902) stubbornly refused to idealize experience and believed that human life was subject to natural laws.

2. In the Bible, Ishmael is the son of Abraham and Hagar and is excluded from God's covenant with Isaac. The name is generally used for an outcast from society because of the prophecy in Genesis 16:12: "And he will be a wild man; his hand will be against every man, and every man's hand against him."

3. Surprisingly difficult to document in view of its importance, the Rhymers' Club of young poets was founded by Yeats and Ernest Rhys and flourished 1890–4, meeting principally at the Cheshire Cheese inn off Fleet Street. Besides Yeats and Rhys, John Davidson, Ernest Dowson, Edwin Ellis,

George Arthur Greene, Selwyn Image, Lionel Johnson, Richard Le Gallienne, Victor Plarr, T. W. Rolleston, and John Todhunter were among those who attended regularly; Edward Garnett, Arthur Symons, and Oscar Wilde appeared less frequently.

4. The "noted verse writer" whom Yeats quotes has not yet been identified.

5. The son of a West Country Methodist minister, Arthur Symons (1865–1945) wrote poetry celebrating decadence and the *demi-monde* of streets and music halls, and in his criticism strove to introduce French Symbolist doctrines into English literature. He and Yeats were to share rooms in 1895–6, and he dedicated his best-known book, *The Symbolist Movement in Literature* (1899), to Yeats. The Scots schoolmaster John Davidson (1857–1909) eventually settled in London to pursue his literary career; his best-known poem is the satiric ballad "Thirty Bob a Week."

6. The men of letters Sir Edmund William Gosse (see note 2.8), Andrew Lang (see note 4.8), and Henry Austin Dobson (see note 2.8) all valued intricate foreign forms of verse, such as the French rondeau and triolet. The "distinguished member" of their school whom Yeats quotes has not yet been identified.

7. The great medieval English poet Geoffrey Chaucer (1343–1400) wrote *The Canterbury Tales* and other works.

8. Yeats quotes from the Prologue to the opening title-sequence of eight poems from *In a Music Hall and Other Poems* (London: Ward and Downey, 1891) p. 2, where there is a stanza break before the last two lines of the quotation. The poem begins, "In Glasgow, in 'Eighty-four, / I worked as a junior clerk."

9. "Selene Eden" forms part of the title-suite "In a Music Hall"; the speaker is a *femme fatale* who dances on the stage.

10. The "radiant poem" is "The Gleeman"; Yeats quotes a passage from p. 22 (*In a Music Hall*); "For Lovers" and "Anselm and Bianca" are longer poems in the volume.

11. Matthew Arnold (1822–88; see note 20.4) used the Old Testament term "Philistine" in *Culture and Anarchy* (1869) to describe uncultured, materialistic aspects of the middle class.

12. The quest romance *Alastor* (1816) by the poet Shelley (see note 1.6) presents a sensitive youth's solitary and unsuccessful quest for an idealized female figure. The poem fascinated Yeats, who regularly (and mistakenly) referred to the anonymous hero as "Alastor."

13. Born in Liverpool, Richard Le Gallienne (1866–1947) moved to London, where he met Wilde, Swinburne, Meredith, and other writers in 1889 and became one of the leading aesthetes. A prolific writer, he published over thirty books; after 1905 he lived mostly in the United States.

14. The *Review of Reviews* included a photograph of Le Gallienne in the Oct 1891 issue (IV, 421) together with a notice of *The Book-Bills of Narcissus* (Derby: Frank Murray, 1891).

15. *Volumes in Folio* (1889) was the first book published by Elkin Mathews and John Lane at their newly founded Bodley Head press.

16. The English Romantic poet John Keats (1795–1821) strongly influenced the aesthetes of the 1890s, who, like Yeats, largely accepted the view of him in Hallam's essay on Tennyson. In "Ego Dominus Tuus" (*PNE* 160)

Yeats later described Keats's luxuriant art as a compensation for his impoverished life.

17. The cousin of Olivia Shakespear, Lionel Pigot Johnson (1867–1902) graduated from New College, Oxford; influenced by Pater, he became one of the leading aesthetic poets of the 1890s. Yeats admired Johnson's learning, mysticism, and love of tradition, all of which helped impel his conversion to Catholicism in 1891. In *Au* Johnson figures as one of the "tragic generation," while in a memorable stanza of "In Memory of Major Robert Gregory" Yeats wrote that "much falling he / Brooded upon sanctity" (*PNE* 132). In the standard modern edition of *The Collected Poems of Lionel Johnson* (New York and London: Garland, 1982) Ian Fletcher lists "Gloria Mundi" as a lost poem. The translator and poet George Arthur Greene (1853–1921) graduated from Trinity College, Dublin, served as Vice-Chairman of the Irish Literary Society (London), and contributed to both of the Rhymers' Club anthologies. Greene's *Italian Lyrists of Today: Translations from Contemporary Italian Poetry* (London: Elkin Mathews and John Lane) appeared in 1893, but his *Dantesques: A Sonnet Companion to the Inferno* (London: Elkin Mathews, Vigo Cabinet Series) was not published until 1903.

18. The English editor and writer Ernest Rhys (1859–1946; see note 3) edited the Camelot (see note 4.12), Lyric Poets, and Everyman's Library series. For Rolleston see note 2.20.

19. *The Book of the Rhymers' Club* (London: Elkin Mathews, 1892) listed the following names as members of the club: Ernest Dowson, Edwin J. Ellis, G. A. Greene, Lionel Johnson, Richard Le Gallienne, Victor Plarr, Ernest Radford, Ernest Rhys, T. W. Rolleston, Arthur Symons, John Todhunter, and W. B. Yeats. *The Second Book of the Rhymers' Club* (London: Elkin Mathews and John Lane) followed in 1894, with the addition of Arthur Cecil Hillier to the list of contributors.

20. *The Banshee and Other Poems* by John Todhunter (see notes 1.3 and 17.1) was first published in 1888 (London: Kegan Paul).

21. For Yeats's extended remarks on "The Children of Lir" and "The Sons of Turann" see his review of *The Banshee* in *PSJ*, reprinted below as item 17 in the present volume. For Ferguson see note 7.19.

14   THE NEW "SPERANZA"

1. John Mitchel (1815–75) was a leader of the Young Ireland movement and a major contributor to the *Nation* (see note 2.27). The opening sentences of Mitchel's *Jail Journal; or, Five Years in British Prisons* (1854; 2nd edn New York: P. M. Haverty, 1868) read as follows: "England has been left in possession not only of the soil of Ireland, with all that grows and lives thereon, to her own use, but in possession of the world's ear also. She may pour into it what tale she will; and all mankind will believe her" (p. 9). Yeats quoted prominently from *Jail Journal* again in section III of his late poem "Under Ben Bulben." The London *Times* was and still is one of the most prestigious newspapers in Great Britain.

2. John P. Leonard (d. 1889) was a friend of John O'Leary and Professor of English at the Sorbonne in Paris.
3. "Speranza" was the pen-name of Lady Jane Wilde (see note 3.2). Yeats also called Maud Gonne "The New 'Speranza'" in a *United Ireland* essay of 16 Jan 1892 (*UP1* 212–15).
4. In the first months of 1892 Maud Gonne (1865 or 1866–1953), the beautiful Irish patriot whom Yeats loved for many years, spoke on behalf of Irish national independence in Paris, Valenciennes, Arras, Rouen, Bordeaux, Cognac, Périgueux, and La Rochelle (*CL1* 295–6n).
5. Maud Gonne addressed the Cercle Catholique des Étudiants du Luxembourg de Paris on 20 Feb 1892. Her account of the occasion appears in Maud Gonne MacBride, *A Servant of the Queen: Reminiscences* (London: Victor Gollancz, 1938) pp. 150–6. The "supplement to *La Revue Catholique*" in which her speech was published remains unidentified.
6. The repeated failure of the Irish potato crop during the 1840s caused widespread catastrophe.
7. Missionaries led by St. Patrick converted Ireland to Christianity in the fifth century AD. King Brian Boru was killed while repelling a Danish invasion at the battle of Clontarf in 1014. By "the English invasion" Yeats may mean any or all of the series of incursions that began with the Norman conquest of 1166. Charles Stewart Parnell died on 6 Oct 1891. Yeats quotes ll. 19–20 of "The Solitary Reaper" (1807) by William Wordsworth; he had quoted them previously in an essay of 9 Oct 1886 (*UP1* 81).

15   THE NEW NATIONAL LIBRARY – THE NATIONAL LITERARY SOCIETY – MR. O'GRADY'S STORIES – DR. HYDE'S FORTHCOMING BOOK – THEMES FOR IRISH LITTERATEURS

1. For the new National Library see note 1.12.
2. The tale of the giant in the egg is type 302 in *The Types of the Folktale* by Aanti Aarne and Stith Thompson (Helsinki: Suomalainen Tiedakatemia, 1961) pp. 93–4. For Irish versions see type 302 in *The Types of the Irish Folktale* by Séan Ó Súilleabháin and Reidar Th. Christiansen (Helsinki: Suomalainen Tiedakatemia, 1963) pp. 63–4.
3. The Irish National Literary Society was founded in Dublin during May and June 1892. The declared objectives of the society were (1) the circulation of Irish literature, (2) lectures and discussions, (3) concerts of Irish music, and (4) the establishment of lending libraries. Plans were also made for a New Irish Library, a series of publications modeled upon the Library of Ireland, a Young Ireland project initiated in the 1850s by Sir Charles Gavan Duffy. Throughout 1892 and 1893 Yeats and Duffy engaged in a fierce battle for editorial control of the New Irish Library, with Duffy the eventual victor.
4. Trinity College, Dublin, was founded in 1592 for Protestants only. Its

graduates include Jonathan Swift, Oliver Goldsmith, George Berkeley, Edmund Burke, Wolfe Tone, Robert Emmet, J. M. Synge, and three earlier generations of Yeats's own family. Thomas of Erceldoune was a Scottish poet and prophet, also known as Thomas Rymour and Thomas the Rhymer (1220?–97?). Many political–historical prophecies were attached to his name after his death.

5. The "men of '48" were the founders of the Young Ireland movement in 1848 (see note 2.27). William Gladstone (see note 5.17) and the Liberals were returned to office with Irish Home Rule Party support in the general election of July 1892. For Yeats's organizing activities in the months prior to this election see note 1.11.

6. The Revd. Thomas A. Finlay (1848–1940) was Rector of Belvedere College, Fellow of University College, Dublin, and Professor of Political Economy in the Royal University of Ireland. For John O'Leary, Sir Charles Gavan Duffy, Dr. Douglas Hyde, and Dr. George Sigerson see notes 2.23, 2.24, 3.8, and 3.13 respectively. Papal Count George Noble Plunkett (1851–1948), poet and art critic, became Director of the Dublin National Museum. For Katharine Tynan and Maud Gonne, see notes 4.10 and 14.4. Richard Ashe King (1839–1932) was a clergyman, novelist, and lecturer. Although Yeats does not mention it, he himself was also a member of the committee and a vice-president of the society. For "the Ossianic days" see note 7 below.

7. For Standish James O'Grady see note 7.14. He appears never to have published a romance about Strongbow (see note 7.15). But the "little stories on events in Irish history" appeared as *The Bog of Stars, and Other Stories and Sketches of Elizabethan Ireland* (London: T. Fisher Unwin, 1893). O'Grady's *Finn and His Companions* (London: T. Fisher Unwin, 1892) was illustrated by John Butler Yeats. The Ossianic age was the legendary era of Oisin, son of Finn, after whom the ancient Fenians were named. Caoilte was one of the chief Fenian warriors. For St. Patrick see note 7.16.

8. For Douglas Hyde see note 3.8. The projected series of books never appeared, and neither did the translations of bardic stories; see *CL1* 286–7n.

9. The National Museum, opposite the new National Library on Kildare Street, opened in 1884. "The stuff that dreams are made on" is a quotation from William Shakespeare's *The Tempest*, iv. i.

16 THE POET OF BALLYSHANNON

1. Yeats was reviewing William Allingham, *Irish Songs and Poems. With Nine Airs Harmonized for Voice and Pianoforte* (London: Reeves and Turner, 1887). For Allingham see note 5.17, and for other essays on his work by Yeats see *UP1* 208–12, 258–61. See also items 5 and 6 in the present volume.

2. *Irish Songs and Poems*, p. 136 (see note 5.20).

3. For Allingham and Ballyshannon see note 6.21.

4. *Irish Songs and Poems*, p. 118; these are the opening lines of "Fairy Hill, or, The Poet's Wedding."

5. *Irish Songs and Poems*, p. 128; these are the opening lines of "The Fairies." Yeats reprinted the poem in *BIV* and *Sixteen Poems by William Allingham: Selected by William Butler Yeats* (Dundrum: Dun Emer Press, 1905).

6. This medley of details is drawn from *Irish Songs and Poems*, p. 33 ("The Pilot's Daughter"), p. 53 ("Invitation to a Painter"), pp. 45–6 ("Abbey Asaroe"), pp. 29 and 27 ("The Winding Banks of Erne"), and p. 61 ("The Music Master"). Yeats reprinted "Abbey Asaroe" and "The Winding Banks of Erne" in *Sixteen Poems by William Allingham*.

7. Heinrich Heine (1797–1856), German poet, and Robert Burns (1759–96), Scottish poet. For Irish poets Thomas Davis and Sir Samuel Ferguson see notes 2.27 and 7.19. In Greek mythology, the Fates were three sisters who spun, measured, and cut the thread of each human life.

8. In the preceding paragraph Yeats refers to Allingham's "The Lady of the Sea. A Legend of Ancient Erin," in *Irish Songs and Poems*, pp. 5–23. The opening lines of "The Music Master" are on p. 60.

9. For Charles Lever and Samuel Lover see note 3.4. Yeats repeats this charge against Lover in *FFT* xv; nevertheless, in *IFT* he uses material from Lover's *Legends and Stories of Ireland* (1832–4).

10. Sir Samuel Ferguson, "The Welshmen of Tirawley," in *Lays of the Western Gael and Other Poems* (London: Bell and Daldy, 1865) pp. 70–88. Emon Lynott, blinded along with the other men of his clan of Welsh settlers, begets a sighted son through whom he wreaks vengeance upon the Barrett clan. Yeats reprinted the poem in *BIV*. Tirawley is one of the baronies of County Mayo.

11. These details come from *Irish Songs and Poems*, p. 61 ("The Music Master"), p. 27 ("The Winding Banks of Erne"), p. 61 ("The Music Master"), and p. 33 ("The Pilot's Daughter").

12. *Irish Songs and Poems*, pp. 104–7 ("The Abbot of Inisfálen. [A Killarney Legend.]"). Yeats reprinted this poem in *BIV* and *Sixteen Poems by William Allingham*.

13. Mount Nephin (elevation 2646 feet) is in the barony of Tirawley, County Mayo. Killarney is one of the principal towns in Kerry, the south-westernmost county of Ireland. The ruined abbey of Innisfallen, dating from the seventh century, occupies an island in Lough Leane, County Kerry. A Jotun is a giant in Scandinavian mythology.

14. "Sassenach" is Gaelic for Saxon; the "strange tongue" is therefore some early form of English. Yeats misquotes Allingham's line "A carven cross above his head, a holly-bush at his feet." The "old ruin" mentioned in the next paragraph may be any of a number in western Ireland. Yeats knew the remains of the monasteries dating from the sixth century on Church Island in Lough Gill (County Sligo) and Church Island in Lough Key (County Roscommon; also spelled Kay, Cay, and Cé). He admired as well the ruins of the thirteenth-century Premonstratentian monastery on Trinity Island in Lough Key.

15. *Irish Songs and Poems*, pp. 150–2 ("Lovely Mary Donnelly"). In Allingham's *The Music Master* (London: G. Routledge, 1855) p. 34, the first line of this song reads "it's you I love the best."

16. For *Laurence Bloomfield* see note 6.22. For William Gladstone see note 5.17.

17. "The Ascendancy" was the Anglo-Irish Protestant ruling class.

17   DR. TODHUNTER'S LATEST VOLUME OF POEMS

1. Yeats was reviewing John Todhunter, *The Banshee and Other Poems* (London: Kegan Paul, 1888). For Todhunter see note 1.3. For another review by Yeats of this book, see *UP1* 215–18. See also item 13 in the present volume. Yeats had read proofs of *The Banshee* before it appeared (*CL1* 63).

2. For Todhunter's *Helena in Troas* see notes 7.8 and 11.2. Helen, according to Greek legend the most beautiful woman in the world, was taken to Troy by Paris, son of King Priam. The Trojan War occurred when Helen's husband, Menelaus, came with an army to regain her.

3. From 1791 to 1817 Johann Wolfgang von Goethe (1749–1832), German poet and dramatist, directed the court theater in Weimar, Germany. Two of his most famous productions were of *Don Carlos* and *Wallenstein* by German poet and dramatist Johann Christoph Friedrich Schiller (1759–1805). German composer Richard Wagner (1813–83) found an "ideal theater" for his operas in Bayreuth, Germany. Where French historian and critic Joseph Ernest Renan (1832–92) described his ideal theater we have not been able to determine.

4. Yeats refers to "The Doom of the Children of Lir" and "The Lamentation for the Three Sons of Turann" in *The Banshee and Other Poems*, pp. 8–83 and 95–116 respectively. We have annotated Yeats's many quotations from the former poem only where they vary from Todhunter's text.

5. For Sir Samuel Ferguson see notes 7.19 and 16.10. The Greek epic poems the *Iliad* and the *Odyssey* are traditionally attributed to Homer (ninth century BC?).

6. According to Todhunter (*The Banshee and Other Poems*, p. 8), the Tuatha Dé Danaan are "one of the great mythical races of invaders of Ireland." They became immortal beings who dwell in lakes, islands, mountains, and burial mounds. Cuchulain (see note 7.11), Conall Carnach, Conary, and Ferdiad are heroes of the Ulster, or Old Red Branch cycle of Irish legends.

7. The Fomorians were another mythical tribe of invaders who became legendary ancestors of the Irish. Their king, Balor of the Baleful Eye, was a giant with one eye in the middle of his forehead and one in the back of his head.

8. For Katharine Tynan see note 4.10. Her poem "The Children of Lir" appeared in *Ballads and Lyrics* (London: Kegan Paul, 1891) pp. 1–5. Yeats reprinted it in *BIV* and *Twenty-One Poems by Katharine Tynan: Selected by William Butler Yeats* (Dundrum: Dun Emer Press, 1907). For Aubrey de Vere see note 2.11. His poem "The Children of Lir" appeared in *The Foray of Queen Maeve and Other Legends of Ireland's Heroic Age* (London: Kegan Paul, 1882) pp. 71–114.

9. Yeats abridges Todhunter's lines (*The Banshee and Other Poems*, p. 12): "'Nay,' said Bov Derg: 'Not so, Lir is a mighty name, / Greater in war than I, dear as my head to me. / Leave Lir, the dragon of our coasts, the lordship of himself, / To daunt Fomorian ships.'"

10. If this is Yeats's wording rather than a *PSJ* printer's error, the sense in which he uses the phrase "muttering a Druid's mage" is unclear.

11. Todhunter (*The Banshee and Other Poems*, p. 33) reads "'A demon of the air!'" and "Pale outlaw of the air." Derryvarragh Lough is in County Westmeath.

12. From the north-easternmost to the south-westernmost corners of Ireland. Fair Head is Beann Mhor (meaning "big peak") in County Antrim; Cape Clear is the southern point of Cape Clear Island in County Cork.

13. For Douglas Hyde see note 3.8. His poem "The Children of Lir" appeared in *The Three Sorrows of Story-Telling and Ballads of St. Kolumkille* (London: T. Fisher Unwin, 1895) pp. 40–80. The Irish lady who "covered the walls of a Dublin hospital with frescoes of the swan children" remains unidentified. The hospital may have been Sir Patrick Dun's Hospital, which had in one of its wards a set of paintings by various artists. Irish painter Nathaniel Hone (1831–1917) executed a large *St. Patrick* for this decorative scheme in 1889, but by 1920 all of the paintings were badly faded. See Thomas Bodkin, *Four Irish Landscape Painters* (London: T. Fisher Unwin, 1920) p. 61.

14. For the triad of Ferguson, Davis, and Mangan see note 2.15. For Ferguson's "Conary" (1880) see note 7.19.

15. In his Preface (*The Banshee and Other Poems*, p. vii) Todhunter explains, "I have made a metrical version of the *Second Sorrow*, 'The Fate of the Sons of Usna;' but I feel that this poem, being longer than the others, and more epic in character, would rather overweight this little book. I therefore reserve it for future publication." He eventually published all three "Sorrows" in *Three Irish Bardic Tales* (London: J. M. Dent, 1896).

16. For the *Nation* in Young Ireland times see note 2.27. Todhunter's "Aghadoe" and "The Coffin Ship" appeared in *PBYI* and "Aghadoe" also in *BIV*.

17. Yeats alludes to "To a Sky-Lark" (1807) by William Wordsworth.

18. This folktale remains unidentified.

18   IRISH WONDERS

1. Yeats was reviewing David Rice McAnally, Jr. (1810–95), *Irish Wonders: The Ghosts, Giants, Pookas, Demons, Leprechauns, Banshees, Fairies, Witches, Widows, Old Maids, and Other Marvels of the Emerald Isle: Popular Tales as told by the People* (Boston, Mass., and New York: Houghton, Mifflin, 1888). For another review by Yeats of this book see *UP1* 138–41. In *CT* 202 Yeats describes *Irish Wonders* as "inaccurate and ill-written."

2. For John Francis Campbell's *Popular Tales of the West Highlands* (1860–2) see note 6.15.

3. *Irish Wonders*, p. 99.

4. For Yeats's collecting of fairy tales see *IFT* 225. Yeats's maternal family came from County Sligo in western Ireland. The village of Coloomey lies between the Ox Mountains and Slieve Deane in County Sligo.

5. *Irish Wonders*, p. 96, For County Donegal see note 4.7.

6. In *CT* 104–5 Yeats identifies "the old man in County Sligo" as "Paddy Flynn." In *IFT* 223–4 Yeats explains that the "Sheeogues proper . . . are

the spirits that haunt the sacred thorn bushes and the green raths." Though sociable, they are child-stealers.

7. In *FFT* 281, *IFT* 227, and *UP1* 135, Yeats draws material from McAnally's chapter "The Leprechawn" (*Irish Wonders*, pp. 139–50).

8. Thomas Crofton Croker (1798–1854), author of *Fairy Legends and Traditions of the South of Ireland* (London: John Murray, 1825–8). Yeats draws material from this source for both *FFT* and *IFT*. County Kerry is in the south-western corner of Ireland. County Monaghan is in the north-central part of the country. County Clare and County Galway are in west-central Ireland, bordering the Atlantic Ocean.

9. *Irish Wonders*, pp. 106–8. Yeats omits some material between the two paragraphs of the quotation. Lough Erne is a large body of water located in County Fermanagh in north-central Ireland.

10. McAnally's translation appears on p. 110 of *Irish Wonders*. The "accomplished Irish scholar" is Douglas Hyde (see note 3.8). For Yeats's inquiry to Hyde see *CL1* 105–6, 112.

11. *Irish Wonders*, p. 110, and Mr. and Mrs. S. C. Hall, *Ireland: Its Scenery, Character, etc.*, 3 vols (London: How and Parsons, 1841–3) III, 106. Yeats reproduces the Halls' notation in *FFT* 321n.

12. *Irish Wonders*, p. 117. The story of the Banshee who followed a branch of the O'Grady family to Canada is told by Lady Jane Wilde in *Ancient Legends, Mystic Charms and Superstitions of Ireland* (1887; new edn London: Chatto and Windus, 1925) p. 136.

13. Charles Carter Blake (1840–97), zoologist, anthropologist, and theosophist, was a founder of the Anthropological Society of London and later its secretary, curator, and librarian. His encounter with the Banshee took place near La Libertad in the Chontales department of Nicaragua. For further details see the version of his report given by Yeats in *IFT* 232.

14. *Irish Wonders*, pp. 110–11. Irish antiquarian John O'Donovan (1809–61) wrote, "When my grandfather died in Leinster, in 1798, Cleena came all the way from Tonn Cleena, at Glendore, to lament him; but she has not been heard of ever since lamenting any of our race . . . ." See "Irish Popular Superstitions. Chapter III. Medical Superstitions. Fairy Lore, and Enchantment," *Dublin University Magazine*, 33 (June 1849) 708. Yeats refers to this passage again in *IFT* 231 and *UP1* 136–7. Cleena plays a major role in Yeats's "The Devil's Book," *National Observer*, 26 Nov 1892, later rewritten as "The Great Dhoul and Hanrahan the Red" in *The Secret Rose* (1897).

15. *Irish Wonders*, p. 111. The *Mahabharata* (*c.*200 BC) is an Indian epic combining history and mythology. The *Inferno* is the first part of *The Divine Comedy* by Italian poet Dante Alighieri (1265–1321). John P. Frayne suggests (*UP1* 141n) that Yeats has canto 13 in mind.

16. This story is told in Ellen O'Leary's poem "A Legend of Tyrone," which appeared in *PBYI* 54–6, and is mentioned by Yeats in item 10 in the present volume. County Tyrone is in Ulster.

17. Yeats lived in Howth, County Dublin, from 1880 to 1883. This ghost story is told at greater length in *CT* 34–8.

18. The Beresford or Tyrone ghost story is recorded by Andrew Lang in *The Book of Dreams and Ghosts* (1897; new edn London: Longmans, Green, 1899)

pp. 164–74. In Oct 1693, while staying at Gill Hall in County Down, Lady Beresford of Curraghmore in Waterford was visited by the ghost of Lord Tyrone, with whom she had made a pact in her youth that the first of them to die "should, if permitted, appear to the survivor" to reveal the truth or falsity of the Christian doctrine of the afterlife. When Lady Beresford asked the apparition for proof of its reality, it touched and withered her wrist, which she thenceforth covered with a black velvet ribbon depicted in the best-known portrait of her. Yeats's story of the stable boy is told in almost exactly the same words in *FFT* 128–9.

19. *Irish Wonders*, pp. 49–50. The Rock of Cashel in County Tipperary is noted for its ecclesiastical ruins, particularly the chapel constructed between 1127 and 1134 by Cormac MacCarthy (d. 1138). Yeats evokes "the grey rock of Cashel" and "Cormac's ruined house" in his poem "The Double Vision of Michael Robartes" (*PNE* 170–2).

20. For Thomas Crofton Croker see note 8. For Yeats's view of the faults of "Croker and his school" see *FFT* xv and *CT* 201–2: "With all his buoyant humour and imagination he was continually guilty of that great sin against art – the sin of rationalism. He tried to take away from his stories the impossibility that makes them dear to us. Nor could he quite desist from dressing his personages in the dirty rags of the stage Irishman." See also *UP1* 187.

21. Alfred, Lord Tennyson (see note 1.6) apparently made a number of statements to this effect near the end of his life. One instance noted by John P. Frayne (*UP1* 253), though too late to be the report Yeats has in mind in item 18, may be found in William T. Stead, "Character Sketch: November: Tennyson," *Review of Reviews*, VI (Nov 1892) 446–7.

22. *Semper eadem* (Latin – "always the same") was a motto of Queen Elizabeth I.

19 *A SICILIAN IDYLL* – DR. TODHUNTER'S NEW PLAY – A NEW DEPARTURE IN DRAMATIC REPRESENTATION

1. For John Todhunter and his play *Helena in Troas* see notes 1.3, 7.8 and 11.2. For the Bedford Park production of Todhunter's *A Sicilian Idyll* see note 7.1. The Queen Anne style of English domestic architecture, first developed in the early eighteenth century, enjoyed a revival in the late nineteenth century.

2. For Alma Murray and the Shelley Society's production of *The Cenci* see notes 1.6 and 8.4. For Winifred Emery, Buchanan's *Miss Tomboy*, Cyril Maude, and William Terriss see note 8.5. For Lady Archibald Campbell see note 11.4.

3. For Louise Jopling Rowe, Mathilde Blind, Marie Bashkirtseff, Mrs. Charles Hancock, Theodore Watts-Dunton, and May Morris see note 8.6.

4. For Alfred Lys Baldry and Arthur Lemon see note 8.8. For Bacchus see note 7.7. Sir Lawrence Alma-Tadema (1836–1912) was a Victorian painter who specialized in Neoclassical scenes. For Theocritus see note 7.1.

5. Todhunter reads "The tedious tragedies of woman's life" (*Sicilian Idyll*,

p. 15); "Whose siege blind Homer sang" (p. 21); "So many centuries old, and not yet grey?" (p. 21); and "My stock I mean" (p. 21).

6. For Arcadia see note 7.6.

7. Todhunter reads "I'll to the wilds and live a savage man, / For there's no truth in woman" (*Sicilian Idyll*, p. 28).

8. Todhunter reads "I am come / To a new wondrous country" and "I am grown a woman in thine arms" (*Sicilian Idyll*, pp. 35, 36).

9. For the Golden Age see note 8.7.

10. For Mrs. Edward Emery (Florence Farr), Lily Linfield, and Edward Heron-Allen see note 1.4. For H. M. Paget see note 8.8. For Bertram Luard-Selby see note 7.4.

20 A SCHOLAR POET

1. Yeats was reviewing William Watson, *Wordsworth's Grave and Other Poems* (London: T. Fisher Unwin, 1890). Watson (1858–1935) was a member of the Rhymers' Club (see note 13.3) but seldom attended its meetings. Yeats praises Watson's work in the Introduction to the *Oxford Book of Modern Verse* (1936). The title of the essay is probably an allusion to "The Scholar Gypsy" (1853) by Matthew Arnold. For William Wordsworth see note 2.25.

2. Victor Hugo (1802–85), French poet, novelist, and dramatist, writes in *William Shakespeare* (Paris: A. La Croix, Verboeckhoven, 1864) p. 272, "'Il est réservé et discret. Vous êtes tranquille avec lui; il n'abuse de rien. Il a, pardessus tout, une qualité bien rare; il est sobre.' Qu'est ceci? une recommandation pour un domestique? Non. C'est un éloge pour un écrivain."

3. For William Blake see note 1.15. Yeats refers to Blake's *The Marriage of Heaven and Hell*, where the Old Testament prophet Ezekiel appears in "A Memorable Fancy" accompanying plate 12.

4. Matthew Arnold (1822–88), English poet and critic, writes in *Literature and Dogma: An Essay towards a Better Apprehension of the Bible* (London: Smith, Elder, 1873) p. 212, "we shall, in general, in reading the Bible, get the surest hold on the word 'God' by giving it the sense of *the Eternal Power, not ourselves, which makes for righteousness.*"

5. Edward Dowden (1843–1913), Professor of English Literature at Trinity College, Dublin, lent Yeats a copy of Watson's *Epigrams of Art, Life and Nature* (Liverpool: G. G. Walmsley, 1884).

6. Dante Gabriel Rossetti (see note 1.5) praised Watson's *The Prince's Quest and Other Poems* (1880). The "famous hedonist" may have been Oscar Wilde.

7. Yeats postulates an elite, secret society of scholars comparable to the Order of the Golden Dawn, a Rosicrucian lodge which he joined in 1890.

8. General Charles George Gordon was killed by Sudanese tribesmen at Khartoum on 26 Jan 1885. Watson's "Ver Tenebrosum: Sonnets of March and April, 1885" appeared in the *National Review*, v, no. 28 (June 1885) 484–9. The political sonnets of English poet John Milton (1608–74) were

written in the 1640s and 1650s. They were inspired by events in the English
Civil War and in religious wars on the continent of Europe. The "evening
Tory paper" remains unidentified.

9. *Wordsworth's Grave*, pp. 29, 34. Yeats quotes ll. 11–14 of "Home-rootedness,"
   in the second line of which Watson confesses, "I own to 'insularity.'"
10. Watson, "Wordsworth's Grave," *National Review*, x, no. 55 (Sep 1887) 40–
    5. The first two volumes in the Cameo series were *The Lady from the Sea* by
    Henrik Ibsen and *A London Plane-Tree* by Amy Levy.
11. Percy Bysshe Shelley (1792–1822), William Wordsworth (1770–1850),
    Walter Savage Landor (1775–1864), and John Keats (1795–1821) were
    English Romantic poets. Christopher Marlowe (1564–93) and William
    Shakespeare (1564–1616) were English Renaissance playwrights. *King Lear*
    (1606) is a tragedy by Shakespeare. Yeats here refers to Watson's poems
    "Shelley and Harriet Westbrook" (*Wordsworth's Grave*, p. 72), the title
    poem, "Wordsworth's Grave" (pp. 11–22), "On Landor's 'Hellenics'"
    (p. 52), "Keats" (p. 71), "After Reading 'Tamburlaine the Great'" (p. 71),
    and "The Play of 'King Lear'" (p. 72). Wordsworth, Shelley, and Keats
    are also mentioned in "To Professor Dowden, on Receiving from Him 'The
    Life of Shelley'" (pp. 73–6).
12. For Goethe see note 17.3, and for Hugo see note 2 above. George Gordon,
    Lord Byron (1788–1824), was an English Romantic poet. All of Yeats's
    quotations come from Watson's poem "On Exaggerated Deference to
    Foreign Literary Opinion" (*Wordsworth's Grave*, p. 47).
13. *Wordsworth's Grave*, p. 65. Wordsworth was known as "the sage of Rydal"
    after Rydal Mount in the English Lake District, his home from 1813 to
    1850.
14. *Wordsworth's Grave*, pp. 68, 69, 70, 72. In Shakespeare's *Antony and Cleopatra*
    (1608) Actium is the site of a naval battle in which a Roman force led by
    Octavius Caesar defeats an Egyptian force led by the protagonists.
15. *Wordsworth's Grave*, pp. 46, 50.
16. Yeats misquotes ll. 85–6 of Matthew Arnold's "Stanzas from the Grande
    Chartreuse" (1855): "Wandering between two worlds, one dead, / The
    other powerless to be born."

21   THE ARTS AND CRAFTS:
AN EXHIBITION AT WILLIAM MORRIS'S

1. Yeats was reviewing the Third Exhibition of the Arts and Crafts Exhibition
   Society, New Art Gallery, 121 Regent Street, London, 6 Oct–6 Dec 1890.
2. For Victor Hugo see note 20.2. During its run at the Comédie Française
   in Paris from 25 Feb to 22 June 1830, Hugo's play *Hernani* provoked a
   passionate controversy between French Romanticists and defenders of
   Classicism. In Act v, the sounding of Hernani's horn on his wedding-night
   summons the young protagonist to his death at the bidding of an aged
   rival.
3. For William Morris see note 1.5. His company – Morris, Marshall,

Faulkner and Co., Fine Art Workmen in Painting, Carving, Furniture, and the Metals – was established in 1861.

4. No. 333 in the Exhibition Catalogue is a "mantel-fitting of teak with relieved intaglio decorations" by Liberty and Co. For Coventry Patmore see note 2.12. The lady who illuminated a copy of his poems is unidentified in the Exhibition Catalogue.

5. In the "Apology" prefacing his poem *The Earthly Paradise* (1868–70), Morris describes himself as "the idle singer of an empty day."

6. No. 88 in the Exhibition Catalogue is a "case containing [seven] specimens of book-binding in morocco and vellum" by Thomas James Cobden Sanderson (1840–1922).

7. No. 8 in the Exhibition Catalogue is "nine cartoons for a window at Jesus College, Cambridge" by Edward Coley Burne-Jones (1833–98), the English painter and designer. Executed in 1873, the cartoons are now in the Birmingham City Art Gallery. The "Oxford windows" which Yeats recalls are probably those of Christ Church Cathedral (1871–8). For D. G. Rossetti see note 1.5.

8. No. 1 in the Exhibition Catalogue is a cartoon of "The Annunciation of [*sic*] the Shepherds" for a window at Lanercost Abbey or Priory in Cumberland (1877). No. 9 is a cartoon of "Lazarus and Mary" for a window of St. Ethelred in Guilsborough, Northamptonshire (*c*.1878). No. 13 is a cartoon of "Rachel and Jacob" for the same church (*c*.1878). All three subjects are taken from the Bible.

9. No. 85 in the Exhibition Catalogue is "Six Sheets of 'The Roots of the Mountains'" by G. E. Renter, printed by the Chiswick Press. Morris's romance was published by Reeves and Turner in 1890.

10. No. 102 in the Exhibition Catalogue is "a chimney-piece in marbles" designed by W. R. Lethaby and created by the firm of Farmer and Brindley. *Undine*, a romance by Friedrich, Baron de la Motte-Fouqué (1777–1843), was published in 1811.

11. No. 113 in the Exhibition Catalogue is an "Irish national banner" executed by Una Taylor after a design by Walter Crane (1845–1915), the English painter, illustrator, and poet. Yeats's description follows that of the catalogue almost verbatim. For Charles Stewart Parnell see note 2.16. The four provinces of Ireland are Leinster, Munster, Ulster, and Connaught.

12. No. 627 in the Exhibition Catalogue is an etching by G. M. and G. W. Rhead of a design (1869) by English painter Ford Madox Brown (1821–93) for a watercolor painting (1871) inspired by Lord Byron's play *Sardanapalus: A Tragedy* (1821). The painting is now in the Bancroft Collection of the Delaware Art Museum.

13. No. 22 in the Exhibition Catalogue is a cartoon in charcoal by Ford Madox Brown for his fresco in the Manchester Town Hall of *The Baptism of Eadwine*. Eadwine was King of Northumbria when Christianity was introduced to that region in the seventh century. Though never a member of the Pre-Raphaelite Brotherhood of young English painters and writers (founded 1848), Ford Madox Brown influenced and encouraged their work.

22   THE POETIC DRAMA – SOME INTERESTING ATTEMPTS TO REVIVE IT IN LONDON – DR. TODHUNTER'S IMPORTANT WORK IN *THE POISON FLOWER*

1. For William Shakespeare see note 20.11. Yeats also refers to George R. Sims, *The Lights o' London* (1881); Henry Arthur Jones, *Judah* (1890); Henry Arthur Jones and Henry Herman, *The Silver King* (1882); and Harry Nicholls and William Lestocq, *Jane* (1890). From 12 Dec 1890 to 4 July 1891 *Jane* was performed 191 times at the Comedy Theatre.
2. For George Chapman see note 8 below. Queen Elizabeth I reigned from 1558 to 1603.
3. Thomas Dekker (*c.* 1572–1632), *The Gull's Hornbook* (1609), ch. v: "How a young Gallant should behave himself in an Ordinary."
4. According to the nursery rhyme, "Jack and Jill went up the hill / To fetch a pail of water. / Jack fell down and broke his crown, / And Jill came tumbling after."
5. See item 19 in the present volume. For Todhunter and the Bedford Park production of *A Sicilian Idyll* see note 1.3.
6. For *A Sicilian Idyll* and *The Poison Flower* at the Vaudeville Theatre in 1891 see note 11.5. The Strand is a major street in central London.
7. For Philistines see note 13.11.
8. Dramatic speeches about love are common to the masques (1605–34) of Ben Jonson (1573–1637), *Bussy D'Ambois* (1607) by George Chapman (1559–1634), and *Old Fortunatus* (1599) by Thomas Dekker (*c.*1572–1632).
9. For *Helena in Troas* and E. W. Godwin see notes 7.8 and 11.2. Edward, Prince of Wales and later King Edward VII (1841–1910), was an ardent patron of the theater.
10. Yeats quotes from the Epilogue of *The Tragicall History of the Life and Death of Dr. Faustus* (1594?) by Christopher Marlowe.
11. For "Rappaccini's Daughter" by Nathaniel Hawthorne see note 11.5. Todhunter has "his new Eden's tree of life" (*Isolt of Ireland and the Poison Flower*, p. 105).
12. For Florence Farr in *A Sicilian Idyll* and *Rosmersholm* see notes 1.4 and 11.10. Actor Bernard Gould (1861–1945) played the role of Giovanni Guasconti in *The Poison Flower* and spoke the Prologue of *A Sicilian Idyll*.
13. For the American revival of Robert Browning's *A Blot in the 'Scutcheon* see note 11.9.

EMENDATIONS TO THE COPY-TEXT

The Textual Preface explains the general principles which govern all emendations to the copy-text made in the present edition. The following list sets out the specific rationale for all emendations except those dictated by the uniform typographical and format conventions adopted for prose volumes in *The Collected Edition of the Works of W. B. Yeats* and specified in the Textual Preface.

The left-hand column gives item and page numbers in the present edition. On the pages listed, each superscript dagger (†) signifies an emendation explained in this list. The center column gives the *unemended* reading of the copy-text, which is HR unless otherwise indicated by a different abbreviation followed by a colon. The right-hand column supplies the authority for each emendation.

Item, page	Copy-text Reading	Authority for Emendation
1, p. 4	*Beckett*	title of play
1, p. 4	*The Lotus Eaters*	title of poem
1, p. 4	and	Yeats's typescript
1, p. 5	Dublin	not in Yeats's typescript
2, p. 10	Willis	proper name
2, p. 11	many of his	*BP*
3, p. 14	*Sgeulaighteachta.* The	title of book; *BP̄*
3, p. 16	dryasdustically	*BP* (name of character)
3, p. 16	*Sgeulaighteachta*	title of book
4, p. 18	he knew only	*BP*
4, p. 19	Cross Road	title of poem
4, p. 20	*Remembrance,*	*BP*
4, p. 20	*and Dreamland*	title of book
4, p. 20	under German eaves,	quotation from poem
5, p. 22	*BP*: and Banim's	authors' names
5, p. 22	*BP*: Sale Sotheby's	typographical error
6, p. 27	*BP*: *Folk Lore*	title of book
6, p. 28	artist	*BP*
6, p. 29	*BP*: Folk-lore	title of book

Item, page	Copy-text Reading	Authority for Emendation
6, p. 29	*Western*	title of book
6, p. 30	*Sgeulaighteachta*	title of book
6, p. 30	re-polishing	*BP*
7, p. 31	*BP:* Idyl	title of play
7, p. 32	stories newer	*BP*
7, p. 33	The Children	refers to characters, not to title
7, p. 33	*The Tain Bo*	title of work
7, p. 33	De Vere	proper name
7, p. 34	fruit of a good quality	*BP*
7, p. 35	names!	*BP*
8, p. 36	a "tragic scene"	*BP*
8, p. 37	*Tom-Boy*	title of play
8, p. 37	Alexander	*BP* (name of character)
8, p. 37	Thertylis [4 times]	name of character
8, p. 39	Thertylis	name of character
10, p. 45	*Friends,*	*BP* (with "Bryen" corrected to "Bryers")
10, p. 45	of the opinion	*BP*
10, p. 46	*Poems,*	*BP*
10, p. 46	*Whisper!* by	*BP*
10, p. 47	might have achieved a style	*BP*
10, p. 48	*The Tain Bo*	title of work
10, p. 49	*Fire,*	*BP*
10, p. 49	*Sgeulaighteachta*	title of book
10, p. 49	seas	*BP*
11, p. 51	made to seem	*BP*
11, p. 51	people needed	*BP*
11, p. 51	with it	*BP*
11, p. 51	*A*	title of play
11, p. 52	*Rosmerholm*	title of play
12, p. 55	*Order.*	*BP*
12, p. 56	and red	*BP*
13, p. 58	*Hall,*	*BP*
13, p. 59	*Book Bills*	title of book
13, p. 59	*Club,*	*BP* (with "Vego" corrected to "Vigo")
15, p. 64	capitol	*BP*

Item, page	Copy-text Reading	Authority for Emendation
16, p. 73	a thorn tree – the piano	*PSJ*
16, p. 74	effects	typographical error
16, p. 75	a solitary valley – isolated	*PSJ*
16, p. 75	Abbott	typographical error
16, p. 75	born. [followed by stanza break]	*PSJ*
16, p. 77	Long blades	*PSJ*
17, p. 79	*PSJ*: Keegan	proper name
17, p. 82	she muttered, pacing a Druid's maze	*PSJ*
17, p. 86	Children	*PSJ*
17, p. 89	adventures	*PSJ*
17, p. 89	lense	typographical error
17, p. 89	same source as	*PSJ*
17, p. 90	for it one	*PSJ*
18, p. 91	*PSJ*: D. A.	proper name
19, p. 98	*PSJ*: "Helena of Troas"	title of play
19, p. 98	*PSJ*: Winfred	proper name
19, p. 98	*PSJ*: *Tom Boy*	title of play
19, p. 98	*PSJ*: Terris	proper name
19, p. 98	*PSJ*: Mr. Jossling	proper name
19, p. 98	*PSJ*: Matilda	proper name
19, p. 98	*PSJ*: Mary	proper name
19, p. 99	*PSJ*: Mediterranian	typographical error
19, p. 99	*PSJ*: Alma Tadema's	proper name
19, p. 99	*PSJ*: Dreseults	name of character
19, p. 101	*PSJ*: revise	typographical error
19, p. 101	*PSJ*: Selby Lingfred's	proper name
19, p. 101	*PSJ*: Heron Allen	proper name
19, p. 101	*PSJ*: Taget	proper name
19, p. 101	*PSJ*: Juan Selby	proper name
21, p. 108	*PSJ*: classicisms	typographical error
21, p. 108	*PSJ*: room	typographical error
21, p. 109	*PSJ*: Reuter's	proper name
21, p. 109	*PSJ*: Roads	title of romance
21, p. 110	*PSJ*: Brindsley	proper name
21, p. 110	*PSJ*: Eadwins [2 times]	title of painting
22, p. 114	tree, this . . . life,	*PSJ*
22, p. 115	*Rosmerholm*	title of play
22, p. 115	Gower	proper name

APPENDIX I
CHRONOLOGICAL LIST
OF ESSAYS

This table is designed to assist readers who wish to view *Letters to the New Island* in chronological order. The left-hand column gives Yeats's dateline or, where none appears, the date of first publication. The center column gives the title of the item and the place in which it was first published. The right-hand column gives the number of the item in the present edition.

APPENDIX II
REYNOLDS'S
INTRODUCTION TO
THE 1934 EDITION

This appendix reproduces Horace Reynolds's Introduction to the original 1934 edition of *Letters to the New Island* for three main reasons. First, Yeats himself sanctioned the inclusion of the Introduction within the volume and even called it "admirable" in the letter to Reynolds dated 24 December 1932. Second, Yeats instigated two changes in the Introduction itself, the typescript of which is found among Reynolds's papers at the Houghton Library, Harvard University. At Yeats's suggestion in the letter of 24 December, Reynolds changed the word "blacks" to the phrase "natives of Ceylon" in the discussion of Florence Farr Emery in section VIII. And as a response to Yeats's objection on the typescript that "Joyce produced 'Ulysses' 700 pages; & perhaps the autobiography [presumably, *Portrait of the Artist*] in exile," Reynolds dropped James Joyce from the discussion of the "sterility which seems to fall on the transplanted Irish" in section II. And, third, Reynolds's Introduction provides a competent commentary from the perspective of 1932 on the main themes of the volume in relation to Yeats's life, as well as information on the evolution of his edition. Because the essay presumably reflects Reynolds's final intentions and because it is reprinted here primarily as a historical document, it has been left in the house styling of Harvard University Press rather than brought into conformity with the styling of Yeats's texts in the present volume.

INTRODUCTION

I

ONE Monday night in Dublin, six summers ago, four of us set out in a cab from The Bailey to call on Yeats in his house in Merrion Square. At Yeats's we had a rather mixed up evening, everyone cutting across the grain of the others' purposes and desires, but in the course of our talk, Yeats asked me a question which I remembered: "Is a paper I used to write for years ago called The Providence Journal still in existence?"

Several years before this I had happened upon a reference to The Providence Journal in Katharine Tynan's *Twenty-five Years*. I knew that she had written for The Journal: indeed it was Alfred

Williams, then editor of that paper, who turned on the tap of her prose and set it flowing; as she herself has said, "Mr. Williams made me begin seriously to write prose." At the time I myself was an occasional contributor to The Journal, and I had meant to look up sometime what my fellow contributor had written forty years before me; but I had never brought myself to the repellent task of handling the very large and very dusty volumes in the newspaper's library.

What Katharine Tynan could not stir me to do, however, Yeats did, and I can still remember the excitement with which I read on the editorial page of The Sunday Journal for May 27, 1888, The Legend of the Phantom Ship, one of the first of Yeats's poems to find the garment of print, and, after it, the five reviews from The Journal here printed. From The Journal the track was well marked to The Boston Pilot—indeed Mr. Allan Wade's bibliography had already pointed out that way—where I found another poem and the fourteen letters to the New Island.

Yeats does not remember how he came to write for The Providence Journal, but it must have been through Alfred Williams, who, in 1887, visited Mrs. Banim, the widow of the Irish novelist, in her house in Dalkey overlooking Dublin Bay. Doubtless then Mr. Williams, whose interest in Irish letters was keen and early, either met or learned about the young Irish poet who had written *Mosada*. As a memento of this relation, Mr. Williams's books, which on his death he left to the Providence Public Library, contain among other Irish books *The Wanderings of Oisin*, "with the author's compliments," and corrections in the young poet's hand. Yeats says he came to write for The Boston Pilot through John O'Leary, the Fenian. Without doubt O'Leary knew John Boyle O'Reilly, then editor of The Boston Pilot, a fellow Fenian, who, like O'Leary, had suffered imprisonment and exile from Ireland for his political activities.

The first of Yeats's contributions to these two papers was a poem, How Ferencz Renyi Kept Silent, in The Pilot for August 6, 1887; the last, a letter from Dublin in The Pilot for November 19, 1892. Yeats reprinted the two poems, How Ferencz Renyi Kept Silent, and The Phantom Ship, with changes, in *The Wanderings of Oisin*. They are not reprinted here.

These years in London, 1887–1892, belong to a distinct period of Yeats's life; they lap but little over the years 1887–1891, the distinctness of which Yeats recognized when he wrote of them thirty years later under the title *Four Years*. They are the curious, receptive, formative years of a young man of genius in his eager twenties, when he is reading the books, making the friendships, feeling about for the ideas that belong to him, which are later to affect his life. These are the years of Yeats's apprentice work; of the early poems which appeared in the anthologies, *Poems and Ballads of Young Ireland* and *The Book of the Rhymers' Club*; of the volumes of Irish folk and fairy tales and Carleton's stories, which Yeats edited for London publishers; of his first play, *The Countess Cathleen*; of *The Wanderings of Oisin*, his first volume of poems to make a stir among those who cared for poetry.

In these youthful years in London the thin, spectacled, black-coated poet was entering earnestly the life of pen, ink, and paper. Against the advice of his father, who wanted him to write stories, Yeats did much critical work and editing. Finally yielding to his father's wishes, he wrote the story *John Sherman*, whose back-ground is Sligo and London, pouring into it, as he did into Innisfree, all his discontent with London and his nostalgia for Ireland. He met Henley and his young men, he chatted with Lady Wilde in her drawing-room, and, with his sister, he joined the circle around William Morris in the old stable in Hammersmith. Two of his father's friends, Dr. Todhunter and T. W. Rolleston, who lived nearby, he influenced to join him in his plans to revive the poetic drama and make Irish literature national. He met the young men and women who were to be his friends, Florence Farr and Maude Gonne, Arthur Symons, Lionel Johnson, Edwin Ellis, MacGregor Mathers, Charles Ricketts, Charles Shannon, and others. He joined the devotees around Madame Blavatsky's green baize table; he was initiated into the Hermetic Students, one of the many societies in which the wave of occult thought that swept through Great Britain and the Continent in the eighties manifested itself. With Edwin Ellis he began the work on Blake; with Ernest Rhys he founded the Rhymers' Club, which met nightly for many years at the Cheshire Cheese. There came Lionel Johnson, Ernest Dowson, John Davidson, Richard Le Gallienne, T. W. Rolleston, Edwin Ellis, John Todhunter, Arthur Symons, and other poets of Yeats's generation. There he could talk poetry to his peers, or, full of race and vision, dream of the awakening of Ireland and the part he was to play in it.

Subordinate to all these interests, when it is not a part of them, is Yeats's passion for Irish letters, his insistence that the proper subject for Irishmen is Ireland. There are many iterations of this belief in these letters, all of which are summarized for us in a brief sentence in A Ballad Singer: "With Irish literature and Irish thought alone have I to do." That is the banner under which Yeats charges, and he has been faithful to it in his fashion: only very occasionally does he allow himself to forget it. Browning dies, and Yeats comments on the relation of his optimism to his thought; the Rhymers' Club publishes, and Yeats devotes a letter in The Pilot to a discussion of the work of some of its members; there is a sale of autographs at Sotheby's, and apropos of that he writes of Blake and what is to him the most beautiful of his letters, one of the last Blake wrote, which contains a passage about the imagination that Yeats has never tired of quoting. But for the most part he sticks close to his last, and the result for us to-day is a body of contemporary comment which takes us behind the scenes of the Irish Renaissance before the curtain has gone up, while the play is still in rehearsal. The articles here rescued from the limbo of newspaper files allow us to see into the mind of the young poet when he is restlessly feeling his way to the ideas that are not only to determine the course of his own work, important as that is to be, but are also to prove of historical importance. The ideas that we find in these letters are to mould a movement, one of the most distinctive in the stream of English letters; brought forth by an unknown young Irish poet in London and printed in New England, they are part of a nation's awakening to intellectual and imaginative energy.

When we scan the ideas that Yeats expressed in these newspaper articles, we see that they all have their roots in five major beliefs. Yeats believed that an Irish writer should be national, should write of Irish life, and take it seriously. He was determined that the treasury of early Irish legend and folk-lore should be unlocked by translation, collection, and publication for Irish reader and writer alike. He realized that Irish poetry needed much discipline; that it must be purged of politics. He sensed that in the study of the occult, man might surprise the secret that would free him from the despotism of unhappiness. He hoped that after Ireland had an imaginative literature, she would be ripe for a national theatre.

II

Yeats testifies in one of his articles in The Pilot that it was his friendship with John O'Leary that awakened national feelings within him: "We of the younger generation owe a great deal to Mr. John O'Leary and his sister. What nationality is in the present literary movement in Ireland is largely owing to their influence—an influence all feel who come across them." It was the influence of John O'Leary that turned Yeats's imagination away from the Swedish princesses, Greek islands, Moorish magicians, Spanish Inquisitors, Hungarian patriots, and Indian scenes of the very early poems, in which Yeats's love of the far-away found expression, to Ireland's national legend and folk-lore. From his fine library of Irish books O'Leary lent Yeats the poems of Mangan, Ferguson, and Davis, and set him reading the other Irish poets who had written in English. It was owing to O'Leary that Yeats could write in The Pilot, "I know our Irish poets pretty thoroughly." It was O'Leary who made possible the publication of *The Wanderings of Oisin*; it was O'Leary, "the irreproachable patriot," who made the Irish Literary Society politically respectable among the Irish people generally; it was through O'Leary, indeed, as we have seen, that Yeats came to write for The Pilot the articles whose matter we are discussing. Yeats and Irish letters are much in debt to the fine old Fenian.

And not only has Yeats decided that Irish legend was to be the matter of his own verse, as *The Wanderings of Oisin* testifies, but he would have all Irishmen write of Irish themes. Irish writers whose subject matter is not Irish are condemned and sentenced to obscurity. Rolleston, who had birched Yeats in his review of *Oisin*, and who, having just translated Whitman into German, was now busy on a life of Lessing, calls forth from Yeats this sentence: "I wish he would devote his imagination to some national purpose." Remarks like "There is no fine literature without nationality" are frequent in these letters: "Allingham had the making of a great writer in him, but lacked impulse and momentum, the very things national feeling could have supplied. Whenever an Irish writer has strayed away from Irish themes and Irish feeling, in almost all cases he has done no more than make alms for oblivion." So John Francis O'Donnell and Miss Frances Wynne both belong to the same school of Irish writers. Instead of steeping themselves in their own national life they "have read much English literature, and have taken from it, rather than from their own minds and the traditions of their own country, the manner and matter of their poetry." So, too, of the newly founded Irish Monthly Illustrated Journal—"an Irish magazine should give us Irish subjects."

So the song goes on with all the repetition of the passionate messiah. It is the same song Yeats is to chant to Synge in 1896 in the rue d'Arras, sending Synge away from Paris and his criticism of French literature back to Ireland and the writing of a drama so national that it is understood by the Russian peasant.

It is a vision the truth of which is attested by the sterility that seems to fall on the transplanted Irish in our own day. Both James Stephens and Sean O'Casey, to take two of the preëminent Irish men of letters of the generation that has succeeded Yeats, have left Ireland, and both have produced little since they left Irish soil and expressed the influences that came to them there. Indeed the cosmopolitanism that Yeats regrets in these articles has lost Irish literature, past and present, much: Irishmen have not only fought, they have written, for other nations; but to lose her men is one of the inevitable tragedies of an unsuccessful country.

The nationalism that the young Yeats had learned at the feet of John O'Leary in his house in Drumcondra, however, was not the political passion that had enslaved the energy of Ireland for hundreds of years. It was not the melodramatization of Ireland's past wrongs, with Ireland the fair heroine and England the dark villain, and all Irish literature one furious hiss. O'Leary was a critical nationalist. He had suffered imprisonment and exile from Ireland, but he could and did say such things as "There are things a man must not do to save a nation." Yeats's nationalism was critical and positive. It was designed not to spit at the Saxon villain but to recover the folk-lore and legend, that rich repository of Irish nationalism which Irishmen had allowed to lie so long neglected. It was out of the seed of this folk-lore and legend that a new literature was to spring.

III

A nation's legend and folk-lore are among its most precious national treasures, and Yeats desired ardently that these Irish treasures should be collected and collected well. And these were the years of their gathering. He himself had edited a collection of Irish fairy and folk-tales in 1888, and he was to do another volume in 1892. In these two books he had selected what interested him in the collections of Croker, Lady Wilde, and Joyce, adding to them stories he had taken out of the Irish novels of Carleton, Lover, and Griffin, with one or two stories collected by himself. Later, in *The Celtic Twilight*, he was to give us a volume of stories all of his own finding. He had done much reading in the Irish folk-tales for his editing, and so he came well armed to the reviewing of new collections for The Journal and The Pilot.

In his review of McAnally's *Irish Wonders*, Yeats complains of the lack of seriousness of McAnally and his predecessors in setting down the stories of the Irish people. He asks the question, "When will Irishmen record their legends as faithfully and seriously as Campbell did those of the Western Highlands?" Then he goes on to discuss McAnally's book in some detail, pointing out that McAnally "is wrong in saying that the Banshee never follows Irish families abroad," lamenting that McAnally fails to give the place and time of his recordings, but complimenting his phrasing, if not his pronunciations, and pleased that, unlike Croker and his school, he does not rationalize. Two or three times, to illustrate a point, Yeats tells stories of his own harvesting. One of these, how the ghost of a woman of Howth appeared to a neighbor woman to demand that her children be removed from the workhouse, Yeats tells again with greater fullness in *The Celtic Twilight*. Another story he has not, so far as I know, retold. Behind it lies what some one has called "the crookedness of the Gaelic mind."

A man at Ballysodare, a Sligo village not far from Colooney, said once to me: "The stable boy up at Mrs. G——'s there met the master going round the yards after he had been two days dead, and told him to be away with him to the lighthouse, and haunt that; and there he is far out to sea still, sir. Mrs. G—— was that mad about it she dismissed the boy."

Six months later Yeats notes the forthcoming appearance of Jeremiah Curtin's *Irish Myths and Folk-Lore*, some of whose advance sheets Little, Brown and Company had sent him from Boston. Of this Yeats expects much. In Curtin's introduction he finds as much science as he had in Campbell and more imagination; his book "promises to be the most careful and scientific work on Irish folk-lore yet published." Yeats promises a full review of this book in The Pilot, but if he ever sent this in, I have not been able to find it.

In the same letter in which Yeats mentions Curtin, he glances at Lady Wilde's second book of Irish folk-lore, *Ancient Cures, Charms, and Usages of Ireland*. He has as yet had time to do no more than turn the pages of the proverbs at the end. Some of these he quotes, and we can see one of them, "The lake is not encumbered by its swan; nor the steed by its bridle; nor the sheep by its wool; nor the man by the soul that is in him," sinking into his memory to be murmured over and over again, as it is his habit to caress and fondle phrases that please his mind and ear. He quotes this proverb in the introduction to his own *Irish Fairy Tales*, dropping out the weakest of the four phrases, "nor the sheep by its wool," so that the quotation there has the symmetry of an Irish triad.

Hyde's *Beside the Fire* followed close on the heels of these collections by Lady Wilde and Curtin, and Yeats speaks highly of this book in The Pilot. In Hyde Yeats finds the folk-lorist he has been looking for, one whose science, learning, imagination, and style answer the question he asked in his review of McAnally's *Irish Wonders*: "If Dr. Hyde carries out his intentions, and continues to gather and write out, in that perfect style of his, traditions, legends and old rhymes, he will give the world one of those monumental works whose absence from modern Irish literature I have been lamenting."

Hyde was to collect *The Songs of Connacht* and little more, alas; and although he was to found in the Gaelic League a movement whose importance it is difficult to exaggerate, Ireland still lacks her monumental collection of Irish folk-lore.

To any one at all familiar with Irish letters the "accomplished Irish scholar, who is also perhaps the best Irish folk-lorist living," upon whom Yeats calls in his review, Irish Wonders, is no less clearly Hyde than is "a certain famous hedonist" who wrote "a letter on scented note paper" praising William Watson's Epigrams, Oscar Wilde. In these articles Hyde appears in a rôle which does him much honor—that of Scholar-in-Waiting to the Irish Renaissance. Yeats, Lady Gregory, and countless others have drawn again and again on the rich deposits of his scholarship, and his help was particularly valuable forty years ago when the Movement was just beginning and poor in scholarship. The notes with which he furnishes Yeats on the Irish word *fearsidh* and the anonymous song Shule Aroon are only two of hundreds which owe their existence to Hyde's generous response to a call for help from some swimmer struggling in the difficult depths of the Irish language and literature.

Yeats, however, did more than read and edit Irish folk-lore, and preach the need of getting it and Irish legend translated and collected: he practiced what he preached; he himself story-hunted among the Irish peasants, and these stories so collected are, and have remained, precious imaginative possessions. To-day in his Norman tower, Thoor Ballylee, Yeats dreams over stories he collected and imagined when he was writing for The Journal and The Pilot; he remembers Red Hanrahan, and Mary Hynes, a peasant girl made famous by Blind Raffery's song, and the "wild old man in flannel" who could change a pack of cards into a hare and a pack of hounds that panted after it. Indeed this sensitiveness to folk-lore, this gift for remembering with pleasure what men to-day no longer care to remember, and making others feel its charm, is one of the primary characteristics of most of Yeats's work, early and late.

It was to this story-hunting, about which Yeats speaks in A Ballad Singer, that we are indebted for the legends set down in *The Celtic Twilight*, a book he wrote, as he tells Ashe King in the dedication to the *Early Poems and Stories*, "when we were founding the National Literary Society." In The Three O'Byrnes we have the first printed version of the story of that name in *The Celtic Twilight*, one of those old stories about the evil of buried treasure that we find in *Beowulf* and all old folk literature.

Yeats's review in The Journal of Dr. Todhunter's *The Banshee and Other Poems* allows us to see the imaginative value that Old Irish legend possessed for Yeats in these years. Writing of the Mythological Cycle of Old Irish romance, Yeats says:

His legends belong to those mythic and haunted ages of the Tuatha De Danaan that preceded the heroic cycle, ages full of mystery, where demons and gods battle in the twilight. Between us and them Cuchulain, Conall Carnach, Conary, Ferdiad and the heroes move as before gloomy arras.

In those mysterious pre-human ages when life lasted for hundreds of years; when the monstrous race of the Fomorians, with one foot, and one arm in the middle of their chests, rushed in their pirate galleys century after century like

clouds upon the coast; when a race of beautiful beings, whose living hair moved
with their changing thoughts, paced about the land; when the huge bulk of
Balor had to be raised in his chariot, and his eyelid, weighted by the lassitude
of age, uplifted with hooks that he might strike dead his foe with a glance—to
these ages belongs the main portion of one legend supreme in innocence and
beauty and tenderness, the tale of The Children of Lir.

"Whose living hair moved with their changing thoughts" is as
beautiful in image and rhythm as anything in *Oisin*. Indeed,
written early in 1889, the whole passage is in the mood of that
poem, a *Götterdämmerung* such as that into which rode Niam and
Oisin, and

> . . . Car-borne Balor, as old as a forest, his vast face
>   sunk
> Helpless, men lifting the lids of his weary and death-
>   pouring eye,

moved by Oisin in his dream.

There is little more of the matter of Old Irish legends in
Yeats's articles. It is not that he was not thinking of them: they
were as much in his mind as the folk-tales, as *The Wanderings of
Oisin* proves, and the references to Goll, Fergus, Conchobar,
Cuchulain, Emer, Diarmuid and Grania, Deirdre, and the Sons
of Usna in the poems from *Oisin* and *The Countess Cathleen*. That
Irish history and legend were even more important as matter for
the new Irish literature-to-be is stressed in several of the letters.
Between the man of letters and Old Irish legend lay the barrier
of a very archaic, difficult, and complicated language. Irish
legend had to wait, in the main, for the scholarship that was to
follow, as it always does, the creative energy that made the
Movement.

IV

What specific use and service Yeats thought the recovery of this
national legend and folk-lore would be to a modern Anglo-Irish
literature is made clear in a long passage from Ireland's Heroic
Age, beginning:

The first thing needful if an Irish literature more elaborate and intense than
our fine but primitive ballads and novels is to come into being is that readers

and writers alike should really know the imaginative periods of Irish history.

Add to the thought of this passage two sentences from the Irish National Literary Society, where, speaking of books such as Hyde's translations of the bardic tales, Yeats says:

It is impossible to overrate the importance of such books, for in them the Irish poets of the future will in all likelihood find a good portion of their subject matter. From that great candle of the past we must all light our little tapers.

These remarks tell us what part the recovery of this legend is to play in Yeats's program for a more "elaborate and intense" modern Anglo-Irish poetry. Yeats felt that the recovery in publication of this epic and folk literature would do for modern Anglo-Irish poetry what the publication of the old English ballads did for eighteenth century English poetry—rescue it from artificiality and bombast, give it substance and subtlety.

And not only must Irish poetry have this background of national epic and folk literature, it must no longer be the handmaid of Irish politics. Since the time of Swift, who on Irish soil first used poetry for political purposes, every strong political movement of the past hundred years, notably those of '98 and '48, had had its poets, and these poets had made a tradition in which the test of a poem was not the truth of its emotion, national or personal, but its patriotic or political hyperbole. This tradition was so deeply ingrained in Ireland as to be almost part of the national character, and Yeats encountered resistance here as he did elsewhere whenever he tried to engender a more critical spirit. Irishmen had made a goddess of Ireland, as the men of the Middle Ages developed the cult of the Virgin, calling Ireland Cathleen ni Houlihan, Dark Rosaleen, and other names of endearment; and poetry, like everything else, was to be her slave. Yeats worshipped at other shrines. The Intellectual Beauty, The Secret Rose, were the names which he and Shelley had imagined for their goddess, and nationalism was to serve her, and by so doing glorify itself. If we look deep into Yeats's mind, we see that for him nationalism was precious not so much because it served Ireland as because it well served Art. Ireland came not before, but after, Art.

Hand in hand with this insistence that Irish poetry be truly national and critical went an inevitable revaluation of the poets of the preceding generation. Just as to-day in their own Renaissance the young Scotch poets, led by Hugh M'Diarmid, are setting Dunbar at the head of the Scotch poets in the place of Burns, so Yeats and his school were putting Mangan and Ferguson into the places formerly held by Moore and Davis. And in these articles it is being done under our eyes. Ferguson, not Mangan, is the touchstone Yeats uses to test the purity of an Irish poet's nationalism; "the poems of Ferguson, Davis, and Mangan," a frequent phrase, is undoubtedly a graded series. When Yeats is writing these articles, Ferguson has passed Davis; it is later that Mangan is elevated above both Davis and Ferguson and placed at the head of the poets of Young Ireland.

In Yeats's review of William Allingham's *Irish Songs and Poems*, the first poet of the new order passes judgment on the last poet of the old, and the verdict is: "These poems are not national." Like McAnally, Allingham does not take the Irish people seriously; to him they and their life are but "a half serious memory." But here the young critic pays for his principles, for the memories are beautiful, and when Allingham writes of his native Ballyshannon, Yeats remembers Sligo, and the pull of sentiment against principle is strong. When, however, Yeats measures Allingham against Davis and Ferguson, Allingham's lack of nationalism becomes too evident to be ignored.

In his review of Todhunter's *The Banshee*, Yeats again sets nationalism against cosmopolitanism, as he had in writing of Allingham; and again Ferguson is the measuring rod of the nationalism of the poet on trial. This time the verdict is for the poet reviewed: "Dr. Todhunter no longer comes to us as an art poet: he claims recognition as one of the national writers of the Irish race." He has done what his fellow exile failed to do—responded to the newly awakened national tradition. A younger man than Allingham, he was able to react to forces that were dominating men twenty years his junior. Three years later Yeats notices in The Pilot a shilling reprint of *The Banshee*, summarizing his long Journal review in a sentence: "Dr. Todhunter follows in the footsteps of Sir Samuel Ferguson and gives us simple and stately versions of The Children of Lir and Sons of Turann."

In Yeats's first note in The Pilot on Miss Ellen O'Leary's poems he writes: "Miss O'Leary's poems . . . are the last notes of that movement of song, now giving place to something new, that came into existence when Davis, singing, rocked the cradle

of a new Ireland." In these words Yeats summarizes fifty years
of Anglo-Irish poetry, from the rhetorical vehemence of Davis
and other poets of The Nation, through the quiet simplicity
of the Fenians, Kickham, Casey, and Miss O'Leary, to the
"something new" that stood affirmed in *Poems and Ballads of
Young Ireland*. And he is quite conscious that he stands between
the waning of one burst of energy and the waxing of another.

The death of Miss O'Leary moved Yeats: her going stood as
a sign of the passing of a generation to whose moral grandeur
and nobility of character he has paid tribute in his poem
with the refrain, "It's with O'Leary in the grave." Yeats had
announced Miss O'Leary's forthcoming volume of poems in The
Pilot for August 3, 1889, praising the Wordsworthian simplicity
of her best poems. Two years later when her posthumous book,
Lays of Country, Home and Friends, finally appeared, he writes of
her again, selecting for praise To God and Ireland True, "a song
in the old sense of the word, that is to say, a singable poem
worthy of good music. The compilers of our songbooks, ballad
sheets and the like, should garner it." Yeats took his own advice
to heart, for eight years later he put it into his *Book of Irish Verse*.

There are also notes on a group of young women who, in the
sociable manner of the Irish, gathered around the fireside of The
Irish Monthly, as the poets of The Nation surrounded their
paper, and the Fenian poets John O'Leary's journal, The Irish
People. A Miss Ryan, who published *Songs of Remembrance* in
1889 and then passed into obscurity, is dismissed with the
succinct comment, "She is too sad by a great deal." I have
already quoted what Yeats said of Miss Wynne's verses—they
were not national, though Yeats is quite conscious that in this
case such criticism is, as he says, a little like breaking a butterfly
on a wheel. To Rose Kavanagh, who also like Miss Wynne died
young, Yeats devotes a whole article. In her much promise was
first dimmed by bad health and then soon quenched by death.
Yeats compares her to Kickham and Casey. She left two or three
poems that have survived in all but the most recent of Irish
anthologies. And Miss Tynan, the best known and most prolific
of all the young women of this group, Yeats praises perfunctorily,
more in gratitude and friendship, it seems to me, than in desire.

These notes are all Yeats has to say of the poetry of his Irish
contemporaries. In writing of them, he is either gently critical
or faint in praise, and this is as it should be, but, like Percy, his

blood beats to a ballad which he buys from a ballad singer in the County Down, with the refrain, "Where the ancient shamrocks grow," of which he quotes three stanzas. I find it pretty commonplace, but then I read in 1933, I do not hear in 1891. The young Yeats is exclamatorily extravagant in its praise: "What infinite sadness there is in these verses! What wild beauty!"

In his Pilot letter for April 23, 1892, Yeats writes of the Rhymers' Club, its members, and their poetry. Notable as are many of these names to-day, when Yeats writes of them they are, like him, unknown, just beginning their work. For mention he selects Arthur Symons, whom he describes as "a scholar in music halls as another man might be a Greek scholar or an authority on the age of Chaucer." Symons, Yeats contrasts with John Davidson, who has also selected the music halls for his material. In both these young men Yeats finds the search for new matter that was as characteristic of the Rhymers as was the search for new forms of the generation of poets just passing. And from what Yeats says here of their wistfulness for their lost Philistinism, it would seem that by 1892, three years before Wilde reached the height of his fame and power, the young Rhymer was already weary of aestheticism, "an Alastor tired of his woods and longing for beer and skittles."

Like Italy in her Renaissance, Ireland in the years when she was discovering her age was alive with the stirrings of her youth: it is not for nothing that Yeats's Cathleen ni Houlihan is both an old woman and a glimmering girl. Passages like the one with which Yeats concludes his notes on the Rhymers are frequent in these letters: "England is old and her poets must scrape up the crumbs of an almost finished banquet, but Ireland has still full tables." It was this same consciousness of Ireland's youth and England's age that in 1899 decided George Moore to answer his echo-augury, "Go to Ireland." No Irish man of letters, least of all Moore, could listen unmoved and unexcited to sentences such as the one at the end of Yeats's letter on The Irish National Literary Society: "If we can but put those tumultuous centuries into tale or drama, the whole world will listen to us and sit at our feet like children who hear a new story." In such remarks lie the seed of Yeats and Moore's *Diarmuid and Grania*, and much of the Anglo-Irish literature that has followed it.

Of the work of William Watson, who joined the Rhymers but

never came to their meetings, Yeats writes at length in The Journal. With the young man's love of strong antitheses he divides the writers of verse into "the poets who rouse and trouble, the poets who hush and console," and then places Watson among the latter.

In this review we have an early affirmation of Yeats's love of "an extravagant, exuberant, mystical" art, which was undoubtedly fostered in him by his father's admiration of intensity. Yeats admires much the art of Watson's verses and pays them the tribute of committing them to memory, but this poetry is too much in the Matthew Arnold tradition to be admired with both the head and the heart by one who had wandered spiritually hand in hand with Ellis down Blake's pathway of excess. Yeats writes of Watson's poems with all the condescension that those who have intensity feel for those who have it not.

But while at this time Yeats admired the art of William Watson, he was not to know him as well as some of the others. Of the Rhymers, Yeats was to know best Davidson, Johnson, and Symons. From the first two he ultimately drifted away because of the irritability bred of frustration in the one, and the great appetite for drink in the other that turned sociability with him into pity and sorrow. Symons, however, became his intimate and influenced his art. Symons had what Yeats lacked at this time, art and scholarship, and Yeats himself has testified how much his theory and practice were influenced by what Symons read him from Catullus, Verlaine, and Mallarmé, in particular how much the elaborate form of some of the poems in *The Wind Among the Reeds* owes to Symons's translations of Mallarmé.

For among the Rhymers Yeats was forming his style. If we look for a moment at the two poems Yeats contributed to The Pilot and The Journal, we can see in what need Yeats stood of criticism in these years. The first of these, How Ferencz Renyi Kept Silent, describes a dramatic moment in which a Hungarian patriot is tortured for information by an Austrian general. His mother, sister, and sweetheart are shot successively in an effort to make him reveal the whereabouts of his countrymen. After the shooting of the sweetheart, Ferencz goes insane and rushes away "rolling from his lips a madman's laugh." In this poem, obviously an imitation of Browning's dramatic dialogues which succeeds only in being melodramatic, all is thin, surface violence, fire without heat or light. The second poem, The Phantom Ship, is equally violent, though it has more academic interest for us, for we can see in it how the poet was beginning to use Irish folklore for the matter of his poems. In Irish Wonders Yeats tells us, "One old man in County Sligo told me a story of a man who saw all who had died out of his village for years, sitting in a fairy rath one night." Make the village a fishing village, and change the fairy rath to a phantom ship crazily riding a squall, while all those ever drowned from that village stand grey and silent under a sky dizzy with lightning, and you have The Phantom Ship. But the Irish quality of the legend is hidden under anonymity: there is nothing more definite than "a pale priest" to suggest that the scene of this poem is an Irish village. And technically the poems are poor; energetic rhythms in iambic pentameter and trochaic octameter, both rhymed with such rhymes as *wine* and the *shine* that is contracted *sunshine*, fall strangely on ears that know only Yeats's later verses.

So much of what has come to be Yeats's poetic ethic is here in these articles, either directly or by clear inference, that it is surprising not to find the hatred of rhetoric which for years so dominated Yeats's judgment that, as he has remarked to me, "I then thought much rhetorical that I should now think otherwise." Certainly if he had developed this scorn for rhetoric by 1890, the admiration for Victor Hugo's *Shakespeare* with which he begins his review of William Watson's poems, to say nothing of "the poets who rouse and trouble, the poets who hush and console," which is pure Swinburne in both rhetoric and rhythm, are very strange. It must have come later.

v

One of the most fascinating folds in Yeats's mind is his love of symbol, mysticism, magic, clairvoyance, hypnotism, cabalistic science—all the occult means by which men seek the Infinite through a study of what seem to them its manifestations. As a young man, fresh from the gentle agnostic influence of his father, John Butler Yeats, Yeats had made himself a little private religion out of the fables of old stories and notable personages from history and literature, really a poet's culture held with the passion of a religious belief. With this as a center of belief he

turned successively to the study of Oriental pantheism through
theosophy, to the worship of Shelley's Intellectual Beauty, to the
passionate mysticism of Blake's Prophetical Books, to modern
Cabalism, to the symbolism of the French Decadents, finally to
the astronomical psychology of his recent *A Vision*, all of which
have ministered to the imaginative intellectualism which is the
passion of his life. And he has approached them all, not as a
true mystic but in the mood in which one says, "Yes, I believe
in ghosts and fairies." He has believed in these doctrines
emotionally, not intellectually, as one believes emotionally, not
rationally, in the ghost of Hamlet's father, or as some men of
agnostic tendencies believe in God. He has sampled all the
imaginative stimulants from table-rapping to Shelley's Intellectual Beauty, and they have been to him what other stimulants
have been to other poets. To trace their succession by means of
the marks they have left upon his poetry and prose will be the
passion of some future scholar in poetry. Now we are attentive
to the traces they have left here in these early articles.

In one of his first letters to The Pilot Yeats mentions Colonel
Olcott's lectures in Dublin on Irish goblins. Colonel Olcott, the
American president of the Theosophical Society, was something
of an expert on ghosts, goblins, and phantoms; he had, among
other studies, translated and annotated Adolphe D'Assier's *Essai
sur l'humanité posthume et le spiritisme*, and he had also the gift of
persuasion. Says Yeats of Colonel Olcott's lectures in Dublin:

He asserted that such things really exist, and so strangely has our modern
world swung back on its old belief, so far has the reaction from modern
materialism gone, that his audience seemed rather to agree with him. He
returns to London at once, where the faithful of his creed are busy with many
strange schemes—among the rest the establishing of an occult monastery in
Switzerland, where all devout students of the arcane sciences may bury
themselves from the world for a time or forever.

Yeats also tells the readers of The Pilot that Madame Blavatsky, "the pythoness of the Movement, holds nightly levees at
Lansdowne Road." It is difficult to judge from what Yeats has
written about this woman just how seriously he took her and
her doctrine. Not very seriously, I am sure: one does not call the
high priestesss of a belief one reverences, a pythoness. Yeats
went to Lansdowne Road to listen to Madame Blavatsky because
"her imagination contained all the folk-lore of the world." Her

belief that there was another globe stuck on the earth at the North Pole, that the shape of the earth was really a dumb-bell— this belief and others like it excited Yeats's imagination. For the same reason he took long walks with Æ in Ireland when Æ was unintelligible with the vision that was in him, "for the sake of some stray sentence, beautiful and profound, amid many words that seemed without meaning." So he read the imaginative algebra of the Cabala, so he studied Blake's symbolical writings, so he sat at the seances of the Hermetic Students. When in these years Yeats wrote to Katharine Tynan of Æ's mysticism: "You must not blame him for that. It gives originality to his pictures and his thoughts," he might well have been apologizing for himself. By these toyings and dabblings around the edges of magic and theosophy and mysticism, Yeats loosened his imagination, thickening the cloud of dreams about him out of which he was to summon the images of his poetry.

Yeats speaks also in The Pilot of his study of the Cabala. In a review of Dr. Todhunter's little play, *The Poison Flower*, he writes, "The copy of the Kabala that lies upon my own desk pleads for him, and tells us that such men lived, and may well have dreamed just such a dream, in the mystic Middle Ages." The malicious Moore has questioned whether Yeats did any more than allow the Cabala to lie upon his desk, but when Moore doubted, Yeats had not yet written *A Vision*. If Moore read that, he no longer could have doubted. The mind that could write *A Vision* could read the Cabala, easily.

I have previously mentioned Yeats's friendship with MacGregor Mathers; it was he who introduced Yeats to the Hermetic Students; it was he, the author of *The Kabbalah Unveiled*, I am sure, who interested Yeats in the Cabala, a book whose form Yeats certainly remembered when, forty years later, he wrote *A Vision*. It was Mather who set the great poet of our generation trying to excite a cat by imagining a mouse in front of its nose, but a man of genius must do something, I suppose, to rid himself of the imaginative turbulence within him, and who dares say where imagination ends and magic begins. Many a thing that in the doing seems foolish yields results at which only a fool can smile.

The interest in Blake that stands revealed in the Ellis and Yeats edition of that mystic is recorded in another early article in The Pilot. Here Yeats quotes a passage from one of Blake's letters, a letter sold at Sotheby's for eight pounds, ten shillings:

I have been very near the gates of death, and have returned very weak, and an old man feeble and tottering, but not in spirits and life, not in the real man, the imagination which liveth forever. In that I am stronger and stronger as this foolish body decays. . . . Flaxman is gone, and we must all soon follow, everyone to his own eternal house.

One wonders how much of this passage Yeats remembered when, forty years later, he calls out in The Tower:

> What shall I do with this absurdity—
> O heart, O troubled heart—this caricature,
> Decrepit age that has been tied to me
> As to a dog's tail?
>   Never had I more
> Excited, passionate, fantastical
> Imagination!

Out of all this preoccupation with the occult and the mystical has emerged one belief which I fancy means something to Yeats and his poetry. Out of his association with Æ and Oriental thought, out of his reading of Shelley and Blake, out of his fellowship with the Theosophists and the Hermetic Students came somehow the belief that every personal imagination is part of the Divine Mind. And every personal imagination, therefore, because it is part of that Divine Mind, can, in favorable moments, receive intuitions of what men, also with a share in that Mind, have felt before it. It is this belief which moves Yeats to say, "People do not invent, they remember"; where to remember is to speak with the voice of the Divine Mind. It is these studies and experiences that prompt Yeats to write, when he himself sums up what he drew from them, "Images well up before the mind's eye from a deeper source than conscious or subconscious memory." A great audacious metaphor, in other words, is a glimpse into a divine order: he who wrote "The spirit of man is the candle of the Lord," saw God. It is this belief which causes Yeats to see in folk-lore and legend a body of metaphor under which may be revealed to men to-day the mind and soul of the past. So in Browning Yeats writes:

To the old folk-lorists, fables and fairy tales were a haystack of dead follies, wherein the virtuous might find one little needle of historical truth. Since then

Joubainville and Rhys and many more have made us see in all these things old beautiful mythologies wherein ancient man said symbolically all he knew about God and man's soul, once famous religions fallen into ruin and turned into old wives' tales, but still luminous from the rosy dawn of human revery.

This is why symbol, whether that symbol be Deirdre or her story, is so precious: it carries the imagination back to all that lies behind it; through it men may recover forgotten truths and unremembered beauty.

VI

"A man's life of any worth is a continual allegory," said Keats, and perhaps in that remark lies the clue to the spectacle of a man who has made it his life's work to evolve a lonely, distant, indirect, aristocratic art, spending ten or more years of his life in the hurly-burly of organization and propaganda. That Yeats was not unconscious of this contradiction of ideal and practice, we have ample evidence. In a letter to Lady Gregory written in 1901 in the midst of the turmoil of the rehearsals of *Diarmuid and Grania*, Yeats says, "I might have been away, away in the country, in Italy perhaps, writing poems for my equals." And once when I spoke to him of it, he said, "It has bothered my conscience." But confession or no confession, we must always remember that every Irishman is a born propagandist, and incorrigible. Has not Yeats only recently organized the Irish Academy and toured America to collect funds for it?

Yeats's review of the poems of John Francis O'Donnell brings us into touch with the Southwark Irish Literary Club and the beginning of the ten years of organization and propaganda. This club, founded in 1883 to take care of the Irish children in South London, had become literary. Yeats had lectured there on Sligo fairies, and the club had collected and published the works of Irish poets, among them O'Donnell's poems. Yeats cared little for O'Donnell's verses, but he saw in the Southwark Literary Club, which was ceasing to function, the nucleus for a society that might do for Irish letters what the Rhymers' Club was doing for the young British poets in London. Accordingly in 1891 he invited the Committee to meet at his father's house in Bedford Square, and out of that meeting grew The Irish Literary Society.

Yeats induced Rolleston and his father-in-law, Stopford Brooke, and others to throw themselves into its work, and the society was joined by most of the Irish authors and journalists then living in London.

A few months later Yeats is in Ireland founding there The Irish National Literary Society, "and affiliating it with certain Young Ireland Societies in country towns which seemed anxious to accept its leadership." He is writing from the new National Library, and, no doubt remembering his father's injunction never to study anything with a practical end in view, he is dismayed by the sight of readers for only what may be turned into pounds and shillings. And then, in this last letter to The Pilot, he calls upon his countrymen to unite literature to their great political passion, to read the literature of their nation which the new Library of Ireland is to bring them, to live as the men of '48 lived, "by the light of noble books and the great traditions of the past."

In this plea Yeats comes dangerously near ideals. Had his father read this, he would have said, "Take care, Willie; ideals thin the blood and take the human nature out of people." But devotion to the cause of Art, not purpose to improve Irish character, is the real motive behind his words here. The political propagandists of the preceding decades of the nineteenth century had made literature the servant of politics. Yeats would reverse that relation, making nationalism the handmaid of Art. He would woo the Irish to an interest in their literature by appealing to their love of Dark Rosaleen. The improvement in the national character that might result from this revived interest in literature is secondary to the call to a disinterested intellectualism.

The disgust of Irishmen with public affairs of which Yeats speaks in this passage:

So far all has gone well with us, for men who are saddened and disgusted with the turn public affairs have taken have sought in our society occasion to do work for Ireland that will bring about assured good,

is a reference to the wave of revolt and self-nausea that swept over Ireland when the Irish people realized that they had allowed their leaders to persuade them to betray Parnell, a mental attitude which, as Yeats points out, had made Ireland receptive to his ideas. Yeats's Movement was a return to the people in the

sense that it was an appeal directly to the people, over the heads
of the leaders who had misled them.

VII

Behind all these plans and interests—this cry to Irish writers to
be national, this passionate desire to see Ireland's legends and
folk-lore revived, rescued, and put into the consciousness of the
Irish race, this purging of Irish poetry of politics, this interest
in the occult, this propaganda and organization—behind all this
is the dream of a national drama for Ireland. At this time it is
not a working plan: Yeats does not immediately urge an Irish
theatre as he does the translation of Old Irish legends and the
publication of Irish books. It exists now as a dream of an ideal
national theatre, to be turned over in the mind until such time
as the foundations for it shall have been laid. Remembering
these years, Yeats writes in *The Trembling of the Veil*, "I had
definite plans; I wanted to create an Irish Theatre; I was finishing
my *Countess Cathleen* in its first meagre version, and thought of a
travelling company to visit our country branches; but before that
there must be a popular imaginative literature." These plans
are set down here in these two New England papers ten years
before the actual beginnings of the Irish Dramatic Movement in
1899.

We find these plans stated in what Yeats wrote about the
London performances of Dr. Todhunter's three plays, *Helena in
Troas*, *A Sicilian Idyll*, and *The Poison Flower*. Yeats was much
interested in these plays and their performance, particularly in
the *Idyll*, a poetical pastoral play, which he had persuaded
Todhunter to write for performance in the little red brick theatre
in Bedford Park. The play was a great success, and Yeats wrote
of its triumph in both The Journal and The Pilot. The next year
the play was put on at the Vaudeville, one of the big Strand
theatres, and for this occasion Todhunter wrote to precede
the *Idyll* another poetic play, *The Poison Flower*, founded on
Hawthorne's Rappaccini's Daughter. Yeats also wrote of these
performances for both papers.

George Moore has described Yeats's original idea of a theatre
(he is writing of the Yeats of 1899) as "a little mist, some fairies,
and a psaltery." That is very witty, and as true as raillery can

ever be. Those were Yeats's foibles, and he knew as little as Ole
Bull about the actual business of conducting a theatre: both were
Don Quixotes charging the technical difficulties of theatrical
enterprise, one with a fiddle bow, the other with a psaltery. But
although Yeats knew little of the technic of the stage, he was
possessed of very definite ideas on the drama. He despised the
contemporary theatre which imitates life for the many. What he
wanted was a drama whose matter was to be the national
legends, a drama revealing through stories that were old enough
to have become symbolical, life that would stir men's imagination
and move their emotions. This drama was to be a poetic one,
and its model was the Elizabethan drama. Its speech, like that
of the Elizabethans, was to be exuberant, vehement, fantastic,
abundant. These plays were to be produced so as to accent the
speaking of the verse, movement was to be stately and deliberate,
scenery impressionistic; nothing was to be allowed to make for
a restlessness that would interfere with the beautiful speaking of
verse. Finally this drama was to be played before a small, select
audience, who should come reverently to the play as if they were
Catholics coming to Mass. Yeats's disgust with the commercial
theatre of his day is the perennial one of the artist with a theatre
that is always so much a lesser thing than he can imagine it to
be. In Yeats's opinion the whole of the spoken drama has
divorced itself from literature, and its falseness stings Yeats into
many a contemptuous phrase. It is the old story of the young
man of taste and talent, his mind full of the masterpieces of the
past, in the presence of machine-made drama for the many.

Loving beautiful speech, Yeats desires a poetic drama, for
which, naturally enough, his model is Elizabethan. He knows
that the days when "everyone, from the pot boys to the noblemen,
thought imagination a high and worthy thing" are gone, that
England has become unimaginative, Puritan, and rich; but the
reception of Dr. Todhunter's poetic plays causes him to believe
that there is a small, perhaps growing, public for the poetic play,
on which such a drama might be founded.

There is in Yeats great scorn, not only for the thought and
action of contemporary drama, but for its language as well.
There are many contemptuous references to its speech of the
street and the tea table. Yeats desires the exuberant, vehement
speech of a drama in which the hero when greatly moved does
not merely stare steadily and silently into an open hearth but

speaks the great poetical oratory of the Shakespearean soliloquy. As yet, however, there is no thought that the speech of the English-speaking, but Gaelic-thinking, Irish peasant of the West can supply that idiom. That is to come later out of Yeats's friendship with Lady Gregory.

It was a woman, also, who drew Yeats's attention to the speaking of verse. Florence Farr, or Mrs. Edward Emery, to give her her married name, played in both the *Idyll* and *The Poison Flower*. She brought to the speaking of Todhunter's lines a monotonous chant-like recitation of verse that gave to each syllable its full volume of sound, and a rhythmic dreaminess of movement and gesture for which Yeats found it difficult to find high praise enough. Heron Allen, another amateur—indeed so much a one that he insisted upon appearing on the program as Mr. Smith—also pleased Yeats greatly. From that day to this Yeats has believed that the cultivated man or woman makes the best performer of poetic plays, and Maude Gonne in *Cathleen ni Houlihan* and Ezra Pound in the London rehearsals of *The Hawk's Well* have done much to bear him out.

It was with Miss Farr that Yeats began his experiments of speaking verse to music in an effort to release poetry from its slavery to music in song. Deaf to the power of music, Yeats sees it when it is combined with words in song or opera as something that destroys the speech balance of consonant and vowel, distorts the rhythms of words, and slows down the speed of the transmission of thought. He would go back to the time before "music grew too proud to be the garment of words," for music developed latest of all the arts and in its early days was humble. What Yeats desires is a musical recitation of words, with little more music in the background than one hears in *recitativo secco*.

The remainder of Yeats's theory of production can easily be inferred if we remember that all the other elements in the ensemble must, like music, be subordinate to the verse. Movement is to be deliberate; gesture restrained and subtle; scenery impressionistic, a vague background, stimulating the imagination, not feeding the eye with imitative detail; even costume must be simple in form and color lest it distract the attention of the audience from the voice of the speaker.

The audience that Yeats sees in the pit of his ideal theatre is not to come to the theatre frivolously, chattering the gossip of the street, but quietly, reverently, like suppliants to an oracle of which the dramatist is the high priest. In The Children of Lir he writes: "We must go to the stage all eagerness like a mob of eavesdroppers and to be inspired, not amused, if modern drama is to be anything else than a muddy torrent of shallow realism." In 1889 Yeats writes in a Providence paper, "We must go to the stage all eagerness like a mob of eavesdroppers"; in the winter of 1932 in a lecture at Wellesley, remembering better than he knew, he said: "I wanted a theatre hard to get into, like a secret society."

Yeats has been faithful to this conception of the drama. He has written plays for the reverent few. And his interest in the old Noh plays of Japan is anticipated here more than twenty-five years before their influence stirred him to invent a form of drama that answers in every detail this youthful dream.

But this meeting with Florence Farr did more than set Yeats theorizing over the details of dramatic production: she has influenced further his life and work. It was with her that he joined the Hermetic Students; it was her image that he saw and her voice that he heard when he was writing *The Countess Cathleen*, *Cathleen ni Houlihan*, and the early dramatic poems; it was for her that he wrote his *Land of Heart's Desire* in 1894, when she was manageress of the Avenue Theatre and needed a curtain-raiser for Shaw's *Arms and the Man*; it was with her that he thought, in 1898, remembering the small club theatre in Bedford Park, of taking a little theatre in the London suburbs for the production of romantic plays; it was she, as we have seen, who was responsible for the experiments in speaking verse to music; it was she, "the lady in the green cloak," whom Moore found at the rehearsals of *The Countess Cathleen* murmuring the line, "Cover it up with a lonely tune," to the accompaniment of the psaltery, while the experienced actress Moore had engaged strode to and fro like a pantheress. It is of her and her art that he has written in his essays and autobiographies; it is she upon whom he calls thirty years later, in All Souls' Night, when in a mood of grave ecstasy he feels the need of a mind freed from all earthly calls outside its own pondering:

> On Florence Emery I call the next,
> Who finding the first wrinkles on a face
> Admired and beautiful,

And knowing that the future would be vexed
With 'minished beauty, multiplied commonplace,
Preferred to teach a school,
Away from neighbour or friend
Among dark skins, and there
Permit foul years to wear
Hidden from eyesight to the unnoticed end.

VIII

These articles also set us thinking about another beautiful woman who was to influence Yeats's life and his art even more than Florence Farr. Ever since the day Maude Gonne stepped out of her hansom cab in Bedford Park on one of her numerous journeys between Dublin and Paris, her beauty has haunted Yeats's imagination, exciting him to write the beautiful love poems in which he has sought for images to express her loveliness.

In The Pilot for July 30, 1892, Yeats reports a long speech Maude Gonne made at the Catholic University of Luxembourg, printed in the supplement to La Revue Catholique. This was one of the many speeches she was making in France on the story of Ireland's wrongs. Yeats tells us that thousands have come "to see this new wonder—a beautiful woman who makes speeches," that "at Bordeaux, an audience of twelve hundred persons rose to its feet, when she had finished, to applaud her with wild enthusiasm." He quotes her description of the famine of 1848, praising the beauty and power of her oratory.

In Maude Gonne was the energy that animated Young Ireland at this time. And she and her image have moulded many a line of the poet's verse. She is Yeats's Laura, and he who would understand much of Yeats's very allusive poetry must learn of her. Both she and Florence Farr scorned the great beauty that was in them, and Yeats has raged at both of them because of it. Florence Farr, neglecting also her gift of beautiful speech, turned to the study of the occult and finally ended her days teaching English to the natives of Ceylon. Maude Gonne, filled with a destroying energy, as Florence Farr was with a destroying curiosity, grew daily more shrill in argument, more violent in action, while Yeats looked on, furious that Demeter, banner in hand, should lead the Dublin lines that picketed the first

performances of *The Plough and the Stars*. But, as Yeats himself
has cried of her in No Second Troy,

> Why, what could she have done being what she is?
> Was there another Troy for her to burn?

IX

It is interesting to see, now that over forty years have passed
since Yeats wrote the first of these letters to the New Island,
how time has turned much of his intuition and logic into fact.

Irish writers have become national, have written out of the
forces, ancient and modern, that have vivified and moulded Irish
life, and have been, or will be, accepted by their countrymen
accordingly.

The legends and folk literature for whose gathering, translation, and reading Yeats plead have been gathered, translated,
and read. The books of Lady Gregory, Rolleston, and others
have restored Irish legend; Cuchulain and Deirdre have been
reborn. *The Tain* has been translated and published. Hyde has
collected the songs of Connacht and the tales of inland Connacht;
Larminie, the tales of the coast of Connacht and Donegal; Curtin,
those of Munster. Scholars in Old Irish, notably Kuno Meyer,
have edited and translated many of the Old Irish texts. These
texts have been used by men of letters, remarkably by James
Stephens.

Irish poetry has been put to school. It has lost its rhetoric and
political passion, and become artistic. In beauty and subtlety of
movement, in the cunning voweling which it inherits from the
Gaelic bards of the seventeenth and eighteenth centuries, it to-
day yields to no poetry in English. It has become "distinguished
and lonely," notably in the poems of Yeats, Lionel Johnson,
Seumas O'Sullivan, Padraic Colum, and James Stephens. The
recent anthologies of Colum and Lennox Robinson will convince
any critic of its fullness and its artistry. It still, however, lacks
its epic masterpiece, but there have been few epic masterpieces
in the poetry of any nation in the last hundred years.

Irish legend has provided the poets of modern Ireland with a
body of symbol through which they have been able to express a
personal emotion. Indeed in the last forty years Deirdre has
grown so deeply into the world's imagination that she has almost

as many lovers among men to-day as have Helen, Dido, Guinevere, to mention only her most famous rivals. And the stories of the Red Branch, which are her *Iliad*, are to-day as powerful an influence in Irish letters as the Arthurian Legend has been in English.

An Irish drama has been born. It has not developed exactly as Yeats planned it, for Dublin has not been made folk-minded and for the most part the plays it has looked upon at the Abbey have not been poetical plays based on the national legends. Yeats and Moore's *Diarmuid and Grania*, Æ's *Deirdre*, Synge's *Deirdre*, and a few small poetical pieces by Daniel Corkery and Austin Clarke are about all the poetical drama, or drama based on national legend, that the Abbey has seen, except the poetical plays of Yeats's own making. Yeats's program of legend and poetry for the drama was too narrow for a living theatre in these days. Synge's peasant plays and O'Casey's plays of the Dublin slum-dweller have been the notable work of this theatre, with many imitations of Synge, and so far no successful ones of O'Casey. Synge's plays, however, while they were not, except for *Deirdre*, based on national legends, or in verse, fulfilled Yeats's desire for "a fantastic, energetic, extravagant art," and O'Casey's speech excites like drink, sending a shock of joy to the blood. As yet the Irish middle classes have had little opportunity to see themselves on the stage of the Abbey, but so much the better for their peace of mind, one who knows Dublin has said, truthfully enough. However, that is the direction in which the Irish drama must spread; that is the highway as yet unbarred by genius that lies open for the coming Irish dramatist.

No man ever shaped a large movement exactly to a pre-arranged pattern, but I think what I have just said shows that Yeats has done almost that. And I come from the contemplation of these facts with a great admiration for the vision, energy of mind, tact, and wisdom of the man who has remade the literature of a nation. Anyone who knows Ireland, its poverty, its pride, and its passion, knows the enormous difficulties that beset Yeats, of which the disturbances over *The Countess Cathleen* in 1899, *The Playboy* in 1907, *The Plough and the Stars* in 1926, are dramatic explosions, the growing-pains of the awakened Irish mind.

The work that Yeats accomplished could only be wrought by an intense energy, and intense energy and concentration are qualities upon which satire is sure to seize: ridicule is the tribute paid them by a lesser energy and a lesser dream. So Moore has snickered maliciously and O'Casey with all the violence of the sentimentalist has growled and snarled from his exile in London, muttering "The Great Founder" under his breath. But we are not deceived; put to the test, these two men would be the first to pay the tribute of praise as they have the tribute of satire.

It is impossible to read these letters without constantly looking forward, as I have done, to what has grown out of them. In their rapid words of the moment are most of the ideas that have shaped the work of the great Irish poet of our time, and much of the Movement with which his name is joined; and it is what the years have made of these ideas that gives these letters their full meaning and their appeal to the imagination. That is their chief value. But they have still another interest. These early letters allow us to see the young poet when he has just emerged from boyhood, when fame has not withered his freshness, when, simple and eager, he is flushed with the ideas that possess him, and writing, as Yeats himself said when he read these letters again recently, better than he knew. The beautiful autobiographical *Four Years* contains the thoughts of youth recollected in maturity; they are the interest on the experiences of which these letters, which complement them, are part of the capital. Beside the reminiscent mood of the *Autobiographies*, the letters are pungent with immediate, living comment; they permit us to come closer than we can elsewhere to a man of genius the undulating rhythms of whose later, formal prose hold us at a distance, so that even in so intimate a form as autobiography, Yeats seems to utter his sentences like a voice in Greek tragedy, speaking unseen from within some great temple.

While the style of these letters lacks the invariable high literary breeding of the later prose—not that the Yeatsian hall mark isn't here somewhere on every piece—they tell us many things for which we are grateful. They were written before Yeats's surrender to the fascination of the difficult, and in them is much of the revealing, accidental self.

INDEX